A Great Day at the Office

10 simple strategies for maximising
your energy and getting the best
out of yourself and your day

Dr John Briffa

FOURTH ESTATE • London

Fourth Estate
an imprint of HarperCollins*Publishers*
1 London Bridge Street
London SE1 9GF
www.4thestate.co.uk

This Fourth Estate paperback edition published 2015
First published in Great Britain by Fourth Estate 2014

A catalogue record for this book is
available from the British Library

ISBN 978-0-00-754793-7

Illustrations by HL Studios
Author photograph © Charlotte Knee

Printed and bound in Great Britain by
Clays Ltd, St Ives plc

MIX
Paper from
responsible sources
FSC® C007454

FSC™ is a non-profit international organisation established to promote
the responsible management of the world's forests. Products carrying the
FSC label are independently certified to assure consumers that they come
from forests that are managed to meet the social, economic and
ecological needs of present or future generations,
and other controlled sources.

Find out more about HarperCollins and the environment at
www.harpercollins.co.uk/green

DISCLAIMER
The information and advice contained in this book should not be used for the
purposes of diagnosis or as a substitute for medical advice. Neither the publisher
nor Dr John Briffa assumes any responsibility or liability for any consequence
resulting directly or indirectly from any action or inaction taken based on the
information contained in this book.

Contents

Introduction

Do you sometimes feel exhausted or overwhelmed by work? Can you find yourself 'putting in the hours', only to find you have little to show for it at the end of the day? At times, do you get the feeling that the bulk of your energies and efforts are going into your career, and that there's not much left over for your loved ones and interests outside work?

If any of these scenarios resonate with you, then you are not alone: they are just the sort of cries I've heard time and again from the individuals I have worked with in the corporate arena over almost two decades. But it needn't be this way: workplace issues such as reduced vitality, faltering focus and sub-par productivity are usually rooted in issues that are not only *identifiable*, but easily *solved* with the relevant knowledge, understanding and practical know-how.

Drawing on cutting-edge but little-known research, as well as the real-world experience of thousands of business professionals, A *Great Day at the Office* equips you with the knowledge required to run your body and brain at maximum capacity. This book explores the fundamental factors that determine our vitality, mental functioning and mood, and how to put them together in a way that will take your energy, performance and sustainability to new heights.

This book offers key insights in wide-ranging factors including diet, physical activity, sound and light exposure, breathing, psychology and sleep. Put even a fraction of the strategies offered here into practice, and you stand to be rewarded with a tangible increase in your energy and vitality, and an ability to get more done more easily.

Solving the Energy Crisis

While most of us acknowledge that our professional lives can be rewarding on many levels, we may also recognize that they usually come with considerable challenges, too. Long working hours and the stresses and strains of a demanding and competitive environment can drain our physical and mental resources. This, in turn, can take a toll on our wellbeing and performance. My experience with organizations around the world tells me that eroded energy, faltering performance and problems with sustainability are common and pervasive issues throughout all business sectors.

The vast majority of the individuals that I have worked with in seminars and workshops clearly have the skillset and knowledge necessary to do their job very well. Some are demons at satisfying the most demanding of clients and have supreme technical knowledge. They may be masters in the principles of effective leadership or know ninja tactics for handling the daily onslaught of email. However, whatever someone's knowledge, skills and experience, they know that none of this counts for much when they find themselves short of energy and struggling for inspiration.

The fact is, without abundant and sustained *energy*, theory tends not to translate at all well into practice, and our talents can easily end up being squandered. Plus, when energy runs low, *more* effort is used to get *less* done (and things usually get done less well, too).

Conversely, in an energized and vital state we are able to get more done more easily, and our work will generally be of superior quality. Combined with professional and business skills, having abundant mental and physical energy is *the* key to success.

The processes in the body that drive energy production are highly dynamic and dependent on several factors. In a way, the human body is no different to a car: for us to get from A to B a few basics need to be in place, such as fuel in the tank (and the *right type* of fuel at that), water in the cooling system, oil in the engine, and for the tyres to be properly pumped up. If these fundamentals are not satisfied, then performance is impaired. This book is essentially a manual for your body, explaining its inner workings and what is required for you to perform at your peak.

A Great Day at the Office offers a wide range of information and advice grouped into seven key areas:

- Diet and nutrition

- Sleep

- Light exposure

- Activity and exercise

- Music and sound

- Breathing

- Psychology

Each area will be explored from a scientific perspective, enabling you to gain valuable insights into the impact specific behaviours have on how you feel and function, as well as on your long-term health and sustainability. In each section, practical guidance is given on the simple and sustainable changes that make a real difference.

But many of us are only too aware that we can sometimes fail to do things we know are good for us, and perhaps persist with habits that hold us back. To this end, the final chapter provides practical tips on how to get healthy habits to stick, as well as unhealthy ones out of our system – with *ease*.

Not every factor this book covers will require action on your part, as my experience tells me that almost everyone is getting some (possibly many) things right. However, hardly anyone has no room for improvement, so there's a good chance that within the pages of this book you will find quite a few nuggets that will make a tangible difference to your ability to achieve your goals, from tasks on your 'to-do' list, to major life ambitions.

Tried and Tested

The information contained in these pages is based on published (but often *unpublicized*) research. But more than this, it's also informed by the collective experiences of literally thousands of people. My work as a doctor, speaker and facilitator has brought me into contact with individuals with diverse wellness and performance issues including fatigue, disturbed sleep, low mood, lack of focus, impaired concentration and burnout. Working with these individuals over time has given me the opportunity to discover what actually works to resolve these challenges and have people brimming with vitality once more.

Much of the information and advice offered in this book is founded in science and published research. As a doctor, I am obviously interested in the underpinnings of the approaches I discuss here, and you may be too. But, as I often tell my clients in talks and workshops, gaining this knowledge is not merely an academic exercise: the focus is always on having individuals leave with practical, sustainable strategies that are effective for improving their condition. Rest assured, the concepts and methods presented here have been tried and tested with countless individuals and have been found to give consistent and predictable results in the real world.

Taking Charge

Anyone who owns a smartphone will know the importance of maintaining charge in its battery. Periodically plugging these devices into the mains is just one of those things we have to do if we want to take advantage of their functionality. The human body is a bit like this, too: we can use it to get stuff done, but we have to put something back. If we drain our 'charge' more than replenish it, we can end up suffering from periods of 'low battery power' that can put a major brake on our productivity. If severe and protracted enough, this situation can ultimately lead people into a state known as 'burnout'.

It's fine to put time and effort into work, even in the long term, just as long as we are regularly doing things that, overall, 'recharge our batteries' and keep them from running flat. In many respects, this is what A Great Day at the Office is about.

↓

↓

'Battery charging' can happen in a number of ways, including making the right food choices and being physically active. However, it can also take place via 'activities' that require little or no effort at all. Examples explored within the pages of this book include getting better sleep, napping, increasing sun exposure, listening to particular types of music, and specific breathing techniques. Other examples of things that might help the 'recharging' process include an evening spent at the cinema or theatre, enjoying time with loved ones and friends, getting a massage, or even indulging in a nice, long soak in the bath.

Some people, though, can view these sorts of activities as distractions from work, and therefore in their minds classify them as 'unproductive' time. However, another way of looking at them is as opportunities to 'plug ourselves into the mains', to ensure we are maximally effective in whatever time we apportion to work. In this way, taking time to 'recharge' through relaxation and recuperation may not now seem 'unproductive', but *essential* to our long-term success.

I am not suggesting for one moment that we should never work in the evenings, at weekends or on holiday (I do all of these things on a semi-regular basis, by the way). The key is to be able to live and work in a way that ensures our energy and effectiveness rarely falter, if at all, and that our personal sustainability is assured too.

Maintaining charge in the battery can be particularly important for those whose work is transactional or seasonal in nature, such as auditors or those involved in business

↓

recovery or mergers and acquisitions. Going into a busy phase already somewhat depleted is 'risky business', to be honest. 'Doing the right thing' in quieter times can provide a store of power that can be drawn on when the pressure is on and the going gets tough.

Working Wonders

Here's a list of the typical benefits to be gained by applying the strategies contained in *A Great Day at the Office*:

- Enhanced energy and vitality

- Increased mental focus, concentration and decision-making ability

- Improved resourcefulness and creativity

- Brighter mood and reduced tendency to anxiety, low mood or depression

- Better sleep and heightened energy on waking

- The ability to function effectively throughout the day with no mid-afternoon slump

- Improved resilience and the ability to maintain high performance, even when the going gets tough

- Weight loss without hunger or the need for extensive exercise

- Resolution of persistent, troublesome health problems including headaches and digestive issues.

Many of these benefits have a direct impact on performance at work, and will significantly enhance your ability to generate high-quality output and 'get the job done' – *consistently*. Moreover, improvements here will likely enrich your professional *relationships* too, from which myriad spin-off benefits can be yours.

It's a plain fact of life that when we are energized and mentally alert, we are able to respond to people with more enthusiasm, resourcefulness and vigour. This, in turn, leads others to respond better to us. If you act on the advice here, do not be too surprised if you end up being held in higher esteem by your colleagues, clients or customers. This can, of course, translate into expanded opportunities and speedier career progression.

And the benefits do not stop when you leave the workplace, either. Typically, individuals will reap the dividends of brighter mood and enhanced energy in their *personal* relationships, too. It's unlikely that anyone close to you will complain about your transformation into a better balanced and altogether happier person.

Occupational Hazards

I have worked with a wide range of organizations around the world and interacted with individuals in varied settings and all levels of seniority – from graduate trainees to CEOs and successful entrepreneurs. Perhaps the most common fundamental issue that my clients express to me is that their performance is, at times, considerably lower than they would like and feel they are capable of. Many people have a sense that they could do more and be more effective – they're just not sure how.

For some people, though, the issues are more acute. They may feel devitalized and swamped with work. A significant minority, no matter how hard they try, feel perpetually 'off the pace' in terms of the jobs they need to do. Work can somehow bleed (or haemorrhage) into personal time, including the evenings, weekends and holidays. All the while, this quite relentless nature of work can leave individuals feeling short of both time and energy.

Ultimately, the quality and quantity of their output tends to suffer, which usually adds to the stress and only compounds the problem. Now blighted by fatigue, some people can struggle to stay afloat and conclude the way they live and work is completely unsustainable. Ultimately, some decide it's all too much for them and it's time to go. For others, their organization makes that decision for them. I've seen the careers of many very talented and experienced professionals end unnecessarily prematurely in this way.

The cost here is not purely personal, of course. When individuals underperform, this has impact on the business too. 'Going off sick' is a potential consequence here, but this is the mere tip of the iceberg. My experience tells me that absenteeism is a relatively confined problem, especially at senior levels within an organization. Much more of an issue, though, can be 'presenteeism': essentially, people enduring long working days consumed with 'busyness', but at the same time simply not getting the results they, and maybe others, expect.

This sort of underperformance saps an organization's productivity, which inevitably knocks on to revenues and profitability. This can eat into the bottom line, as will the increased costs relating to staff turnover: many organizations have considerable people 'churn', and substantial sums can be spent recruiting and training replacements. Healthcare costs associated with wellness issues can be a significant financial drain, too.

All organizations need to justify the resources they put into learning and development. It's clear, though, that whatever is spent on making tangible improvements to the wellness, effectiveness and sustainability of its people pales into insignificance compared to the cost of not making this investment.

Opportunities Knocked

Another major unseen cost of impaired performance and 'unwellness' relates to missed opportunities. When vitality is depleted, fewer calls are made and emails sent, and less creative thinking and planning may go into, say, product development or service improvement. The acquisition and retention of clients and customers can be similarly neglected.

If you pitch for business, not being fully on top of your game or appearing 'spent' will do little to inspire confidence in your prospective customers. The inability to be mentally agile and spontaneous in your thinking won't help matters, either. The winning or losing of work can sometimes come down to very small margins, and if a client does not have complete confidence in those doing the selling, it can cost you (and your business) dearly.

Also, if you are in a position of some seniority, then it's inevitable that some will look to you as a role model. If you appear 'bent out of shape' to your junior colleagues, what sort of message might they take from that? I've worked with human resource professionals who tell me they have serious sustainability issues in their organization because increasing numbers of staff look at the sort of lives senior colleagues lead and decide it's just not for them.

Of course, in the age of the internet, word is out about the organizations that are best avoided if one wants to enjoy a rewarding career *and a* decent quality of life. If an organization gains a reputation for driving its people ever harder, without giving much back, this can make recruiting top talent that more challenging (and costly).

Taking Care of Business

Of course, the reverse is also true, and I have worked with organizations that use the fact that they provide wellness and performance programmes for their people as a major selling point in the recruiting process. Some organizations even 'advertise' these initiatives to their clients. After all, the fact that an organization takes steps to support its people in meaningful ways only helps to convince clients that this is a company with whom they should do business.

Occasionally, some will go a step further and invite existing or prospective clients onto wellness programmes they sponsor. This endeavour provides value and meaning to people in a way that eclipses traditional corporate hospitality and the finest of dining.

One such delegate was the CEO of an international public company, who came as the guest of one of my corporate clients. The usual stresses and strains of running a sprawling, shareholder-owned company, coupled with an insane travel schedule, had led to some fatigue and wellbeing issues, as well as an ever-expanding waistline.

Inspired by what he learned on the programme, he changed some behaviours and found his lost energy was quickly restored. As an added bonus, he shed over 35 pounds in weight without any additional exercise or cutting back at all on business lunches or dinners. In a few short months, his diminishing proportions had required him to twice renew his wardrobe. While costly, he did not begrudge a penny of this additional expense. So changed was he by the experience that he sponsored a wellness programme for his own executive board.

This particular CEO's experience is not by any means extraordinary, either – it's typical. Again, all that is usually required to make a tangible difference to someone's wellbeing and how they feel and function is some small but targeted changes in key areas. Many of the strategies in this book are simple and easy to apply, yet they pack considerable punch.

It was actually some significant personal benefits gained from some simple self-applied strategies that inspired me to shift my focus from conventional medicine to approaches that can transform wellbeing and health.

All Change

When I was a young hospital doctor, I had a pressing problem with fatigue. Some sleep deprivation no doubt contributed to this, but even when I snoozed my sleep debt away I felt I lacked the zip someone in his mid-twenties should have. In particular, I would find my energy levels were highly variable, and I was prone to catastrophic 'energy crises' at certain times. A major danger time for me was the mid to late afternoon: often at around 4 p.m., I would feel the life drain out of me. Sometimes, I would even struggle to stay awake.

It's perhaps easy to imagine that these symptoms were the inevitable consequence of the often hectic schedule I worked back then. But, in truth, my unreliable energy and afternoon slumps started many years before I ever set foot on a hospital ward in a professional capacity. When I look back, I remember regularly 'zoning out' during lectures and tutorials while at medical school. However, it was when I started work as a doctor that my deflating energy became much more evident and inconvenient.

Seeing a long list of people in an outpatients' clinic can be challenging at the best of times, but it was made infinitely harder when my overriding desire was to lie down on the examination couch in the corner of the room and go to sleep. Even in the operating theatre, I remember occasionally having to press hard with the heel of one foot on the toes of the other just to spark some life into my wilting body.

One morning, I was doing the necessary checks on an elderly man who was due to have a minor operation later that day. I was struck by the fact that he had an energy and vitality considerably greater than my own, despite being almost fifty years my senior. My curiosity was piqued enough for me to remark: 'Whatever you're on, I'd like some of it.' He responded by telling me that he set great store by eating healthily, as well as regular cycling and keeping up his interests through reading and listening to the radio.

As a junior doctor, I did not feel in need of any more mental stimulation, and lack of activity was not my problem either (I was a keen runner back then), but it did occur to me that maybe my diet might be a bit of a blind spot. In my six years of study at medical school, I recalled not one single lecture on nutrition, and what I knew about this subject would have fitted comfortably on the back of a postage stamp.

Later that evening while out shopping, I found myself drawn to a carousel of books I had spied from outside a health food store. I bought a book on nutrition and read it over the next couple of days. Getting through the book quite quickly was a breeze because what I was reading appeared to make perfect sense to me. I became convinced that although I had previously thought my diet to be perfectly sound, conventional nutritional 'wisdom' had led me off in the wrong direction. I resolved to make some immediate changes to my diet.

And I was very glad I did, because the impact this had on me was profound. My sense of wellbeing improved quickly and steadily to the extent that, within two weeks, I felt I had more energy than ever before in my adult life. However, the benefits did not end there, because just a few days into adopting my new diet, the itchy, red rash under my arms and on my torso that had plagued me on and off for many years disappeared (never to return).

Another happy side effect of my new diet was that the additional weight I'd acquired through six years' worth of a pretty rubbish diet (I was a typical student, and no stranger to fast food like KFC, kebabs and Kronenbourg 1664 in those days) was shed in about six weeks. This happened, by the way, without hunger or deprivation, nor any increase in my activity levels. If you're wondering what sort of dietary changes could possibly have led to this transformation in my energy, wellbeing and weight, all is revealed in Chapter 1.

So changed was I by all this that I ended up leaving the traditional career path I was on to devote myself to helping people take their health into their own hands using natural self-applied means. In the beginning, I was principally interested in dietary approaches, but quickly my interest expanded into other areas too, including sleep, activity, light exposure and psychology. I witnessed countless individuals liberate themselves from long-term health issues such as fatigue, anxiety and depression, weight issues, joint and muscle pain, skin conditions, digestive discomfort and headaches – and all without recourse to medication or conventional means.

But I discovered something else too: when individuals took approaches that addressed the underlying nature of their health issues (rather than merely treat their symptoms), not only would these issues often resolve, but they would usually experience benefits in terms of their energy, general wellbeing and mental functioning too. Many would report that they felt more mentally and physically alive than they had in years (just as I had).

I began to wonder if there existed people who, although not sick enough to be called truly *sick*, were not well enough to be called truly *well* either. Might many people be wandering around in a sub-par state as a result of lifestyle factors that could be simply rectified?

My curiosity was satisfied when, in 1996, I was asked to facilitate on a wellness programme for a global professional services firm. The delegates were senior members of the organization, almost all of whom suffered from the sorts of wellbeing and performance issues that I now realize are endemic in the corporate arena. Some simple, sustainable changes in areas such as diet, activity, psychology and sleep reaped significant dividends for them in terms of enhanced vitality and performance. The results from the early programmes were so good that the initiative was rolled out nationally and, subsequently, internationally. The programme became part of the culture of the organization and continues to run to this day.

Since the mid-1990s, I've been privileged to work with many different organizations in the UK and abroad. While there are certainly things that set businesses apart from each other, I have found the issues that this book addresses are common the world over and in all settings in which I have worked.

Uncommon Knowledge

If you read this book from cover to cover you will find in it many examples of information and advice that run counter to conventional opinion. You'll discover, for instance, evidence that challenges the ideas that starchy carbohydrates are ideal for ensuring sustained energy, that saturated fat causes heart disease, that sunlight causes melanoma, that controlling cholesterol levels is inherently important, and that the key to losing weight is simply to 'eat less and exercise more'.

While some of the concepts presented here may come as a surprise or even a shock, I will present the evidence that supports them (the numbers in the text refer to specific scientific studies that are listed at the back of the book). If it's any consolation, every myth I explode in this book I previously believed myself. Only by taking nothing at face value (however seemingly credible the source) and going back to published research have I discovered that much of what is described as conventional 'wisdom' is anything but.

But, how could it be that we have managed to have been so misled about health – something that affects not just our lives, but our livelihoods? How do things so often get stated as fact, even though the facts don't stack up at all?

A Great Day at the Office is not political or a polemic, but I do think it is worth bearing in mind that health information and advice can be influenced by economic and commercial concerns. Quite simply, there is often money to be made in misinformation (be it deliberate or unwitting). A classic example of this includes low-fat and cholesterol-reducing foods, for which there is not a scrap of evidence that they benefit health (see Chapter 1).

The commercial aspects of health advice can, unfortunately, have another unwanted side effect: they can keep useful and important information from our attention. Just as some erroneous ideas become popularized because there's money in them, some highly valuable ideas and strategies may not get the attention they deserve because there isn't.

For example, you'll see that sunlight exposure, overall, is linked with significant health benefits and relative protection from many conditions including heart disease and several different forms of cancer. However, these facts are often drowned out by relentless stories about the supposed hazards of sunlight with regard to skin cancer. At the risk of sounding unduly cynical, could the explanation for this disparity be due, at least in part, to the fact that while sunlight is *free*, considerable commercial potential exists in sunlight *protection* (particularly sunscreens)? In Chapter 5, you can find evidence that suggests this is exactly how it is.

Other aspects of health that have limited potential for commercial exploitation and are therefore perhaps similarly neglected include certain breathing techniques, the impact of music on our mental state and performance, walking as an activity, and many of the tips that will help you get sound, restorative sleep. In fact, the great majority of the strategies contained in this book can be yours for little or no cost, but they have tremendous power to transform your health and efficiency.

Make It Easy on Yourself

For some of us, the idea of lifestyle adjustment and 'being healthy' conjures up images of restricted eating and exhausting and unsustainable exercise regimes. Relax: the recommendations in this book are not of that nature at all. For example, you will discover approaches that will enable you to be functionally fit and strong with relatively little effort and minimal time investment. You'll also see how hunger actually jeopardizes weight loss, and also makes practically every aspect of life harder to boot.

Not only are the methods here generally easy and sustainable, many are downright enjoyable. You will see how some activities that you may have hitherto regarded as the height of indulgence and perhaps laziness, like getting an early night, taking a nap, listening to music, or snoozing in the sun, have the capacity to help you be fitter, healthier and more productive.

Sometimes, people imagine that putting even a little time and effort into their work–life balance and wellbeing just cuts into work time and detracts from their productivity. Let me assure you that nothing could be further from the truth. Each of the many strategies in this book is designed to optimize your energy and effectiveness in a way that ensures you are significantly more productive than you are right now. What you put in is likely to be returned to you many times over in terms of enhanced output and the satisfaction you derive from your job. The potential 'return on investment' of these strategies is enormous.

A Great Day at the Office is about how to incorporate some simple tips, tricks and tools in your life that will enable you to get more done more quickly, but with less effort – and who wouldn't like that?

How to Use This Book

There's a lot of information in *A Great Day at the Office*, and some parts will be inevitably more relevant to you than others. One way to approach this book, therefore, is to go first to the chapters that pique your interest. The short descriptions of each chapter in the next section are there to help guide you to the parts of the book that you feel you'll get the most out of.

As you read, you'll see that many of the areas covered interconnect. For example, what we eat can affect our sleep. Sleep can also be influenced by light exposure, and both of these can have an impact on our mood. Certain mood states can affect sleep, of course, and lack of sleep can actually drive hunger and food choices. And these are just a few examples.

I've added cross-references throughout the book, so starting in one place may point you to other information that perhaps had no special interest for you to begin with. However, if you have been led somewhere by the text, then the chances are you'll find something useful for you there, so I suggest 'going with it'.

Another approach, of course, is just to read the book from cover to cover. Even if you feel 'sorted' in a particular area, it would be unusual if you did not gain a tip or two in each chapter that could make all the difference.

Each chapter includes a summary in bullet-point form. These are designed to help you remember key learning points. If you like, you might return to these summaries from time to time so that they may serve as useful reminders.

↓

↓

Do bear in mind, though, that you do not need to do *everything* suggested in this book and get it all right to derive major benefits in terms of your energy and effectiveness. I recommend starting with the things that seem most relevant to you and that you feel inspired to act on. You could, if you wish, always add new strategies later.

Chapter Summaries

Here's a summary of the ten chapters that stand to transform your work and life for the better:

Chapter 1: Energy to Burn

Food provides us with *fuel*, and what we choose to eat can determine whether we are highly energized and raring to go, or feeling as though we're wading through treacle. The first part of the opening chapter explores the science of the conversion of food into energy, and how to eat to ensure sustained levels of vitality throughout the day.

Most of us have an eye on the long term too, so the second section of this chapter conducts an evidence-based examination of how to eat in a way that aids our personal sustainability. Here, you will learn which foods are best for staving off health issues such as weight gain, heart disease and diabetes. The final part of the chapter provides practical guidance on how to put all this theory into practice.

If you're imagining that this chapter is all about bran-based breakfast cereals, skinless chicken breasts and low-fat spreads, then you're in for a treat. As the research reveals, most conventional nutritional 'wisdom' is fundamentally flawed. Using up-to-date science (and a healthy dose of common sense), the chapter clears up dietary confusion and puts a slew of nutritional myths to bed. Read this chapter to learn why 'healthy eating' may actually be holding you back, and how to release yourself to a state of optimal energy and wellbeing, with ease.

Chapter 2: Fluid Thinking

Ensuring peak performance is not just about what we eat, but also what we drink. In this chapter, we explore the critical importance of hydration, and reveal the single best guide to whether your needs are being met here or not.

This chapter examines the health aspects of not just water, but also soft drinks, fruit juice, smoothies, coconut water, coffee and tea. The chapter ends with an assessment of alcohol's influence on wellbeing. Here, you will also discover three deceptively simple strategies that often lead to dramatic reductions in alcohol intake, but without the need for conscious restriction or feelings of deprivation.

Chapter 3: Movable Feast

As with advice regarding what to eat, recommendations regarding when and how often we should eat are prone to mixed messages. Traditionally, three square meals a day has been advocated, though in recent times there has been a vogue for 'intermittent fasting' – the practice of consuming very little on certain days, or going for extended periods of time without eating. In contrast, others recommend eating frequent, small meals as the best way to maintain energy and effectiveness.

This chapter examines the benefits and pitfalls of different eating patterns and provides guidance on how to ensure the optimal feeding strategy for *you*.

Chapter 4: Dream Ticket

For some, sleep can seem like 'unproductive time', and they will often relegate it in favour of work and other endeavours. Research shows, however, that not only does sleep prepare the body physiologically and psychologically for the next day, it promotes better health and even assists weight control.

This chapter explores how scrimping on sleep can cause our energy levels, performance and general health to suffer. It also offers a range of simple but highly effective strategies for ensuring the sort of deep, restful sleep that leaves us feeling properly revived and ready for action each morning.

Chapter 5: Light Relief

Most of us don't usually think of light as a lifestyle factor but, as this chapter reveals, it can play a vitally important role in how we feel and function. The chapter starts with an exploration of light's impact on mood and mental functioning, and the practical steps we can take to make full use of this natural commodity, particularly in the winter.

This chapter also reviews the value of sunlight regarding physical health and wellbeing, specifically through its ability to stimulate the production of vitamin D in the skin. We will see how this nutrient is linked with protection from a wide range of health issues and conditions including heart disease and several different forms of cancer. The chapter ends with advice about how to use 'safe tanning' and perhaps supplementation with vitamin D to optimize health and wellness in the long term.

Chapter 6: Fit for Business

We've all heard that exercise is good for us, but some can nonetheless struggle to find the time to 'fit it in'. This chapter looks at how we can meet our needs for physical activity in as practical and time-efficient a way as possible.

The chapter starts by exploring the benefits to be had from incorporating walking into our lives, and provides everyday guidance here. The importance of *resistance* exercise is also highlighted, and the chapter outlines a brief but effective routine that requires venturing no further than your home or hotel room.

For those who are already active and looking for something more advanced, this chapter also discusses 'high-intensity intermittent exercise' – a form of physical training that offers significant benefits for health and fitness, but with relatively small time investment.

Chapter 7: Sound Effects

Many people will know what it's like to have a favourite song boost their mood and put a spring in their step. This chapter explores the scientific basis for this phenomenon, as well as how something as simple and enjoyable as listening to music may improve our wellbeing and performance, both in and outside work.

This section also introduces a technology known as 'binaural beats' – the playing of specific frequencies of sound into the ears to induce desired states such as mental focus or relaxation.

Chapter 8: Breath of Life

Breathing is one of those bodily processes we tend to take for granted. This chapter reveals, though, that many of us can breathe quite inefficiently from time to time, and how this can impair our energy and mental functioning.

The chapter also provides practical guidance on breathing techniques that can calm the mind, optimize our physical and mental state, and promote general good health over time.

Chapter 9: Mind Control

Our success depends not just on balancing and optimizing our physiology, but also our *psychology*. Unfortunately, we can sometimes get caught in negative thought patterns that may block our mental processes, creativity and inspiration.

In this chapter, we explore some simple and effective tools for changing our thinking in ways that can very quickly boost our mood, brain functioning and productivity. Specifically, this chapter explores the research that shows that the key to mastering our mind can often be to focus on another organ entirely – the *heart*.

Chapter 10: Habit Forming

This book offers a range of highly effective strategies for boosting energy, productivity and sustainability. But many of us can sometimes resist things that we know are good for us, and may persist with things that we know are holding us back.

This final chapter show how *motivation* is the key to changing behaviour, and reveals a way of thinking that makes good habits stick (and bad habits easy to break) – *for good*.

The Appliance of Science

Throughout this book I refer to scientific research, and it makes sense to get clear on what we can (and can't) learn from different types of evidence from the start. Research relevant to human health comes in two main forms: so-called 'epidemiological' research and 'intervention' studies:

Epidemiological Studies

Epidemiological studies look at *relationships* between things, such as the drinking of red wine and the risk of heart disease. Such studies can tell us that two things are *associated* with each other, but not that one is necessarily *causing* the other. So, those studies you've perhaps heard about linking red wine drinking with a reduced risk of heart disease cannot be used to conclude that red wine is good for the heart (sorry about that!). It might be, for instance, that red wine drinkers eat more healthily or smoke less than imbibers of other forms of alcohol. It could be these or other factors, not the red wine *per se*, that account for the apparently superior heart health of red wine drinkers.

Factors that may queer the pitch in this way are referred to as 'confounding factors' or simply 'confounders'. In some studies, researchers attempt to take account of these factors when data is analysed. The problem is, though, this is a very inexact science, and in the end we still end up with results that cannot prove *causality*.

If epidemiological studies cannot be used to provide a definitive answer, why do them at all? Well, apart from keeping a lot of researchers in jobs, this sort of evidence is good for generating ideas (also known as 'hypotheses') that can be tested more definitively using what are termed 'intervention studies'.

Intervention Studies

Intervention studies involve exposing individuals to a specific intervention and comparing their outcomes to a 'control' group not exposed to this intervention. Examples include the testing of the effects of low-fat diets on weight loss and the impact of exercise on fitness.

Intervention studies are far less plentiful than epidemiological studies, mainly because they are much more labour-intensive and costly. However, the fact remains that they are generally much more illuminating than any number of epidemiological studies, and this is why I focus on them quite a lot throughout the book.

Single intervention studies can be insightful, but sometimes it helps to take a wider view by grouping several similar studies together in the form of what are known as 'meta-analyses'. For example, the results of studies that have tested the effects of exercise on weight loss can be pooled together to get a good overview of the effectiveness of this approach.

Meta-analyses are not perfect, but they are generally more useful than, say, selecting single studies in isolation, particularly if these are taken out of the context of wider evidence that is contradictory in nature.

↓

Science: What is it Good For?

One thing I think science is undoubtedly good for is to discern whether a 'fact' is genuinely 'evidence-based' or not. Quite often, as you'll discover as you read this book, many pieces of health advice we are given by doctors, dieticians, health bodies and government agencies (and we perhaps take for granted) simply do not stand up to scientific scrutiny. For example, you'll see how research reveals low-fat diets are ineffective for both weight loss and for staving off heart disease.

A Great Day at the Office does not primarily exist to expose what does not work, but reveal what *does*. Published scientific evidence can inform us here too, of course, but sometimes we need to look beyond this. The reality is many potentially useful strategies have not been subjected to systematic study. I've seen countless people, for instance, benefit hugely from choosing something other than a sandwich at lunch, or from going to bed a bit earlier than they habitually do. These approaches have not been the focus of properly conducted trials, but they have been tried and tested with countless individuals and been found to produce consistent and reliable results.

So, the information and advice in this book is based on the available evidence, but it's also informed by thousands of hours of consulting with real individuals in the real world. There is nothing quite like this wealth of experience, I think, for giving us perspective on what really works to help us be the best we can be, both in and out of the workplace.

Chapter 1

Energy to Burn

In the Introduction to this book, I briefly likened the body to a car. All cars require a few fundamentals to be taken care of to get us efficiently from A to B, one of which is to have fuel in the tank. But it has to be the *right* fuel: it's no good filling up a petrol-driven car with *diesel*. Yet, my experience tells me that a surprising number of us are unwittingly doing something akin to this, and are getting spluttering performance as a result.

In the first part of this chapter, we're going to explore the nutritional causes of symptoms such as fluctuating energy, the mid-afternoon slump and mental sluggishness, and how to correct these issues with ease. In the chapter's second part we are going to take a longer view, and examine the sort of diet that will best support our personal sustainability and stave off chronic health issues such as heart disease and type 2 diabetes. The final part of the chapter then gives constructive advice on how to convert nutritional theory into practice in your everyday life.

Nutrition is a big subject, and one in which competing theories and misinformation abound. For these reasons we're going to be referring to much scientific theory and literally dozens of research studies as the chapter unfolds. The size and complexity of this subject is reflected in the fact that this is the most sizeable chapter in the book. If you like to understand things properly and are keen to explore the science of optimal eating then there's plenty in this chapter for you. However, if you don't need the level of detail provided here then fret not, because within this chapter I'll be revealing a simple way of thinking about food that will allow you to make quick, accurate and future-proof decisions about the best foods to eat for optimal health and wellbeing (no flicking ahead, now).

We're going to start by exploring the physiology relevant to how the body converts food into our most valuable resource of all: *energy*.

PART 1: FROM FOOD INTO ENERGY

Almost all our energy needs are met through the activity of tiny capsule-shaped structures in our body's cells known as 'mitochondria'. Essentially, mitochondria take 'fuel' (from food) and convert it into energy. You can think of the mitochondria as tiny engines that drive the processes in the body – everything from our mental energy to the speed and strength of our muscles. Energy production in the mitochondria is dependent on two main factors:

1. How effectively the mitochondria are supplied with fuel

2. The appropriateness of the fuel supplied to the mitochondria

Much of this chapter is dedicated to optimizing these factors to get the best performance out of our body and brain.

There are essentially two fuels the mitochondria can use to create energy. One is *sugar*; the other is *fat*. Later on in the chapter we'll be exploring the role of fat (in all its forms) in the diet, but for now, let's focus on sugar.

There are different types of sugar in the diet, but the one that the mitochondria utilize to generate energy is known as 'glucose'. Some foods contain actual glucose, including certain fruits and sugary soft drinks. Glucose can also be derived from 'table sugar' ('sucrose'), which consists of a molecule of glucose joined to a molecule of another sugar known as 'fructose'.

Glucose   Sucrose

Another important (but sometimes under-recognized) source of glucose is *starch* (found in foods such as bread, potato, rice, pasta and breakfast cereals). Starch is, essentially, made up of a chain of glucose molecules.

Starch

From Starch into Sugar

Conventional nutritional wisdom tells us that starchy foods such as bread, potato, rice, pasta and breakfast cereals take time to be broken down, and therefore deliver a *slow* release of sugar into the bloodstream for sustained energy.

We are also usually warned that fat is an inferior source of energy as, supposedly, it 'burns more slowly' than sugar. Plus, the official line is that fat is *fattening*, and certain fats (particularly 'saturated' fat found in foods such as red meat, eggs and dairy products) can clog the arteries and lead to heart disease.

It is these essential 'facts' that have been the major drivers of the traditional dietary advice for us to eat a *low-fat, high-carbohydrate* diet, replete with foodstuffs such as wholemeal bread, wholegrain breakfast cereals, rice and pasta, supplemented with fruit and vegetables. This sort of diet, according to official sources, is nutritional nirvana.

The concepts used to support low-fat, high-carbohydrate diets may look utterly persuasive on the surface, but in this chapter you're going to see how eating this way can actually play havoc with your energy, concentration and sleep. There's also good evidence that 'healthy eating' may even jeopardize your ability to control your weight and keep yourself free from chronic conditions such as heart disease and diabetes. Key to understanding all this is an awareness of the importance of maintaining stable levels of sugar in the bloodstream.

A Question of Balance

Imagine you take conventional dietary wisdom to heart and base your diet on 'starchy carbs' such as bread, pasta and breakfast cereals. When you eat these foods the starch in them is broken down into glucose through the process of digestion, which is then absorbed into the bloodstream.

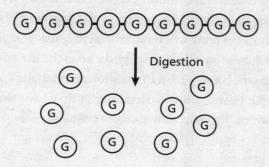

This means that whether we eat sugar, starch, or a combination of both, blood sugar levels rise. In healthy individuals, the body responds to this by secreting the hormone 'insulin' from the pancreas. One of the chief functions of insulin is to facilitate the uptake of glucose from the bloodstream into our cells where it can be 'burned' in the mitochondria to generate energy. It could be said, then, that blood sugar stability is key to ensuring sustained levels of energy. The figure below represents relatively stable blood sugar levels after eating over a few hours.

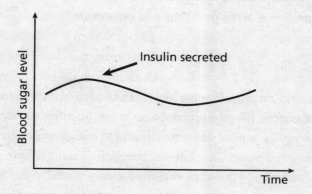

However, imagine for a moment we eat a food that releases substantial amounts of sugar quite quickly into the bloodstream. In response, the body will tend to secrete copious quantities of insulin. Gluts of insulin are not good news for the body in the long term (see below). Even in the short term, though, surges of insulin risk pushing blood sugar levels down to 'subnormal' levels (termed 'hypoglycaemia') some time later.

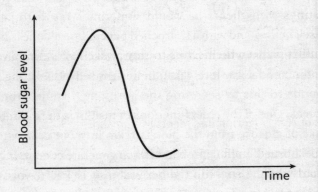

When sugar levels dip too low, our cells can end up seriously under-fuelled, compromising their ability to function optimally. Here are some of the problems that can ensue:

Fatigue and lethargy

Sugar tends to provide ready fuel for the body and if supply stalls, so can energy. Blood sugar imbalance can manifest as fluctuating energy during the day, with the mid to late afternoon being a common low point. The slump of energy that many people experience at around 3 or 4 p.m. is almost always rooted in this issue.

In the corporate arena, I find this one of the most frequent drains on productivity of all, and I estimate it affects about 60 per cent of people to a significant degree. If you have come to recognize that the mid to late afternoon is typically your least productive time of day, then there's a good chance you have some blood sugar balance issues going on.

Some people are so badly affected by this that they have to pinch themselves under the desk in meetings (or stand on their own toes in operating theatres) to stay awake and alert. One senior lawyer once told me he could be so sleepy in afternoon meetings with clients he would sometimes resort to jabbing himself in the hand with a sharpened pencil. If someone is having to inflict pain on themselves to stay awake in front of a valued client, it's usually a sign that something is seriously wrong.

Loss of concentration and mental sluggishness

The brain is only about 2 per cent of our weight, but it uses about a quarter of the sugar in the body at rest. In other words, the brain is one *sugar-dependent* organ. If it's not adequately fuelled, it tends to malfunction. Common ways this plays out include poor concentration, loss of focus, and a mind completely devoid of fresh ideas and inspiration.

Brain Drain

While facilitating a wellness programme for a group of partners in a financial services firm, one of the delegates recounted a story that aptly demonstrated the hazards of low blood sugar with regard to brain function. He had travelled to a regional office to give a presentation to a large group of colleagues in the late morning. When he got up to speak, though, 'gibberish' (in his own words) came out of his mouth. He composed himself, started again, but the result was the same.

He excused himself and recommended that everyone reconvene in ten minutes. During that time he ate some biscuits. Almost instantly, his mental powers were restored. It turns out he had eaten nothing since dinner the night before and, in all likelihood, had unwittingly allowed his blood sugar levels to sink too low. He remarked that it was a good job the meeting was internal, and that his brain freeze did not happen in front of a key client.

Mood issues

Proper fuelling of the brain is important for maintaining our mood too. For some people, low blood sugar can cause people to experience 'glass half empty' syndrome. I remember a banking executive who told me he always knew when his blood sugar level was on the slide as he would inexplicably start seeing the world through 'shit-tinted spectacles'. At least he had a sense of humour about it.

In others, low blood sugar can wind them up like a top. This is partly because it has the ability to activate the body's *stress response* and cause surges in hormones such as adrenaline and cortisol that can bring on feelings of anxiety or aggression. Low blood sugar also ramps up the production of a chemical known as 'glutamate' in the brain, which can increase our sense of agitation and irritability.

A common danger time for these issues is the end of the day, when someone may return home in a too-hungry state. The chemical imbalances induced here can cause the most insignificant things – be it some apparent untidiness or an ambiguous comment – to trigger a mini-meltdown. If you want to know the simple measure you can take to stop yourself making a right nuisance of yourself when you walk through the door (and perhaps save your relationship, too), read Chapter 3.

Food cravings

When blood sugar levels drop, it's common for this to induce cravings for foods that replenish sugar quickly into the bloodstream. A lot of people find themselves irresistibly drawn to the vending machine or some stray biscuits in the mid-afternoon. I once heard a delegate refer to this time as 'Twix o'clock'.

Some people imagine succumbing to such foodstuffs is down to a weak will, lack of self-control, or an inadequate personality. The reality is when someone is finding it difficult to resist something stacked with sugar, the underlying problem is almost always not psychological, but *physiological*.

Disturbed sleep

Low blood sugar can happen not just in the day, but at night too. Typically, blood sugar levels will fall at around three or four in the morning. Activation of the stress response and rushes of glutamate (see above) do nothing to aid restful sleep. Many individuals will be tripped into wakefulness, and may find it difficult to drop off again until about half an hour before the alarm goes off.

Once rudely awakened in this way, these poor unfortunates usually feel utterly dreadful. And the thought will normally occur to them as to why this level of zombie-like tiredness was not possible a few hours before.

Waking up feeling as if you've not really slept at all is obviously not the ideal way to start the day. Again, though, this feature of blood sugar imbalance is quite common, and it affects about half of my patients and clients on at least a semi-regular basis.

Sugar Highs

As we've learned, low blood sugar levels are best avoided for those of us seeking to optimize our energy, focus, sleep and eating habits. However, *raised* blood sugar can be a huge problem too. Spikes in blood sugar are known to provoke changes in the physiology and biochemistry of the body that predispose us to chronic (long-term) illness. Known effects include:

- Increased *inflammation* (a key underlying process in chronic disease including so-called 'cardiovascular diseases' such as heart disease and stroke)

- Increased *oxidative stress* (also known as 'free radical damage' – another potential driver of chronic health issues such as cardiovascular disease)

- Protein *glycation* (the binding of glucose to proteins in the body, thereby damaging them)

- Increased *coagulation* (essentially, making the blood 'stickier' – a risk factor for heart attacks and strokes)

- Raised levels of fats known as '*triglycerides*' in the bloodstream (a recognized risk factor for cardiovascular disease)

There is compelling evidence that eating foods that are disruptive to blood sugar levels actually *causes* heart disease.[1] One review found that such foodstuffs were associated with up to a doubling in risk.[2]

Another problem with elevated blood sugar levels relates to insulin: the higher blood sugar levels rise, the more insulin tends to be secreted. This poses others hazards for the body, particularly with regard to *weight control*.

Insulin: The Fat Controller

Do you remember how insulin stimulates the uptake of glucose into the cells? It does this for *fat* too. Not only does insulin encourage the uptake of fat into fat cells, it also *inhibits fat's release* from them. In fact, insulin is the body's chief 'fat storage' hormone, and taking steps to lower levels of this hormone is a good strategy for those seeking to attain and maintain a healthy weight.

Moreover, lowered insulin levels can help circumvent other problems. If, over many years we secrete relatively high levels of insulin, tissues and organs such as the muscles and brain can eventually become relatively *unresponsive* to insulin – a situation referred to as 'insulin resistance'. But if our muscles and brain are not responding properly to insulin, and are not taking up sugar efficiently, they can be *starved of fuel*. When this happens, physical and mental energies usually suffer, and hunger and food cravings can be triggered too.

With insulin not doing its job properly, blood sugar levels will tend to be on the high side, causing the body to secrete more insulin in an effort to keep sugar in check. Remember, though, insulin drives *fat storage* – so the more insulin we secrete, generally the harder it is to maintain a healthy weight.

Ultimately, the body may become so unresponsive to insulin that sugar levels remain elevated no matter how much insulin is secreted and a diagnosis of *type 2 diabetes* may be made. Gluts of sugar and surges of insulin may also eventually cause the cells in the pancreas that make insulin to 'burn out', eventually causing levels of this hormone to fall. Some researchers have suggested that inadequate levels of poorly functioning insulin (what some are calling 'type 3 diabetes') is a significant underlying cause of Alzheimer's disease.[3]

In Part 2 of this chapter we're going to be looking at other important nutritional factors that can impact on our long-term health and sustainability, including the different forms of fat in the diet. However, at this stage, what is clear is that if we want a long, healthy, energized and productive life, it pays to have decent control over blood sugar levels. So, what to do?

On Balance

There are two main considerations if we're looking to optimize blood sugar levels: *when* we eat, and *what* we eat.

The timing of eating can be important because irregular eating can lead to us consuming too little at some times and too much at others. Imagine skipping breakfast, having a snatched sandwich at lunch, and then getting so hungry by the evening that you proceed to eat about half your weight in food washed down with some wine or beer. Irrespective of what you eat, this sort of pattern of eating is far from ideal for blood sugar stability.

Some smoothing out of the eating pattern can be important for some people. This does not necessarily mean eating strictly by the clock or perpetually grazing through the day, but it does generally require eating regularly enough to be able to quell any drive for eating big meals. In Chapter 3 we'll be exploring eating patterns in more depth.

In this chapter, though, we're going to focus mainly on *what* to eat, and specifically the sort of diet that stabilizes blood sugar levels.

Key, here, is acknowledgement of the fact that different foods disrupt blood sugar levels to different degrees. The extent to which a food does this can be measured and is referred to as its 'glycaemic index' or 'GI'. Pure glucose (obviously, very disruptive indeed) is assigned a GI of 100, against which other foods can be compared. The higher a food's GI, the more it disrupts blood sugar (and insulin).

Earlier on, we touched on the fact that conventional wisdom tells us that starchy carbohydrates such as bread, potato, rice, pasta and breakfast cereals give a slow, sustained release of sugar into the bloodstream. Let's see if that stacks up.

The following table provides a list of a wide range of carbohydrate-based foods and their GI values.[4] Before looking at the table, just bear in mind that sucrose (table sugar) has a glycaemic index of 68.

Looking at the foods in the table and their corresponding GI values, one thing is clear: many starchy carbohydrates we're

Glycaemic indices of common carbohydrate foods

Bread

baguette ('French stick')	95
bagel – white	72
wheat bread – white	70
bread – wholemeal	71
rye bread – wholemeal	58
rye bread – pumpernickel	46
bread – spelt, wholemeal	63

Crackers

rye crispbread	64
cream cracker	65
water cracker	71
rice cakes	78
corn chips	63
potato crisps	54
popcorn	72

Pasta, rice and related foods

brown rice	55
basmati rice	58
rice – Arborio (risotto rice)	69
rice – white	64
pearl barley	25
pasta – corn	78
gnocchi	68
pasta – durum wheat	44
pasta – wholewheat	37
couscous	65

Sweet foods

digestive biscuits	59
croissant	67
crumpet	69
doughnut	76
muffin – bran	60
scone	92
shortbread	64
ice cream	61
Mars bar	65
muesli bar	65

Snickers bar	55
honey	55
sucrose (table sugar)	68

Beverages

apple juice – unsweetened	40
cranberry juice	56
orange juice	50
Gatorade	78
tomato juice	38
Coca-cola	53
Fanta	68
Lucozade	95

Breakfast cereals

All-Bran	42
Bran flakes	74
cornflakes	81
muesli	40–66
porridge – home-made	58
porridge – instant	66
Special K	54–84
Shredded wheat	75
Raisin bran	61

Fruit

apple	38
apple – dried	29
banana	52
mango	51
grapes	46
kiwi fruit	53
cherries	22
peach	42
pear	38
pineapple	59
plum	39
watermelon	72
figs – dried	61
apricots – dried	31
sultanas	60

raisins	64	**Vegetables**	
prunes	29	parsnips	97
strawberries	40	potato – baked	85
		potato – boiled	50
Legumes (beans, lentils, peas)		potato – new	57
baked beans	48	chips (French fries)	75
black-eyed beans	42	potato – mashed	74
butter beans	31	potato – instant mashed	85
chickpeas	28	potato – sweet	61
hummus	6	yam	37
kidney beans	28	carrots – raw	16
lentils – green	30	carrots – cooked	58
lentils – red	26	pumpkin	75
peas – dried then boiled	22	beetroot	64
peas – boiled	48		

Note: non-starchy vegetables are predominantly carbohydrate, but have very low GI values (often under 20). Examples include cabbage, kale, broccoli, cauliflower, lettuce, tomato, cucumber, bell peppers, aubergine and artichoke. Low-sugar fruits such as avocado and olives are relatively fat-rich, and also have low GIs.

encouraged to have our fill of turn out to be very disruptive to blood sugar levels. Several of these staples, notably cornflakes, porridge, wholemeal bread and baked potatoes, have GIs about the same or even higher than table sugar. Some are almost as disruptive as pure glucose. Other potentially problematic food-stuffs in this respect include beverages such as sugary soft drinks and fruit juices, and we'll be examining these in more depth in the next chapter.

Within the GI list, you will see that some fruits and vegetables, including beetroot, pineapple and watermelon, have high-ish GIs too. Does that mean that these foods are equivalent to foods with similar GIs such as sugary soft drinks and Mars bars?

Actually, while the GI is an important measure of the appropriateness of a food, another is its offering of nutrients such as vitamins and minerals (see below). Also, though, the relevance of the GI needs to be taken in the context of how much we eat of a food. The more we eat of a disruptive food the worse it is for us. Conversely, if we only eat a little of it, it's unlikely to matter. Not much harm can come from us eating a single Ferrero Rocher. If we eat a whole box, though, that's clearly more of a problem.

Let's see how this concept plays out in the real world. The GI table tells us that basmati rice and kiwi fruits have similar glycaemic indices (in the 50s). But are they likely to be similarly disruptive to blood sugar in real life?

Answer this: Have you ever come home very hungry, needed something quite quick to eat, and then polished off a meal with a big serving of rice – say a chilli or curry? If you have, then this meal will have contained quite a lot of a food that is generally disruptive to blood sugar levels. In nutritional parlance, this would be a meal of significant 'glycaemic load'.

On the other hand, however hungry you have been, have you ever come home and polished off a big bowl of kiwi fruits? When people are hungry, kiwi fruits are not usually their go-to food. And when people do eat them, they may eat one or two (if they're really going for it), but the fact remains that there is not much volume here, and the end result is unlikely to be particularly disruptive to blood sugar levels.

Another example is the potato. This is a generally disruptive food, but in its favour is the fact that potatoes usually make only an accompaniment to a meal, rather than the basis for it. So, some new potatoes alongside a piece of fish and French beans, or a few roasties accompanying a nice roast and some veggies, are not really an issue. However, meals that are based on generally disruptive starches that have considerable glycaemic load (such as most breakfast cereals, sandwiches, bowls of pasta and dinners containing mounds of rice) are generally best avoided.

Are Grains the Staff of Life?

Not everyone agrees with these established facts about grains and their impact on the body's blood sugar and insulin levels, though, and will remind us of their supposed 'essential' nature for energy and life itself. Is this actually true?

Here's an official list of the established *essential* elements in the human diet:[5]

- Water

- Energy

- Certain amino acids (termed 'essential amino acids')

- Certain fats (termed 'essential fats')

- Vitamins (such as vitamins A, C, D, E, K and B vitamins)

- Minerals (such as calcium, magnesium and iron)

- Trace minerals (such as zinc, iodine, selenium and chromium)

- Electrolytes (sodium, potassium and chloride)

However much we scrutinize this list, we will find no mention here of sugar, starch or carbohydrate. Part of the reason for this is that the mitochondria can burn alternative fuels (such as fat) for energy (more about this later).

It is true, though, that some of the body's cells are totally dependent on glucose as they can burn no other type of fuel. However, glucose can be made from other things (notably, certain amino acids – the building blocks of protein) in the liver. It's believed that the body can produce about 200g of glucose a day in this way – considerably more than we actually need. The fact is, technically speaking, the absolute requirement for glucose in the diet (from either sugar or starch) is *none at all*.

This does not necessarily mean that we should eat no carbohydrate, and it can play a role in the diet. For example, people engaged in certain forms of exercise and sports may benefit from carbohydrate (see Chapter 6 for more about this). However, basic physiology reveals that the idea that starchy carbohydrates are 'essential' for energy is simply wrong.

Some will still maintain, nonetheless, that grains are good for us because they provide 'vital nutrients'. Again, does the evidence support this?

One way to assess the nutritional value of a food is to compare its nutrient content with the calories it contains. The idea here is that the best foods will be those of higher nutrient content but lower in the calorie department. This has led researchers to develop a concept known as the 'nutrient density score'.[6]

Let's compare the nutrient density scores of grains with those of other carbohydrate-based foods: fruits and vegetables. This figure represents the scores for fruits and veg. The healthiest foods are those that are positioned low (low energy density) and to the right (high nutrient levels) on the graph. Looking at the table we can see that fresh fruits and vegetables, with the exception of the potato, rate generally very well indeed.

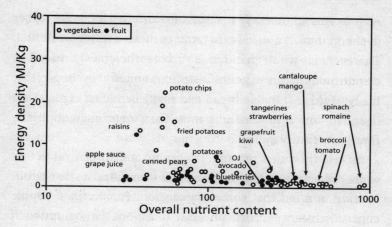

Relationship between energy density and the
nutrient score for fruits and vegetables

Now, let's take a look at the nutrient density scores for grains.

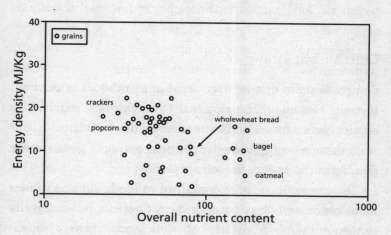

Relationship between energy density and the
nutrient score for grains

As you can see, generally speaking, grain-based foods are higher in energy density and lower in terms of their nutritional offering. This includes wholegrain foods such as wholemeal bread. The un-nutritious nature of grains is strongly hinted at by the fact that many of them (notably bread and many breakfast cereals) are 'fortified' with additional nutrients. If they were inherently nutritious, why fortify them?

In reality, grains provide us with no nutritional value that cannot be acquired more healthily elsewhere. And it's also worth bearing in mind that some grains, notably unrefined wheat, contain substances called 'phytates' that block the absorption of nutrients such as calcium, magnesium and iron. Phytates compromise not only the nutritional value of grain, but also foods we eat with them.

The bottom line is that while many starchy carbohydrates are technically food, many are perhaps better described as *fodder*.

Clutching at Straws

Some will claim that we need some of this fodder in our diet, though, if for no other reason than to provide fibre required for efficient bowel function. This is another common claim we hear from those who argue for the essential nature of grains in the diet. Again, what does the science show?

The main sort of fibre contained in foods such as wholemeal bread and high-bran breakfast cereals is technically termed 'insoluble' fibre (also colloquially referred to as 'roughage'). Insoluble fibre is said to be important to give the bowel 'something to grab onto' and ensure waste moves nicely along our large bowel to be expelled with ease. But is insoluble fibre really essential for bowel regularity and health? There is, in fact, some evidence that suggests it can do more harm than good.

In one study, more than sixty adults with persistent constipation for which no medical cause could be found were asked to take a quite unconventional dietary approach: instead of being asked to eat more fibre, they were asked to eat *none at all*.[7] Study participants were instructed to eliminate breakfast cereals, wholemeal bread and brown rice (as well as fruit and vegetables) from their diets for two weeks. They were asked to continue eating as little fibre as possible if this helped their symptoms.

Six months after the start of the study, the majority of patients had persisted with the 'no-fibre' diet and had seen their bowel frequency increase from an average of once every few days to once every day. In contrast, in the minority of individuals who remained on a higher fibre diet, bowel function had not improved at all.

In other words, the results showed that the more fibre there was in the diet, the more constipated individuals tended to be. Here's how the study authors attempted to explain their findings:

> The role of dietary fiber in constipation is analogous to cars in traffic congestion. The only way to alleviate slow traffic would be to decrease the number of cars and to evacuate the remaining cars quickly. Should we add more cars, the congestion would only be worsened. Similarly, in patients with idiopathic constipation [constipation of no known cause] and a colon packed with feces, reduction in dietary fiber would reduce fecal bulk and volume and make evacuation of the smaller and thinner feces easier. Adding dietary fiber would only add to the bulk and volume and thus make evacuation even more difficult.

It's difficult to argue with the logic here, nor the results achieved in this study. And the results mirror my own experience in practice, where I find stripping out grains from the diet (and leaving fruits and vegetables in) usually improves constipation and other symptoms such as bloating and abdominal discomfort. Scientific research supports this approach in management of 'irritable bowel syndrome'.[8]

'Roughage' does not seem to be essential for regular bowel function, but some claim it helps prevent colon cancer. The truth is, though, the best evidence does not support this idea at all.[9–11] In fact, in a review of the evidence relating to fibre and bowel health, the authors concluded that: 'there does not seem to be much use for fiber in colorectal diseases.'[12]

The evidence shows that we simply do not need grains for energy, 'vital nutrients' or fibre. But, in addition to their non-essential nature, there are reasons for positively avoiding them. We know, for example, just how disruptive they can be to blood sugar and insulin levels, and how they can impair the nutritional value of food because of the phytates they contain. But grains pose others additional hazards, too, specifically through a mechanism known as 'food sensitivity'.

Sensitive Issues

It's well-recognized that specific foods can sometimes trigger unwanted reactions in the body. In their most extreme form, these can take the form of allergic reactions known as 'anaphylactic shock' that can be life-threatening. However, other types of reactions to food can occur too that, although not as obvious, can nonetheless have debilitating effects on wellness and health. While any foodstuff may do this, grains are a common cause of problems in practice.

Grains contain proteins known as 'lectins' that are difficult to break down in the gut and can trigger problems with food sensitivity. This situation is made worse by the fact that grains also contain what are known as 'protease inhibitors' that impair proper breakdown of proteins, including lectins. The end result is that lectins can remain relatively intact and can then be absorbed into and even through the gut wall, subsequently to be recognized as something 'foreign'.

This can cause the body to react in ways that may manifest themselves in the form of digestive strife (including pain and bloating), or problems beyond the gut such as headaches, asthma and eczema.

Of the grains, the one that I find particularly troublesome in this respect is *wheat* (found in, among other foodstuffs, most forms of bread, breakfast cereals, biscuits, cakes, pastries, pasta and pizza). Wheat is particularly rich in *gluten* – a protein that can trigger adverse reactions in the body. Some individuals have extreme sensitivity to gluten in the form of what is known as 'coeliac disease'. However, there is good evidence that it is possible to be sensitive to gluten even if tests for coeliac disease have proven negative.[13,14]

In my experience, sensitivity to wheat and/or gluten is quite common, and frequently manifests itself as *fatigue*. This, in addition to a tendency to disrupt blood sugar levels, is another reason why eating something bread-based at lunch might lead to someone feeling tired or possibly 'knocked out' in the afternoon. If you ever find yourself wondering why you are struggling to get any real work done at this time, it might have something to do with that sandwich or foot-long baguette you ate at lunch. I once got chatting to a nutritionist at an obesity conference I was speaking at, and the subject strayed into the problems that can ensue for working people who eat something bread-based for lunch. 'Death on the high street' she called it.

To summarize, grains:

1. Are generally disruptive to blood sugar levels in a way that predisposes to fatigue, mood problems, waking in the night, hunger and sweet cravings

2. Tend to induce surges of sugar and insulin that predispose to issues such as weight gain, type 2 diabetes and heart disease in the long term

3. Are generally un-nutritious

4. Don't seem to have an important role in maintaining bowel health and regularity

5. Contain phytates that impair the absorption of key nutrients

6. Can be rich in lectins and gluten that may provoke a range of symptoms including digestive discomfort, bloating and fatigue

With all this in mind, does it really make sense for these foods to form the cornerstone of our diets, as governments and health professionals usually advise?

Does all this bad news mean we should eat no grain at all? Not necessarily. Some individuals do seem to tolerate grain products reasonably well, in my experience. But, overwhelmingly, I find that when individuals eat less of these foods (or none at all), they are almost always rewarded with benefits in terms of changes such as weight loss, improved disease markers (see below) and, crucially, a sense of heightened vitality.

Beans and Lentils

Beans and lentils (collectively referred to as 'pulses' or 'legumes') represent potential alternatives to grain at certain meals. Like grains, though, they are relatively rich in lectins and enzyme inhibitors that impair the digestion of food.[15]

On the plus side, there is evidence that these substances can be reasonably well deactivated through thorough soaking and cooking prior to eating. Also, another plus is that legumes are usually eaten in a 'whole' form, in stark contrast to the refined, nutrient-stripped forms of grain that are commonplace in the diet. Generally speaking, legumes are less disruptive to blood sugar and insulin levels than grains, too.

I'm not a particularly enthusiastic advocate of legumes on account on their tendency to cause digestive symptoms (such as bloating and wind), but I do believe they can be included in moderation in the diet as a potential substitute for grains and as an ingredient in, say, soups and stews.

What to Eat?

A diet that does not feature grains leaves fruit and vegetables as our main sources of carbohydrate. You may actually quite like spinach and broccoli and the odd piece of fruit, but the thought of subsisting on these sorts of foods for long periods is unlikely to appeal much.

Don't lose heart yet, though, as there are plenty of foods that we have not even touched on yet, because they contain little sugar or starch, and therefore cannot disrupt blood sugar levels to any significant degree. These foods, which are primarily composed of protein and/or fat, include *meat*, *fish*, *eggs*, *nuts* and *seeds*. So, if we were thinking of eating a diet with the express purpose of stabilizing blood sugar levels and keeping insulin levels in check too, then these foods, accompanied by some vegetables and perhaps some fruit, will fit the bill.

The final part of this chapter provides instruction on what this sort of diet looks like in terms of easily sourced and practical meals and snacks. However, it may have occurred to you that foods such as red meat and eggs may be fine from a blood sugar balance perspective, but will only lead us down a ruinous path to heart disease and premature death. In Part 2 of this chapter, we're going to explore this idea, as well as how we might eat to optimize our health and wellbeing in the long term.

PART 2: EATING TO LIVE

In this second part of the chapter, we're going to use science and published research to determine the best foods for sustaining ourselves long into the future. Just for a moment, though, let's step away from the science and introduce some old-fashioned *common sense*. At the beginning of this chapter, I promised you I would reveal a way of thinking about food that allows us to make quick, accurate and future-proof decisions about the best foods to eat. So what is it?

What's the Big Idea?

What should be the best diet for us humans? The answer, theoretically at least, is one based on the foods we've been eating the longest during our time on this planet. These are the foods we *evolved* to eat, after all, and are therefore those that we're the best adapted to. It's these foods, evolutionary biology dictates, that will likely suit our innate physiology and biochemistry the best, as well as our nutritional needs. Relative nutritional newcomers, on the other hand, are more likely to create a 'mismatch' with the natural order within us, and therefore compromise our wellbeing and health over time.

Evolutionists generally agree that our first truly human ancestors emerged about two and a half million years ago in Africa. From there, our earliest forefathers are believed to have made their way into colder regions lacking much in the way of edible vegetation, making meat-eating a necessity for survival. Direct evidence for meat-eating comes from patterns of wear and tear in the teeth of our early ancestors,[16] as well as the discovery of stone tools and bones scored by cut marks which indicate that butchering of meat went on some two million years ago.[17]

Things changed when our ancestors began to settle in communities and cultivate grain crops such as wheat and corn. But *when* did this happen? The palaeolithic record tells us that agriculture began only 10,000 years ago. That sounds like a long time ago, but is it *really* in the context of the whole of human evolution?

One way to get a good overview of the timing of the addition of grains to the human diet is to imagine our evolution spread out over the course of a calendar year, with the first origins of human life starting on 1 January, stretching to the present day at midnight on 31 December. According to this scale, we were exclusive hunter-gatherers from 1 January until about midnight on 30 December. It was only on the last day of the year that we added grains to our diet.

Genetic change is generally a very slow process, and our genes have altered only a fraction over the last 10,000 years. In this context, one could rationalize that perhaps, theoretically at least, grains do not represent ideal foods for human consumption. But it's not just a theory, because we've seen how grains are often highly disruptive to the body's chemistry, and can contain substances such as phytates, lectins and gluten that pose other hazards for our health.

Actually, we have evidence from the very dawn of civilization that grains were not the best way to go from a nutritional perspective. For example, the addition of these foods into the diet was accompanied by a significant deterioration in our dental health[18] and led to a sudden drop in height of some 4–6 inches.[19]

What On Earth Did We Eat?

We cannot know for sure what our oldest ancestors ate prior to the invention of agriculture, and this no doubt would also have varied quite a bit according to geography: individuals from colder climes would generally have had to rely more on hunted and fished foods than those living in warmer parts of the world where edible fruits and vegetables were more abundant.

One way to get a more precise picture of our ancestral diet is by looking at the diets of traditional, modern-day hunter-gatherers. When this has been done, it turns out that the percentage of calories coming from hunted and fished foods ranges from about 50 per cent in, say, areas of tropical grassland, to about 90 per cent in the cold and relatively barren tundra.[20] Also, in this research of over 200 hunter-gatherer populations, not one was found to be vegetarian.

It seems that flesh foods, including red meat, are a fundamental part of the human diet. Yet we are usually warned off red meat, as well as another 'primal' animal food – *eggs*. The case against these foods is based on the fact that they are rich in cholesterol and so-called 'saturated fat', which are said to 'clog the arteries'. Saturated fat, along with other fats, is also said to be inherently *fattening*.

While red meat and eggs have been some of the most vilified foods of all, wouldn't evolutionary theory suggest that there is little to be concerned about here? Either this concept holds true, or these foods are genuinely unhealthy: it can't be both. So, which is it?

As we did with carbohydrate, let's assess the impact of dietary fats and cholesterol on health using science and published research.

Is Fat Fattening?

Conventional wisdom tells us that weight gain follows when we consume more calories than the ones we metabolize. A gram of fat contains about twice as many calories as either carbohydrate or protein. So, logic dictates that the more fat we eat, the more likely we are to consume calories that are surplus to our requirements, which then end up being stored as fat in our bodies. Another thing that adds to dietary fat's fattening reputation is its name (it is called *fat*, after all).

These facts do, on the face of it, seem to incriminate dietary fat as something inherently fattening, and appear to justify a somewhat joyless life replete with low-fat foods and an absence of butter and bacon.

However, the propensity for fat to be stored in the body is not purely determined by the balance of calories going into and out of the body, but also by the impact foods have on *hormones* that regulate weight. A key player here, as we learned earlier, is insulin. Insulin is secreted readily in response to glucose (from sugar and starch in the diet), but dietary fat has minimal, if any, insulin-inducing effects. In theory at least, this means that fat has limited fattening potential.

The supposedly fattening effects of fat were comprehensively assessed in an extensive review of the evidence conducted by researchers from the Harvard School of Public Health in the US.[21] After evaluating a mass of epidemiological studies, the authors concluded that: 'diets rich in fat do not appear to be an important cause of body fatness.' This epidemiological evidence fails to support the idea that fat is fattening, but the acid test here comes from intervention studies in which low-fat diets are tested for their effectiveness for weight loss.

The most comprehensive review on the subject found that low-fat diets led to small weight losses over time, and after eighteen months individuals were, on average, the same weight as when they started out.[22] This review was subsequently withdrawn some years later, but only because there were no plans to update it. Since its publication, no other good new evidence supporting the effectiveness of low-fat diets for weight loss has surfaced. The review cited earlier [21] also assessed the evidence from intervention studies, where again low-fat diets were found to be ineffective, leading the authors to conclude that: 'lowering fat in the diet will not be a solution for overweight and obesity.'

There's perhaps something counterintuitive about the fact that eating fat is not fattening, and that eating less fat does not lead to us shedding bodily fat of our own. However, all becomes much clearer when we consider that fat has little or no effect on the secretion of the chief fat storage hormone: insulin. For a complete discussion of the science of weight control and how to achieve success here without semi-starvation or unsustainable amounts of exercise, see my book *Escape the Diet Trap*.

A key point I make in this book is that for any dietary approach to be successful, it needs to be *sustainable*. This essentially means people need to enjoy eating it and not have to endure undue hunger. Most individuals will simply not tolerate being hungry for extended periods of time (hunger also makes life harder in myriad other ways that are explored in Chapter 3).

So, what should we eat to keep the appetite nicely in check and make healthy eating *easy*?

Appetite for Change

Theoretically, a diet lower in sugar and starchy carbohydrate might help control our appetite because of its ability to guard against blood sugar lows that can cause hunger and food cravings. Also, lower-carb diets tend to be richer in protein which, calorie for calorie, has been found to be more satiating than either carbohydrate or fat.[23-25]

Another proposed mechanism for the ability of relatively low-carbohydrate diets to quell appetite concerns their impact on insulin. Low-carb diets help to lower insulin levels that facilitates fat loss. When fat is lost, where does it go, though? The answer is that it makes its way into the bloodstream, via which it can be transported to our tissues, including the muscles. Here, it can be taken up into the muscle cells and be metabolized for energy.

In this way, then, the body is using stored fat as 'food' (that is what it's there for, after all). The ability to utilize stored fat efficiently may reduce hunger because the body isn't actually 'starving'. Like a hibernating bear, the body is now living happily off its stored fat, just as it's designed to do. This state, though, is nigh impossible to achieve with a standard 'carb-fuelled' diet, but is facilitated by one that lowers insulin levels.

Satisfaction Guaranteed

The ability of protein-rich, fat-rich, lower-carbohydrate diets to sate the appetite was well demonstrated in a study of obese men.[26] At the beginning of the study, men ate a low-fat, high-carbohydrate diet designed to maintain a stable weight (about 3,000 calories a day on average).

Then, on separate occasions, the volunteers ate two different diets, each for a period of a month. Both diets were protein-rich (30 per cent of calories) but differed in terms of the amount of carbohydrate and fat they contained. In one of the diets, 35 per cent of calories were contributed by carbohydrate (moderate carbohydrate and moderate fat) while in the other just 4 per cent of calories came from carbohydrate (low carbohydrate and high fat).

The test diets were 'ad libitum' in nature, which means that the men were allowed to eat as much of them as they liked.

One of the most notable things about this study was that when men switched to either of the protein-rich test diets, they naturally ate less than the amount of food calculated to maintain a stable weight. Actually, they ate about 40 per cent fewer calories, despite having no restriction placed on the amount they were allowed to eat. This finding supports the idea that relatively protein-rich diets have generally superior appetite-sating properties.

↓

However, there were differences noted *between* the two test diets as well. On the low-carbohydrate, higher-fat diet, hunger levels were lower compared to a medium-carbohydrate, lower-fat diet, and about 150 fewer calories were consumed on average, too.

What this study shows is that emphasizing protein in the diet can lead to a spontaneous reduction in food intake, and this effect is even more potent when the diet is low in carbohydrate and rich in fat.

Other research has assessed the appetite-quelling effects of diets based on natural, unprocessed foods. For example, in one study, men were asked to eat either a diet based on 'primal' foods or a 'Mediterranean' diet for a period of twelve weeks.[27] The primal diet emphasized meat, fish, fruit, vegetables, eggs and nuts. The Mediterranean diet was based on wholegrains, low-fat dairy products, vegetables, fruit, fish, vegetable oils and margarine. Both diets were *ad libitum*.

Those eating the Mediterranean diet ate an average of over 1,800 calories per day to satisfy themselves properly. On the other hand, the 'primal eaters' were satisfied with significantly less (under 1,400 calories a day). This is evidence that a diet based on natural, unprocessed, nutritious foods really does have the capacity to satisfy and promote weight loss without hunger.

The fundamental ability of lower-carb diets to quell the appetite naturally and allow individuals to eat less without hunger makes them generally effective for the purposes of weight loss.

Nevertheless, conventional advice is for us to avoid eating in this way, lest it jeopardizes our health. In particular, this sort of diet is said to load us up with 'artery-clogging saturated fat'. The idea that saturated fat is bad for us is generally accepted as fact. But where did this idea come from, and is it actually based on sound evidence?

The Heart of the Matter

The concept that saturated fat causes heart disease first gained traction back in the 1970s on the publication of a seminal study that purported to show a clear association between the amount of saturated fat consumed in seven countries, and the risk of heart disease in those countries.[28] The findings of this study are summarized in the figure below.

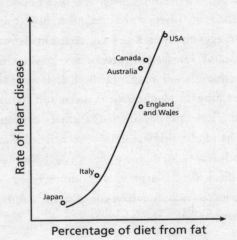

This study has been cited extensively since its publication as convincing evidence that eating saturated fat causes heart disease, and is widely recognized as a major driver of the fear of saturated fat that persists to this day. Yet, while it represented quite a turning point in our beliefs about saturated fat, one of this study's major weaknesses is that it is epidemiological in nature, which means it can only tell us about the *relationship* between saturated fat and heart disease, and not that saturated fat *causes* heart disease.

Differences in heart disease may, possibly, have been due to differences in so-called 'confounding' factors (such as smoking or levels of activity) that tend to differ a lot between countries. Also, the study drew on very limited data (from just seven countries). What happens when we take a wider view?

Data from other countries available at the time has been added into the graph below.

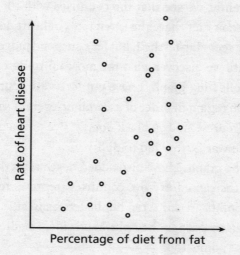

As you can see, the clear relationship that existed before has now disappeared. The original use of data was selective (and misleading), and we can be similarly selective, too, if we wish. How about if we choose the points on the following page instead?

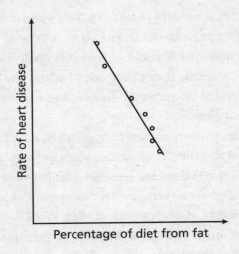

Now, apparently, we see that the countries with the most saturated fat in their diets have the *lowest* rates of heart disease.

This may seem far-fetched, but let's suspend judgement for a moment until we discover what the most up-to-date data turns up. In the following graph, I have put forty-five countries from the European region in order of ascending levels of saturated fat in the diet (represented as black dots).[29] I've put in a trend line too (going upwards from left to right).

Within the graph, I have also added death rates due to heart disease for the same forty-five countries (represented by white dots). The points are scattered on the left-hand side, but notice how they cluster *down* to the right-hand side. I've drawn a trend line for these points too.

Taking as wide a view as possible, this graph shows that as saturated fat intake *rises*, deaths from heart disease *fall*.

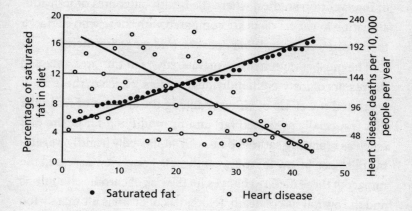

- Saturated fat   ○ Heart disease

Much as this evidence supports the evolutionary theory of nutrition beautifully, it is still epidemiological in nature, and can therefore only tell us about the relationship between saturated fat and heart disease (and not whether or not saturated fat causes heart disease).

That said, the facts are:

- It was epidemiological evidence that was originally used to incriminate saturated fat back in the 1970s

- The original data was very selective in nature

- More recent and complete data show the polar opposite finding: that higher intakes of saturated fat are associated with lower risk of heart disease

For what it's worth, all recent reviews of the epidemiological evidence have simply failed to find an association between saturated fat intake and risk of heart disease.[1,30,31] All this weight of epidemiological research, however, will never trump the results of intervention studies, where the health outcomes of individuals eating lower-fat diets are compared with those who eat fat to their heart's content. What does the evidence show here?

The most comprehensive meta-analysis in this area amassed the results of forty-eight individual studies.[32] Each of these studies tested the effect of either reducing the amount of fat in the diet (especially saturated fat) and/or modifying fat in the diet (such as replacing saturated fat with supposedly healthy 'vegetable oils' (see below for more on these). The review assessed the impact of these dietary changes on the risk of chronic conditions and the overall risk of death. (Note: risk of death is ultimately 100 per cent for all of us, of course, but in these studies risk of death is assessed over a finite period of time. This allows researchers to compare the numbers of deaths in different groups over this set time period.)

This biggest and best review of the evidence revealed that when individuals eat less saturated fat and/or replace it with 'healthier' fats, there is:

- No reduction in risk of heart attack

- No reduction in risk of stroke

- No reduction in risk of diabetes

- No reduction in risk of cancer

- No reduction in risk of death from cardiovascular disease (e.g. death from heart attack or stroke)

- No reduction in overall risk of death

In other words, no benefits are found at all. If eating less saturated fat or replacing it with supposedly healthier fats does not improve health or extend life, one might ask what's the point of eating this way? The point is: there is no point.

Bearing in mind just how often and vociferously we've been told that saturated fat gums up our arteries, this notion may come as a shock. Yet it is utterly in keeping with the primal principle: saturated fat is a component in red meat and has been part of the human diet for as long as we have been, well, human.

The Question of Cholesterol

Before we leave the subject of saturated fat, there's just one more attribute of this foodstuff that demands our attention: the idea that it raises blood cholesterol levels. The thinking here is that higher cholesterol levels cause heart disease, so if saturated fat raises cholesterol, it must cause heart disease.

Actually, the bulk of the evidence does not find a strong relationship between saturated fat levels in the diet and cholesterol levels in the bloodstream at all. One recent review of the literature concluded that: 'The influence of dietary fats on serum cholesterol has been overstated.'[33]

And even if eating saturated fat does raise cholesterol levels, it's irrelevant anyway. This is because the impact anything (e.g. a food or drug) has on cholesterol levels is not the important thing – it's the impact it has on *health* that really matters. With regard to this, here are the facts:

- Eating more saturated fat is not linked with an increased risk of heart disease (some evidence suggests that it's quite the reverse, actually)

- Eating less saturated fat and/or replacing it with 'healthier' fats has not been found to have benefits for health

Any data that exists regarding the impact of saturated fat and cholesterol levels is now completely redundant.

These facts, rooted in research and not rhetoric, will not stop food companies marketing cholesterol-reducing foods with the promise that they are good for the heart (see section 'Spreading the Risk' below). The idea that eating in a way that reduces cholesterol will cause our heart disease risk to come tumbling down is actually based on studies in which cholesterol-modifying medications have been found to reduce the risk of heart disease. However that's quite a leap of faith, because the mechanisms of a drug's action are, generally, entirely different to those induced by dietary change, and the benefits may not transfer at all.

Also, while cholesterol reduction with certain medications has been found to reduce the risk of cardiovascular disease, a more important measure of benefit is their impact on *overall risk of death*. That's because, while a medication may reduce the risk of one condition, it may increase the risk of others (low cholesterol is associated with an increased risk of cancer, for instance) and possibly have side effects that pose hazards for health. So, just how effective are cholesterol-reducing agents at saving lives?

When the Drugs Don't Work

The most commonly prescribed cholesterol-lowering drugs are known as 'statins', and these have been shown to reduce the risk of death in individuals who have had a previous heart attack or stroke (and who are therefore at relatively high risk of future problems). However, statins do not appear to save the lives of individuals without this sort of history and who are, essentially, healthy.[34] These people, by the way, represent the great majority of people prescribed these drugs.

Also, many other cholesterol-modifying treatments have not been found to reduce the risk of death at all, even in individuals with a prior history of heart disease.[35] Failures here include classes of drugs known as 'fibrates' and 'resins', as well as the drug 'torcetrapib'. This last medication had to be withdrawn because it was actually found to *increase* the risk of death. A similar drug ('dalcetrapib') was also removed from the marketplace when it was found to be ineffective.

We also have a rather bizarre situation in which drugs can be licensed because of their ability to 'improve' cholesterol, despite the fact that they have never been shown to benefit any aspect of health. An example here is the drug 'ezetimibe', which is widely prescribed by doctors, but has never been shown to prevent a single heart attack or save a single life.

A look at the wider body of evidence reveals there is considerable reason to question the notion that taking medication to improve cholesterol levels has broad benefits for health.

It seems that statins are the standout winners in terms of benefits, but just how effective are they really? One way to assess the effectiveness of a drug is to calculate what is known as the 'number needed to treat'. For example, we might ask how many people need to be treated with statins over a defined period of time to prevent one of them from having an event such as a heart attack.

Here are some stats from studies conducted on individuals without a prior history of cardiovascular disease.[36] If such individuals were to be treated with a statin drug for five years:

- 1 in 60 would avoid a heart attack (meaning that only 1 in every 300 people treated is spared a heart attack each year)

- 1 in 288 would avoid a stroke (1 in 1,440 people each year)

The evidence also shows that no one will have their life saved during five years of treatment and 98 per cent of people will derive no benefit whatsoever.

The fact is, the great majority of people taking statins will just not benefit, but up to 20 per cent will suffer from one or more of the recognized side effects of statins such as muscle pain, fatigue, mental confusion, liver damage, kidney damage and diabetes.

The fact that statins stand to do more harm than good for many may seem like heresy, but it's a fact that has been recognized by some in conventional medical circles. For example, the editors of the *Archives of Internal Medicine* concluded that the use of statins in people without known heart disease has: 'known adverse effects despite the absence of data for patient benefit'.[37] In a subsequent piece,[38] the editors of the journal concluded that: 'For a medicine to be recommended to healthy patients for a lifetime of use, there should be robust evidence that this regime will reduce suffering or extend life, and evidence that the benefit outweighs adverse effects. Until there is such data for statins for [people with no history of cardiovascular disease], we will continue to classify it as an intervention without known benefit, but with definite risks.'

Statins might be the right option for some people, particularly those with a prior history of heart attack or stroke. But it's clear from the evidence that, for many, the chances of benefit are very slim indeed, and there is considerable risk of harm.

The Essential Nature of Cholesterol

Many people imagine that the primary source of cholesterol in the bloodstream is foodstuffs such as butter, eggs, meat and seafood. Actually, most of the cholesterol in the bloodstream is not derived from the diet, but is manufactured in the liver. One wonders why the body would do that. Is it somehow intent on committing some form of slow suicide?

While we may have been given the impression that cholesterol's role in the body is simply to clog up our arteries, this substance is actually an essential body constituent. For instance, it is a basic building block in the membranes of all the body's cells, while also being an integral substance within the brain. Cholesterol is essential for the production of several hormones in the body including cortisol (our major stress hormone) and testosterone. In addition, cholesterol is the fundamental component of vitamin D, a critically important health-boosting substance (see Chapter 5). Bearing all this in mind, does it really make sense to be attempting to drive cholesterol to ever lower levels?

Spreading the Risk?

In recent years, health claims have been made for margarines that have the capacity to reduce cholesterol. These margarines contain substances known as 'stanols' and 'sterols' derived from vegetable oils and wood pulp that block the absorption of cholesterol from the gut, and produce modest reductions in blood cholesterol levels.

As we've learned, cholesterol reduction is, in and of itself, of dubious value at best. But even if cholesterol reduction

↓

↓

had been proven to be beneficial to health, does this assure that something that reduces cholesterol is automatically good for us? Put another way: if arsenic and cyanide were effective cholesterol-reducing agents, would it make sense for us to drink these each day?

The fact is, stanols and sterols have never been demonstrated to benefit actual health in terms of protection from heart disease or stroke or anything else. Worse, there is genuine evidence that sterols can have adverse effects here. This was the subject of a comprehensive review published in the *European Heart Journal*.[39] The review cites several studies in which higher levels of sterols in the body (sterols can be absorbed from food) were found to be associated with an *increased* risk of cardiovascular disease.

Perhaps most worrying, though, is the evidence showing that sterols have the potential to damage living cells. In one study, exposing rat heart cells to sterols reduced their metabolic activity and growth.[40] The review also refers to other evidence in which sterols were found to damage and even kill the cells that line the inside of our blood vessels.[41] Sterols have also been found to shorten the lifespan of animals prone to cardiovascular disease.[42] It's difficult to reconcile sterols' healthy image with these apparently toxic effects.

The idea that stanols and sterols and the food products that contain them do not provide benefits for health may seem controversial, but it's grounded in science and is a view shared by the National Institute of Health and Care

↓

↓

Excellence (NICE), the body that informs medical practice in the UK. Here's what NICE has to say about these substances:

> Randomised controlled trials are needed to test the effectiveness of advising people who are at high risk of experiencing a first [cardiovascular disease] event to include food items containing plant sterols or stanols in a low-fat diet.

In other words, any presumed health benefits offered by stanols and sterols are unsubstantiated. And NICE issues this edict, too: 'People should not routinely be recommended to take plant sterols and stanols for the primary prevention of [cardiovascular disease].'

Most people, including doctors and dieticians, are seemingly unaware of the official line on stanols and sterols and the completely unproven nature of these compounds. Now you are, you can decide whether or not to put your faith in food products 'enriched' with these substances.

So, in summary, it seems concerns about saturated fat are simply unfounded. Again, this is consistent with evolutionary theory: the evidence suggests we've been eating meat, and the saturated fat it contains, for more than two million years. Saturated fat really is something we ought to be well adapted to by now.

A Change for the Better?

For probably as long as most of us can remember, we've been enthusiastically encouraged to swap carbohydrate for saturated fat for the sake of our heart health. But, as we know, there is no good evidence that saturated fat causes heart disease. And, as we learned earlier, there are good, science-backed reasons to be wary of certain carbohydrates that disrupt blood sugar levels. So, what might happen when individuals follow advice to cut back on saturated fat and eat more carbohydrate instead?

In one study, eating habits and risk of heart disease were assessed in more than 53,000 individuals over more than a decade.[43] The researchers found that substituting high-GI carbohydrates for saturated fat was associated with a 33 per cent increase in risk of heart attack. Another study, this one, a meta-analysis of eleven studies, found that this dietary change was associated with an enhanced risk of 'coronary events' such as heart attack.[44]

This evidence is epidemiological but, remember, it's underpinned by research that finds that high-GI carbohydrates induce processes in the body that would be expected to increase cardiovascular disease risk (such as inflammation and oxidative stress). Taken as a whole, the research shows that taking saturated fat out of the diet and putting carbohydrate in its place stands to do us more harm than good.

Saturated fat is but one major type of fat in the diet. What does science tell us about the others?

Monounsaturated Fats

So-called 'monounsaturated' fat is found in foods such as nuts, avocado, olives and olive oil. This type of fat enjoys a healthy reputation, on account of evidence linking its consumption with a reduced risk of cardiovascular disease.[2] Monounsaturated fats are not just found in plant foods, but those derived from animals too. For example, about half the fat in a steak is monounsaturated in nature, and it's actually the predominant fat in lamb and eggs. Also, the next most plentiful fat in butter after saturated fat is monounsaturated in nature.

Polyunsaturated Fats

'Polyunsaturated' fats come in two main forms: 'omega-6' and 'omega-3'. The main omega-6 fatty acid in the diet is known as 'linoleic acid', rich sources of which include so-called 'vegetable oils' derived from corn (a grain), seeds (e.g. sunflower, safflower and sesame) and beans (e.g. soya).

The major omega-3 fatty acids in the diet come in the form of alpha-linolenic acid (from plant sources such as flaxseed), as well as eicosapentaenoic acid (EPA) and docosahexaenoic acid (DHA) that are found in oily varieties of fish such as mackerel, herring, sardine, trout and salmon, as well as some meats, particularly from wild and grass-fed animals.

In general terms, omega-6 fats tend to encourage inflammation, blood vessel constriction and clotting in the body – all of which are disease-promoting if left unchecked. On the other hand, omega-3 fats generally have opposite, disease protective effects. Because omega-6 and omega-3 fats have broadly opposing action within the body, a 'balance' in these fats appears to be vital for optimal health.

A glut of omega-6 fat in the modern-day diet may have important implications for our health, at least in part because of its potentially inflammatory and other disease-promoting effects. Higher omega-6 to omega-3 ratios in the diet are associated with enhanced risk of heart disease and stroke[45] and type 2 diabetes,[46] as well as inflammatory conditions such as rheumatoid arthritis[47] and the 'inflammatory bowel disease' known as 'ulcerative colitis'.[48]

The evidence suggests that the substantial increase in our intake of omega-6 fats is a potent force in the rise of many modern-day maladies. In this light, it seems the conventional nutritional advice to emphasize 'vegetable' oils in the diet is misguided. In fact, the evidence suggests it may even be harmful to health (see section 'Pass (on) the Marge' below). Higher intakes of omega-3, on the other hand, have generally been associated with a reduced risk of chronic diseases including heart disease.[2]

While it appears that, ideally, we should have roughly equal quantities of omega-6 and omega-3 fats in the diet, the typical ratio of omega-6:omega-3 in the diet is somewhere between 10:1 and 30:1.[49]

A major source of omega-6 fats are vegetable oils used in cooking (such as sunflower oil), but these fats are also used in the manufacture of many processed foods including margarine and baked goods, and they are usually present in high amounts in fast food, too. Eating less of these foods is probably a generally wise move, as is eating more omega-3 fats (e.g. oily fish) to balance their effect.

Partially-Hydrogenated and Trans Fats

Omega-6-rich vegetable oils are liquid at room temperature, which is a problem for food manufacturers who may require something more solid or spreadable. This can be achieved through a process known as 'hydrogenation', where hydrogen is added to the fat under conditions of high temperature and pressure. This process produces 'partially-hydrogenated' fats that may have the physical characteristics food companies desire, but unfortunately have chemical characteristics that are completely alien to nature.

The processing of fats can also alter not just the chemistry of fats, but their *shape*. What happens here, in essence, is a straightening out of fat molecules to form what are termed 'trans fats'. Industrially-produced trans fats appear to have particular potential for toxicity, and are linked with an increased risk of conditions including heart disease[2,48–53] cancers of the breast and colon[54] and type 2 diabetes.[55–57]

Partially-hydrogenated fats can be found in a wide range of processed foods including margarine, biscuits, bread and other baked goods. Some scrutinizing of labels may be required. However, eating a diet based on 'primal' and unprocessed foods makes this endeavour largely redundant, as partially-hydrogenated and industrially-produced trans fats simply don't occur naturally in food.

Trans fats can be found in small quantities in more natural foods such as butter. However, the chemical structure of these fats is very different to those that are industrially-produced. More importantly, though, while industrially-produced trans fats have links with heart disease, naturally occurring ones do not.[58,59]

Pass (on) the Marge?

Margarine is marketed as a 'healthy' alternative to butter. Initially margarine was sold to us on the basis that, compared to butter, it is 'low in saturates' (saturated fat). This selling proposition is based on the assumption that saturated fat is bad for health. As we now know, there really is no evidence for this.

More recently, some stanol- and sterol-enriched margarines have been vigorously promoted on the basis that they help to reduce levels of cholesterol in the blood. As we discussed above, stanols and sterols have no proven benefits for health and there is research suggesting that sterols actually pose hazards here.

But another reason to be suspicious of margarine relates to its highly processed and chemicalised nature. The vegetable oils that are the base ingredient in margarine are usually extracted using heat, pressure and chemical solvents that can damage and impart unhealthy properties to them too. The resultant oil is then treated with sodium hydroxide to neutralize unstable fats in the oil that may cause spoilage. After this, the oil is bleached, filtered and steam-treated to produce what is essentially a colourless, flavourless liquid.

To convert this into margarine, this oil is subjected to hydrogenation (see above) or 'interesterification' (which involves the use of high temperature and pressure, along with enzymes or acids, to harden the oil). After this, the solidified fat is blended with other fats, which can be of vegetable or animal origin.

↓

↓

But, we're not done yet, though, as the product now needs colouring and flavouring (using yet more chemicals), as well as emulsifying agents to stop it separating out. And finally, the end result is extruded into a plastic tub and sold to us as something healthy. *Really?!*

Margarine's nature is, obviously, very unnatural. Butter, in comparison, is a quite natural food. It may not be a 'primal' food, as such, but its constituents (primarily saturated and monounsaturated fat) have been in the diet *for ever*.

So, what does the research show regarding the relationship between margarine and butter and health?

In one study in men, while butter consumption was not associated with heart disease risk, margarine was.[60] In the long term, for each teaspoon of margarine consumed each day, risk of heart disease was found to be raised by 10 per cent. Other evidence links margarine consumption with a heightened risk of heart disease.[61]

This is epidemiological evidence, and cannot be used to prove that margarine causes heart disease. However, these findings become more incriminating when we consider that margarine consumers are generally more health-conscious than those who eat butter. By rights, these individuals would be expected to have a lower risk of heart disease compared to generally less health-conscious butter-eaters.

What is more, some researchers have raised considerable doubt about the supposed wisdom of replacing saturated fat with omega-6 fats (which is a central proposition of the

↓

↓

'benefits' of replacing butter with margarine). The relevant evidence was reviewed in the British Medical Journal.[62] This review examined several studies in which saturated fat had been at least partially replaced with omega-6 fats. When all the studies were analysed together, no benefits for health were found.

The authors of this review did turn up some troubling data from a study known as the 'Sydney Diet Heart Study'. In this research, men aged 30–59 were instructed to reduce saturated fat intake and increase omega-6 fat intake in the form of safflower oil and safflower oil-based margarine. A similar number of men got no dietary instruction and acted as a comparison. Men eating the 'heart-healthy' diet complete with omega-6-rich oils and fats saw a 62 per cent increased risk of death, and a 74 per cent increased risk of death from heart disease.

The authors of the review concluded:

Advice to substitute polyunsaturated fats for saturated fats is a key component of worldwide dietary guidelines for coronary heart disease risk reduction ... In this [group of people], substituting dietary [omega-6 fat] in place of saturated fats increased the rates of death from all causes, coronary heart disease, and cardiovascular disease. An updated meta-analysis of [omega-6 fat] intervention trials showed no evidence of cardiovascular benefit. These findings could have important implications for worldwide dietary advice to substitute omega-6 linoleic

↓

acid, or polyunsaturated fats in general, for saturated fats.

There is nothing in the research that gives me confidence that margarine is healthier than butter. In fact, more than one line of evidence points in completely the opposite direction. For me, the best place for margarine is not our mouths, but the bin.

The evidence from the scientific literature shows:

- Fats found naturally in the diet (including saturated fat) pose no threats to health and some have health-giving properties

- Processed fats are damaging to health and should be avoided

Bad Blood?

You'll see diets relatively low in carbohydrate described by many doctors and dieticians as a 'fad' and hazardous to health. But can a diet akin to the one that fuelled us for the vast majority of our evolution really be described as a *fad*? And what evidence do we have that such a diet is fundamentally unhealthy?

Much of the rhetoric around the supposed hazards of eating this way centres on the idea that red meat, say, is full of 'artery-clogging' saturated fat. Yet, as we saw earlier, the evidence reveals that saturated fat has no links with heart disease (and neither does the eating of fresh meat).[63]

We can also gauge the potential health effects of diets lower in carbohydrate by assessing their effects on 'disease markers' such as blood fat levels and blood pressure.

Here's a summary of the metabolic changes typically seen on low-carbohydrate diets.[64] After each effect, I've added in brackets whether the change would traditionally be regarded as a good or bad thing from a disease risk perspective:

- Improved insulin sensitivity (good)

- Reduced blood pressure (good)

- Reduced triglyceride levels (good)

- Raised levels of HDL-cholesterol – the form of cholesterol said to be associated with protection from cardiovascular disease (good)

- Raised levels of LDL-cholesterol – the form of cholesterol said to be associated with increased risk of cardiovascular disease (bad)

Low-carbohydrate regimes richer in fat seem to win out over higher-carb ones for almost all disease markers, though the one potential fly in the ointment (albeit from a conventional perspective) is the raised level of LDL-cholesterol these diets can sometimes induce.

Traditional wisdom tells us that LDL-cholesterol is responsible for the artery-narrowing process that is at the root of cardiovascular disease known as 'atherosclerosis'. But how is it that this one marker tends to worsen on low-carb diets, while everything else improves? Is there something else we need to know?

It turns out that the relationship between LDL-cholesterol and heart disease is not nearly as straightforward as we have been led to believe. LDL-cholesterol comes in a range of sizes, varying from small, dense particles, up to larger, less dense ('fluffy') ones. It appears that the size and density of LDL particles have an important bearing on the apparent risk of heart disease. What the evidence shows is that small, dense LDL particles are associated with an increased risk of heart disease, while larger LDL particles are not.[65] So, what effect does diet have on the size of LDL particles?

In one study, individuals were fed a low-fat, high-carbohydrate diet for four weeks on one occasion, and a low-carb, higher fat diet at another time.[66] Compared to the low-carbohydrate diet, the low-fat one led to a reduction in the size of the LDL-cholesterol particles (not a good thing). Also, in another study, adopting a low-carbohydrate diet was found to increase LDL-cholesterol particle size.[67]

In other words, low-carbohydrate diets induce healthy increases in LDL-cholesterol size. Put this together with the other effects of lower-carbohydrate diets, and we can see they improve disease markers *across the board*.

So How Come We're Living Longer?

If a change from our indigenous diet to a more modern one is so potentially damaging to our health, how is it that we're living longer now than ever before? In the palaeolithic age, average lifespan is estimated to have been thirty to thirty-five. That doesn't compare at all well with, say, the current life expectancies of about seventy-five and eighty for men and women respectively.

One explanation for our enhanced longevity has to do with the fact that our ancient ancestors were more at the mercy of factors such as warfare, starvation, extreme climate and animal attack than we are now. Also, advances in medicine, hygiene and sanitation have been massively instrumental in reducing the risk of death due to, say, infectious disease and the complications of childbirth.

The scientific evidence points strongly to the fact that relatively recent dietary changes pose very real risks for our health. What is more, there really is nothing to be feared in consuming natural and unprocessed foods. The logical conclusion is that our increased life expectancy has not been because of recent changes in our diet, but in *spite* of them.

Dairy Products

One last major food group we have yet to cover are dairy products such as milk, cheese and yogurt. Where, if anywhere, do they fit into a healthy diet?

Milk and other dairy products represent staples in the 'standard Western diet', and their importance for growth and bone health has been impressed on us by health agencies, doctors and dieticians. Yet, for the vast majority of our time on this planet we drank no milk other than human breast milk early in life: the record shows before our ancestors started to keep and milk animals (about 5,000 years ago) they had strong and healthy bones. Does it really make sense that we need milk now?

While dairy product consumption has been widely advocated to combat the bone-thinning disease known as 'osteoporosis', the evidence as a whole does not support this. Two meta-analyses have found no evidence of reduced hip fracture risk from greater intakes of milk in either women or men.[68,69] The second of these reviews found that calcium supplementation actually *increased* the risk of hip fracture by 64 per cent.

The value of dairy products for children is not nearly as nailed-on as we have been led to believe, either. In one review, the great majority of studies found no evidence that calcium or dairy consumption has a significant influence on bone health in children.[70] Of the small number of studies that did find benefit, any apparent benefit was small. An accompanying editorial highlighted the lack of evidence for the supposed benefits of dairy products for bone health.[71]

The research shows that dairy products, and the calcium they provide, have limited benefits for bone health.

Sensitive Information

Earlier, we explored how grains, particularly wheat, pose hazards as a result of 'food sensitivity'. Dairy foods are a fairly frequent factor in food sensitivity issues, too. For instance, in childhood,

I find dairy products are a common cause of ailments such as asthma, eczema, ear infections, 'glue ear', frequent colds and recurrent tonsillitis. In adults, some of the most common problems associated with dairy sensitivity include excessive catarrh, sinus and/or nasal congestion, asthma and eczema.

A possible provoking factor here is the incomplete digestion of proteins found in milk and other dairy products, particularly one known as 'casein'. Pasteurization is believed to make milk proteins particularly difficult to digest, and therefore more problematic. This idea is certainly consistent with my experience in practice: many individuals who react to pasteurized dairy products seem to tolerate raw (unpasteurized) products just fine.

If someone is sensitive to dairy products, then they will normally have a problem with milk, though I find that yogurt is generally much better tolerated. This might have something to do with the fact that the bacteria deployed in the fermentation process that forms yogurt partially digest milk proteins,[72,73] making it more likely that they will be fully digested in the gut and rendering them less problematic. An added benefit of yogurt is that it contains less lactose than milk and is generally better tolerated by individuals who suffer from 'lactose intolerance'.

In addition to helping the digestibility of dairy products, studies suggest that the organisms found in 'live' and 'bio' yogurts have the potential to help alleviate gut-related issues such as constipation, diarrhoea and 'irritable bowel syndrome'.

In practice, cheese and cream seem to have similar potential to cause food sensitivity issues as yogurt, and while they can be problematic, they are generally better tolerated than milk. Butter, I find, is generally very well tolerated indeed, and this may have something to do with the fact that it is low in both protein and lactose (it's almost all fat).

Another common finding is that individuals who have problems with cow's milk-based products do not react as badly, and may not react at all, to milk and dairy products derived from other animals such as sheep and goats. It has been suggested that milk from these animals is, compared to cow's milk, more similar to human breast milk, thereby making it easier to digest and more appropriate for our consumption.

Are Dairy Products Fattening?

Dairy products are often recommended as part of a healthy diet, but usually in the same breath we are warned to opt for 'low-fat' versions such as semi-skimmed milk and low-fat yogurt. This advice is based on the ideas that the saturated fat in dairy products is potentially fattening, and can increase the risk of heart disease – neither of which stands up to scrutiny.

Theoretically, dairy products might have some impact on weight through a known ability to stimulate insulin secretion.[74] However, the protein in dairy products also stimulates the secretion of another hormone called 'glucagon', which has actions that counteract the fat-forming effects of insulin (glucagon, for instance, stimulates 'lipolysis' – the release of fat from fat cells).

Another factor that mitigates the fattening potential of dairy products relates to their calcium content. Increased calcium levels in the blood have been shown to accelerate the breakdown and release of fat (lipolysis).[75] There is evidence linking higher intakes of calcium and dairy products with reduced body fat levels,[76] and supplementing the diet with yogurt has been found to enhance fat loss in some studies.[77,78]

While dairy products have theoretically fattening potential due to their influence on insulin, the evidence suggests their incorporation in the diet is unlikely to be a barrier to weight loss, and in fact may even help here.

Dairy and the Primal Principle

Dairy products are relatively recent additions to the diet and cannot, therefore, be described as 'primal' foods. However, for those who tolerate them, they do have something going for them from a nutritional perspective in that they are relatively rich in protein and fat, and relatively low in carbohydrate. In this sense, their nutritional make-up reflects one that we know tends to be the best for blood sugar stability and general health.

Another important attribute of dairy products is that they're generally effective at sating the appetite. The relatively protein- and fat-rich nature of dairy products such as full-fat yogurt and cheese probably has something to do with this.

Parts 1 and 2 of this chapter have provided a scientific and evidence-based account of diet and nutrition, and the conclusion is that the best diet for us is one based on foods that are as natural and unprocessed as possible. In the final part, we're going to explore how to convert the theory of healthy eating into practice – easily and sustainably. So, what are we going to eat?

PART 3: MAKE A MEAL OF IT

Breakfast

We're often told that 'breakfast is the most important meal of the day', but I actually don't think this holds true for all people. Some people are simply not hungry in the morning and may be better off delaying eating to later or even skipping breakfast altogether (see Chapter 3 for more on this). However, if you are going to eat breakfast, the chances are that speed and convenience will be priorities for you in the working week.

Toast and cereal are out if optimal eating is a priority for you, but one option that works well for most people is a yogurt-based breakfast. I recommend full-fat Greek yogurt as the base, to which can be added some berries (e.g. fresh strawberries, blueberries and raspberries or defrosted berries) and maybe some nuts (e.g. chopped almonds and walnuts). Certain berries (e.g. blackberries) can be a bit tart, so you might allow yourself a faint drizzle of honey. Other than the honey, there's no need to limit quantities at all, so you should eat enough to sate your appetite. This does not mean eating gratuitously, though. Eat enough to be pleasantly satisfied. More about this can be found in Chapter 3.

One of the good things about this breakfast is that it can travel well. If you commute to work, you may get up and leave home at a time that is too early for you to feel like food. The yogurt mix can be taken in a container to be eaten en route to work or even once you're there. If you don't get hungry until mid-morning or later, there is no issue at all with delaying your breakfast until then, as long as you do not allow yourself to get very hungry (see Chapter 3, again).

Another breakfast option that can be had outside the home is an omelette or frittata (basically, a thick omelette). Goat's cheese and chorizo or goat's cheese and spinach work well here. Another option is to make 'breadless Scotch eggs' ahead of time. All this entails is wrapping minced pork (or other meat) around a hard-boiled egg, leaving them in the fridge to chill, after which they can be deep- or shallow-fried.

At the weekend, I generally recommend cooked breakfasts/brunches. Smoked salmon and scrambled eggs is a good combination, or even just some poached eggs with fried mushrooms and tomato. Wilted spinach can make a good accompaniment here too. Just wash some spinach leaves, shake and add to a heated frying pan or saucepan and keep moving until the spinach has softened. Add some butter, salt and pepper (if you like) and serve.

If you're feeling a little more adventurous you might like to whip up a hollandaise sauce. There's a quick and easy way of doing this: take a couple of egg yolks, add some lemon juice, and whizz with an electric hand blender while you add very hot melted butter little by little.

A 'full English' or variation on a cooked breakfast is another option, and this can work well at weekends or when staying at a hotel (I suggest avoiding the bread and pastries on offer).

Are Processed Meats OK?

Concerns have been expressed about the health effects of processed meats such as bacon, sausage, ham and salami. These meats are linked with an increased risk of health problems, notably bowel cancer.

This evidence is epidemiological in nature, so cannot be used to conclude that processed meat causes bowel cancer. For a start, people who eat a lot of processed meat (such as rubbishy pork pies, sausage rolls or pasties) may well be doing other things in their lives that could jeopardize the health of their large bowels and other body parts.

However, processed meats usually contain preservative chemicals called 'nitrites' that have been said by some to have cancer-inducing potential. Some evidence, however, disputes the role of nitrites in cancer formation,[79] and other evidence even points to their potential to keep the body free from undesirable organisms.[80]

Also, the majority of the nitrite that finds its way into our gut does not come from processed meat, but is found in vegetables and even our own saliva. Anything is possible, but these facts do not point to nitrites as a major issue for health. As a result, I eat some good quality processed meat such as bacon, sausage, ham and chorizo, though the great majority of the meat I eat is unprocessed.

Some people simply don't need much food in the morning, and find a couple of handfuls of nuts and maybe a piece of fruit is all they need, say, in the mid or late morning. As long as this allows you to maintain good energy and brain function throughout the morning and does not leave you famished by lunch, there's nothing wrong with it at all.

Lunch

Often the biggest challenge for lunch-eaters is avoiding sandwiches or something else bread-based. One alternative is salad, and many sandwich bars and shops that specialize in prepared food will have these already made. If you're not vegetarian, I suggest opting for salads that include meat, fish or seafood. For vegetarians, egg, avocado and cheese are ingredients to look out for. The protein and fat in these foods generally help to *sustain* people through the afternoon in a way that a 'pile of leaves' usually won't.

Sandwich bars and cafés often offer soups at lunch, usually in the form of both meaty and vegetarian options. Again, unless you have reason not to, I suggest opting for the meat variety. If you're not going to eat bread (you're not going to eat bread, are you?) then, say, a bowl of carrot and coriander soup probably is not the ideal option. After all, this basically offers you a couple of carrots, half an onion and some water. Where's that going to get you? The answer is: probably not very far.

If you're at home for lunch, as long as you've got the right food to hand, there are plenty of easy options. Examples include:

- Omelette and salad

- Grilled chops or fish with salad

- Reheated stew or casserole

- Meaty fresh soup (shop-bought or home-made)

Remember, it's very important not to be too hungry before lunch, as having your appetite under control is what makes eschewing bread and other carb-rich accompaniments (such as chocolate, cereal bars and crisps) easy.

And also bear in mind that what you eat at lunch does not need to get you through to dinner; if you get hungry again then by all means munch some nuts in the late afternoon or early evening. The thinking behind this strategy is described in Chapter 3.

How Much?

Many people wonder about 'portion control' and how much food it is healthy to eat. This is an obvious question if, for instance, you are concerned to keep your weight under control. In theory, though, there should be no need to consciously restrict portion sizes if the *right food* is being eaten. In populations eating indigenous diets, overweight and obesity are essentially unknown, despite the fact that no one consciously restricts the amount they eat nor counts calories. What I've found to be overwhelmingly true is that when individuals concentrate on eating the right food, they don't generally need to concern themselves with how much of it they eat.

In fact, conscious restriction of food can, almost inevitably, leave us hungry, which can make healthy eating unnecessarily challenging and also sap willpower. But, while it's important not to get too hungry, food should not be eaten when *not hungry* either, for the most part. The importance of appetite control and how to eat enough but not too much is covered in Chapter 3.

Dinner

Dinner is generally the easiest main meal to manage: the key is to think 'primal'. The lunch options referred to above all work as dinners, for instance. Another quick and easy option is some cold meat (e.g. cold chicken, cold roast beef) and/or fish (e.g. smoked salmon, smoked trout, peppered mackerel), served with salad, perhaps with some hummus or other 'deli' items such as roasted red peppers or Greek salad.

One of the beauties of this sort of dinner is that no one needs to cook – the food just has to be pulled out of the fridge and put on a plate (and minimal washing-up is required, too).

If you're vegetarian, perhaps think about something like an omelette or frittata or a nice big salad, preferably with some avocado, egg or cheese for nourishing and sustaining protein and fat.

The trick to making these sorts of meal work is not being too hungry when you sit down to them. Ensuring your appetite is under reasonable control is also important when eating in a restaurant as it takes the challenge out of resisting the urge to 'fill up' on bread, risotto, rice, pasta or a side order of chips. Not being unduly hungry makes it so much easier to make choices based on primal principles and what you like, rather than what you believe you need to satisfy your now rampant hunger. So, you may perhaps choose something salad-based to start (e.g. smoked duck salad, smoked salmon salad, or tomato, avocado and mozzarella salad), and then follow this with some meat or fish with vegetables, perhaps with a few potatoes.

Some people are concerned about eating too late. Personally, I think the real problem is not eating too late; it's eating *too much too late*. There's an argument for eating smaller evening meals than we traditionally do. Appetite control is key here, again, and eating well during the day and grabbing a snack in the late afternoon/early evening can be critical.

Get Ready For Ready-Meals?

There's a strong theme in these recommendations that the diet should be made up, as much as possible, of natural, unprocessed foods. However, we don't always have the time to cook foods from fresh ingredients, and this is one reason why some of us may be tempted by convenience foods and ready-meals. A lot of these, for example, microwaveable lasagne and other pasta dishes, are highly unlikely to get you closer to your health goals. However that does not mean to say that all ready-meals are off limits.

A ready-meal made up of a piece of fish or meat accompanied by some vegetables is, to all intents and purposes, no more processed than something you might prepare at home. Yes, it might have a bit more salt than you would use, but it's essentially quite unprocessed food cooked in a factory (rather than your kitchen). The trick is to stick to ready-meals that are made from ostensibly primal ingredients. Such meals are a good compromise between healthy eating and convenience, I think, and can provide practical options for those with limited time to cook or who just don't like cooking.

Takeaways don't need to be a nutritional disaster area, either. The first rule is not to be too hungry when you do the ordering (or eating). Grabbing a takeaway late on the way home from work when lunch was eight or more hours ago ↓

↓

or when staggering back from the pub are not situations that lend themselves to making the best choices.

Ordering a takeaway on a weekend night in a non-famished state is much more compatible with healthy eating. The key, again, is to think 'primal'. So, for instance, if Indian food is the order of the day you might opt for a meat- or prawn-based curry, or tikka dish, plus vegetables say in the form of sag paneer (Indian cheese and spinach) and some dahl (lentils). If you're not too hungry, you won't miss the rice and naan that stand to do the most damage. If Chinese food is in the offing, opt maybe for a beef, prawn or chicken dish (e.g. beef with ginger, spicy prawns, chicken with cashew nuts) and some stir-fried vegetables. Again, just avoid filling up on rice and noodles.

Snacks

While 'snacking' does not have the healthiest of reputations, I explain in Chapter 3 why it can be a very smart tactic for those who want to eat healthily, work efficiently and perhaps even save their marriage (I'm only half-joking).

Fruit is often recommended as the healthy snack of choice, but I'm not a particular fan. The point of the snack is to sate the appetite effectively, and for most people, fruit does not really do the job, here. Raw vegetables such as carrot and cucumber sticks suffer from the same fundamental deficiency, though they may be OK if coupled with something more sustaining such as some hummus or guacamole.

For ease, though, here are some snack options that usually work well:

- Nuts (see Chapter 3 for more on the best forms of nuts, as well as the evidence that shows nuts, despite their intensely calorific nature, have limited potential to drive weight gain)

- Seeds (e.g. toasted pumpkin seeds)

- Olives

- Biltong (dried meat – this keeps and travels very well)

- Cold meat (e.g. roast beef, chicken)

- Hard-boiled eggs

Sweet Nothings

By their very nature, desserts tend to be loaded with sugar, and eating them can accustom the taste buds to intensely sweet tastes and can perpetuate a desire for more of the same. In the long run, it can be easier (not to mention healthier) to cut out dessert-eating, apart from odd occasions such as part of a celebratory meal or if you find yourself in a particularly swanky restaurant and simply want to indulge yourself. Any treat of this nature should be savoured and is nothing to feel guilty or regretful about; put its eating in the context of your diet as a whole and see it pale into insignificance.

At other times, if you want a little something, you may find you get what you need from a couple of squares of

↓

dark chocolate (70 per cent or more cocoa solids). This sort of sweet treat will not overload you with sugar, and there is evidence the cocoa may benefit cardiovascular health via its content of 'polyphenols'[81] (health-giving plant chemicals that are found in other foodstuffs too including coffee and tea – see the next chapter).

Another feature of dark chocolate is that it's not nearly as moreish as sweeter chocolate (e.g. milk chocolate) can be. People can often eat a square or two and have little or no desire for any more.

An alternative 'dessert' if more volume is required is some full-fat yogurt with some berries.

THE BOTTOM LINE

- Stable blood sugar levels are key to ensuring buoyant and sustained levels of energy throughout the day

- Spikes of blood sugar are disease-promoting, and also encourage the storage of fat via the action of the hormone insulin

- Many starchy carbohydrates (including bread, potato, rice, pasta and breakfast cereals) are disruptive to blood sugar levels

- Blood-sugar-stabilizing foods include meat, fish, eggs, nuts, seeds, and non-starchy vegetables

- Dietary fat does not appear to be inherently fattening, and low-fat diets are generally ineffective for weight control

- Saturated fat is not linked with heart disease, and eating less of it does not reduce heart disease risk or other chronic health issues

- Monounsaturated fats (found in foods such as nuts, avocado, olive oil, meat, eggs and butter) appear to be good for heart health

- Excesses of omega-6 fats found in 'vegetable' oils, margarine and many processed foods have the potential to harm heart and general health

- Partially-hydrogenated and trans fats, found in margarine and processed foods, appear to be particularly toxic to heart health

- Omega-3 fats found in oily varieties of fish such as salmon, mackerel, herring and sardine support heart and general health

- Diets lower in carbohydrate and richer in protein and fat than is traditionally advised generally lead to improvements in a range of disease markers

- Dairy products are a quite common cause of food sensitivity, though yogurt is generally better tolerated than milk (and butter is rarely a problem)

- There is abundant scientific evidence that the best diet for us is one based on natural, unprocessed, 'primal' foods such as meat, fish, eggs, nuts, seeds, vegetables and fruit

- Thinking 'primally' with regard to our diet helps us make quick, accurate and future-proof judgements regarding the best foods for optimizing our energy, effectiveness and general health

Chapter 2

Fluid Thinking

In the previous chapter, we explored the best foods for optimizing our energy, effectiveness and sustainability. But, of course, our health and wellbeing is not just influenced by what we eat, but also what we drink. This chapter highlights the importance of hydration in vitality and performance, and also provides information on beverages such as soft drinks, fruit juices, coffee and tea. The chapter ends with information and advice about the beverage many of us hate to love: alcohol.

Water, Water, Everywhere

Because water is a fluid, it's sometimes forgotten that one of its key functions in the body is actually *structural* in nature[1] – it makes up about two-thirds of the body's size and weight. Dehydration can compromise the physical form and function of our tissues and cells. For example, dehydration in the muscles has been found to lead to significant losses in power[2] and endurance.[3]

Water is the major constituent of blood in the circulation, and has a role in delivering oxygen and nutrients to our tissues, as well as the removal and elimination of waste products. Dehydration can lead to a reduction in the volume of the blood, which compromises the functioning of the body's organs and tissues. Other functions of water include temperature regulation (through sweating, which dissipates heat from the body), and as a lubricant and shock absorber for the joints.

Drying Down

In practice, I find some of the most common symptoms of dehydration affect the head. I think dehydration is perhaps the most frequent underlying cause of headaches, for instance. But I find for many of my patients and clients dehydration manifests itself as *mental sluggishness*. My experience tells me that dehydration is quite simply one of the biggest, under-recognized drains on performance in the workplace.

Is there any scientific basis for this phenomenon? Interestingly, research has discovered that cells that are dehydrated do not take up glucose very efficiently.[4] If our brain cells were to be starved of fuel, one could imagine this might drain our mental powers, and make it harder for us to 'get the job done'.

There is some other relevant research in this area, too. In one study, the effects of dehydration were tested in a group of young men.[5] The study participants were subjected to each of three test conditions at different times:

1. Forty minutes of treadmill walking at a temperature of 28°C (82°F). In addition, the men were treated with the drug 'frusemide' (a 'diuretic' that speeds urine production)

2. Same conditions as 1, but instead of being given frusemide, the men were treated with a placebo

3. Same conditions as above, but the hydration status of the men was maintained with fluid (in other words, they were not allowed to become dehydrated)

Conditions 1 and 2 were designed to induce dehydration of two severities (condition 1 – with the diuretic drug – being the more severe), and condition 3 was designed to act as a 'control' (where individuals exercised to the same degree and in the same heat, but did not suffer dehydration). The study participants were subjected to a range of tests of mental function, fatigue and mood.

Individuals suffering from at least 1 per cent dehydration (e.g. an 800 ml fluid deficit in an 80 kg male) saw deficits in vigilance and working memory (the ability to actively hold information in the mind – required for complex tasks such as reasoning, comprehension and learning). Other notable findings were increases in feelings of tension, anxiety and fatigue. A similar study to the one above, this one conducted in young women, also found detrimental effects from dehydration.[6] In women with an average fluid deficit of about a litre, both mood and concentration were impaired, and headaches were more common, too.

Liquid Engineering

In the field of nutrition, we'll often be urged to drink 2 litres or 8 glasses of water each day. The problem is, as with many things, a 'one-size-fits-all' approach doesn't necessarily work.

Are we really saying that a sedentary individual weighing 60 kg needs the same amount of water each day as someone physically active who tips the scales at 120 kg? Also, our fluid requirements can be influenced by other factors including temperature and air-conditioning. People can clearly have very different fluid requirements from each other that can vary according to conditions too.

What's required is a *personalized* gauge of our fluid requirements. Some people rely on thirst, here. The problem is, by the time we are thirsty we might already be 1–2 per cent dehydrated.[7,8] From the studies described earlier, we know that this level of dehydration is enough to induce performance problems, particularly with regard to brain function.

You may know the limited value of thirst in judging fluid needs if you engage in endurance exercise and have been told: 'Once you're thirsty, it's too late.' That's right, I think, and it's true not just during a long cycle ride or marathon, but also when we are sitting at our desk. Ideally, we want a guide that is going to prevent us from becoming dehydrated to the extent that it impacts on our performance.

Colour Coded

A more sensitive and altogether better guide as to our state of hydration is the *colour of our urine*.[9] If you want to know how much water to drink each day, the answer is not 2 litres or 8 glasses or any specific amount, but: enough to ensure your urine remains *pale yellow* in colour throughout the course of the day.

If your urine should stray into darker tones, and particularly if it becomes noticeably odorous, then you can take that as a sure sign that you have run low on fluid. The chances are your vitality and performance will have dried up a bit too.

Here's the good news, though: I find that in almost every case, when individuals respond to the passing of some dark and pungent urine by drinking more water, they usually feel significantly revived within about twenty minutes (yes, it's usually that quick).

Just Add Water

I've found that the vast majority of people will drink water quite happily and automatically as long as it is *in front of them* or, at least, very close to hand.

The trick to getting enough water into ourselves is usually to keep a bottle of water and a glass or cup on our desks, and in front of us in meetings. Just the tactic of having water around is usually all that is required for people to maintain their hydration and keep energy levels buoyant throughout the day.

My experience is that almost everyone intuitively knows that hydration is important, but that a minority will complain that water is 'boring'. I have noticed that when people are looking for more 'flavour' or perhaps sweetness from their drink, dehydration is usually an underlying issue. If someone tends to be dehydrated and on the thirsty side, then soft drinks, fruit juices, squashes, beer and wine tend to be infinitely more attractive options than 'plain old water'. However, I find when individuals hydrate themselves properly, and particularly if they keep thirst at bay, they are usually quite content with water as their stock drink.

So, if at this time you think water is too boring, maybe just make a conscious effort to drink more of it for a few days and see what happens. You might be pleasantly surprised to find that any resistance you have to water just dissolves away.

Another option is to inject a little flavour with a squeeze of natural lemon or lime (some people keep a little squeezable bottle of citrus juice in or on their desk for this purpose). This works particularly well in sparkling water, if you like it. The one potential issue with sparkling water is that it is quite acidic (especially if some citrus juice has been added), and it has some potential to cause erosion of tooth enamel. It can be better to drink sparkling water through a straw as this helps to bypass the teeth.

Soft Drinks

Understanding the place these beverages have in the diet requires us to have a knowledge of the health implications of consuming sugar and artificial sweeteners. Let's start with sugar.

When a lot of us think of 'sugar' we conjure up an image of the white, granulated stuff we might add to a cup of coffee or tea or bowl of breakfast cereal. You may remember from the preceding chapter that this form of sugar (sometimes referred to as 'table sugar') is sucrose, comprising two sugars (glucose and fructose) joined together. When sucrose is consumed, it is digested down to its constituent sugars prior to absorption into the bloodstream.

Glucose derived from sucrose undoubtedly has the ability to disrupt blood sugar levels and cause surges in insulin (see Chapter 1). In that chapter, we also explored how spikes in blood sugar can provoke disease-inducing processes including inflammation, glycation, oxidative stress and coagulation. In short, we need to be careful regarding our consumption of glucose and therefore sucrose.

What About Fructose?

In contrast to glucose, fructose has traditionally enjoyed a healthy reputation, mainly on the basis that it does not raise blood sugar levels directly. Fructose is also the predominant sugar in some fruits – something that tends to bestow on it an image of healthiness.

In recent years, though, a mass of evidence has accumulated that while fructose does not immediately elevate blood glucose levels, it can nonetheless have toxic effects on the body (see below). Interest here has been sparked, at least in part, by the fact that an increasing amount of the sweetening agent 'high fructose corn syrup' (HFCS) is making its way into the diet, principally in the US (in Europe, legislation forces food manufacturers to use sucrose, from sugar beet, as the prime sweetener). HFCS is made cheaply by the chemical treatment of corn and, similar to sucrose, contains fructose and glucose in roughly equal measure.

Once fructose is absorbed into the body it is transported directly to the liver where it is metabolized. Some fructose is converted into glucose here. Fructose can, ultimately, cause glucose levels in the bloodstream to rise, albeit indirectly.

In the liver, fructose can also be converted into *fat*. Some of this fat can get 'stuck' in this organ which can lead to what is known as 'fatty liver' over time.[10] Fructose has been implicated in obesity and type 2 diabetes, too.[11,12]

There is, therefore, good evidence that fructose has considerable capacity to harm health. A similar claim could, though, be made for any element of the diet (*anything* can cause us problems if we consume enough of it). In the studies in which fructose has been fed to animals or humans, relatively large doses have been used which may not reflect normal levels of intake. Do we have any idea how much fructose is too much?

How Much Is Too Much?

Fructose levels vary a lot between foodstuffs. An apple, for instance, contains about 6 g of fructose, compared to about 20 g found in a can of cola. One review concluded that fructose at levels of 25–40 g per day appears to be safe.[13] Another suggested that the safe limit is most probably something under 90 g per day.[14]

My tendency would be to shoot for more conservative intakes, partly on the basis of a study that found giving people just 40 g of fructose each day in the form of a sweetened drink for just three weeks was enough to induce unhealthy changes including raised markers of inflammation, weight gain and unfavourable changes in the size of LDL-cholesterol particles (discussed in the preceding chapter).[15]

With all this in mind, here are a few generalities about fructose that I believe hold true:

- Fructose may not raise blood sugar levels directly, but is most certainly not benign in terms of its effects on health

- There is convincing and consistent evidence in animals and humans that fructose has the potential to contribute to health issues including weight gain and type 2 diabetes

- Relatively small amounts of fructose in the diet are likely to be safe for the majority of people, particularly when found naturally in food such as fruit

I mentioned before that a can of soft drink (sweetened with HFCS or sucrose) contains about 20 g of fructose. But it contains essentially the same amount of glucose, too. The total sugar content in a 330 ml serving is about 9 teaspoons. Just imagine spooning that much sugar into the same volume of coffee or tea (anyone witnessing you do that might imagine you had taken leave of your senses). Soft drinks, I think, are best avoided.

Are Artificial Sweeteners a Better Bet?

Artificial sweeteners such as 'aspartame', 'sucralose' and 'saccharin' offer sweetness with few or no calories, and would seem the obvious choice over sugar for those seeking to lose weight and optimize their health. There is some evidence, even, that many people regard artificial sweeteners as 'health food'.[16]

However, to know if the theoretical benefits of artificial sweeteners materialize in the real world requires them to be subjected to 'randomized controlled trials'. These trials, often used to assess pharmaceuticals, are generally regarded as the 'gold standard' for determining the effects of a medication or other intervention. The scientific literature does not contain one single properly conducted trial that demonstrates weight loss benefits for artificial sweeteners. In fact, artificial sweetener consumption has been linked in many studies with an *increased* risk of obesity.[17]

A potential explanation here, though, is that overweight individuals may be more likely to choose artificially sweetened drinks rather than sugary ones. In other words, excess weight may lead to an increased intake of artificial sweeteners, rather than the other way round.

One way to get a better picture here is to follow people over time who start out at the same weight. Here, the weight of individuals should not influence whether or not they choose artificially-sweetened foodstuffs. Several studies show that under these circumstances, individuals who choose artificially sweetened drinks are still more likely to end up heavier and in poorer health. This finding throws up the possibility that artificial sweeteners might actually *cause* weight gain and other chronic health issues.

Further evidence to support this idea comes from laboratory studies, albeit in animals. In one study, rats were fed with either saccharin- or sugar-sweetened yogurt together with their normal diet.[18] Compared to those eating sugar-sweetened yogurt, the rats eating artificially-sweetened yoghurt consumed more calories and got fatter, too. The authors of this study concluded that: 'These results suggest that consumption of products containing artificial sweeteners may lead to increased body weight and obesity by interfering with fundamental homeostatic, physiological processes.'

In another study, rats were given unlimited amounts of standard rat food (chow) and water.[19] The animals were split into three groups, in which the diet was supplemented with yogurt sweetened with saccharin, aspartame or sucrose. Rats eating the artificially-sweetened yogurt ate more chow than those eating the sugar-sweetened yogurt. In the end, overall calorie intakes were the same. This suggests that when reduced-calorie foodstuffs are consumed, there can be a natural drive to seek those 'missing' calories elsewhere.

One intriguing aspect of this study was that the rats consuming artificial sweetener gained weight at a faster rate than those eating the sugar, even though their calorie intakes were the same. What mechanisms might be at play, here? Normally, after eating, there is a little boost in the body's metabolism. In one study, this effect was observed after rats ate sugar-sweetened food, but not if it was artificially sweetened.[18] A comprehensive review paper detailed the considerable evidence that artificial sweeteners may upset the metabolism and drive weight gain and advised that we should be cautious about their use.[20]

In addition to these potential effects on weight, there is evidence linking artificial sweeteners with other health risks too. All the three elements of the artificial sweetener aspartame – aspartic acid, phenylalanine and methanol – have toxic potential,[21] particularly on the brain. Aspartame has been linked with a range of adverse effects including headache[22,23] and depression.[24]

One of aspartame's constituents – methanol – can convert in the body into *formaldehyde*. This is what is used to preserve dead bodies, but it's also a known cancer-causing agent (carcinogen). Aspartame consumption is associated with an increased risk of specific cancers in humans.[25] These studies are epidemiological in nature, and therefore cannot be used to conclude that aspartame causes cancer in humans. However, studies have shown that aspartame has the capacity to cause similar cancers in animals, and at levels of intake permitted in the human diet (scaled down to reflect the size of the animals).[26]

In a way, one might predict the potential for problems with aspartame from the fact that it is not a naturally occurring foodstuff, but one that is synthesized in industrial laboratories and introduced into the human diet very recently. The likelihood, therefore, is that we don't have the metabolic and biochemical machinery to deal with this effectively. This makes the chances of benefits low, but the risk of toxicity high.

I don't advise the consumption of artificial sweeteners. I never take them myself, and once people are aware of the research in the field, I find they usually don't either.

Sweet Mercy?

One sweetening agent that is popular in some quarters because it is plant-extracted and therefore perceived as 'natural' is *stevia*. There exists evidence that stevia is safe and may even have health-promoting effects.[27] If I were to choose between drinks sweetened with stevia or an artificial sweetener, I'd take the former.

My only real reservation about stevia is that it can 'feed' a desire for intensely sweet foodstuffs. For some, sweet tastes can cause parts of the brain called 'reward centres' to light up, which can drive further desire for sweet-tasting foodstuffs. Anyone so affected would generally do well to deal with what can be an unhealthy attachment, and foodstuffs sweetened with stevia (however natural and safe) may not help, here.

I'm relaxed about the idea of people consuming occasional sweet foodstuffs (including those sweetened with stevia), as long as this does not appear to perpetuate a drive for unhealthy foods.

Fruit Juice and Smoothies

We learned in the previous section that regular soft drinks are intensely sugary. So are fruit juices. In fact, the sugar content of fresh squeezed orange juice (so, no added sugar) is essentially the same as cola. When asked about fruit juice and I impart this fact, people often look as though I have just delivered the most devastating news to them.

Now, I am not equating fruit juice to cola or any other soft drink. If I had to drink one, I'd take the juice, because at least there's some nutritional value to be had in it. But if the choice were juice or water, I'd take the water, because I think the sugar content of the juice is simply too much to be healthy for most people. This is particularly the case, by the way, for people who are looking to lose weight or, say, have diabetes.

Smoothies, I think, are slightly better, in that they are usually based on whole fruit (rather than merely juiced fruit) and therefore offer a bit more from a nutritional perspective. They are, however, still very sugary, and I would recommend them only in very limited amounts. It's perhaps not such a bad thing that they usually come in very small bottles.

Coconut Water

Coconut water sales have skyrocketed since its introduction as a mass-produced beverage several years ago. Its sugar concentration is about half that of fruit juices and regular soft drinks, and comes as a mix of naturally occurring glucose, fructose and sucrose. Coconut water also contains useful quantities of potassium and magnesium, two minerals that help a range of processes including muscular function and blood pressure control.

I drink a little of this myself, but I would not go big on it (drink it habitually and that sugar can certainly rack up). Perhaps the best time to take it is immediately after exercise. It will help with rehydration, of course, but also provides some sugar and potassium for replenishment and recovery. I think there's some truth in the claims some make about it being a natural 'isotonic' drink.

Coffee and Tea

Coffee and tea don't have particularly healthy reputations, something that I think has to do with the fact that they contain caffeine and other stimulants. Yet both of these beverages are linked, overall, with benefits for health. Let's take a look at this evidence now and see if we can explain it.

Tea comes in two main forms: black (regular tea) and green. Basically, black tea is made by allowing green tea to undergo oxidation (through fermentation). Tea contains disease-protective compounds known as 'polyphenols' that have 'antioxidant' activity. This means they have the capacity to neutralize the effects of damaging, disease-provoking molecules called 'free radicals' that contribute to 'oxidative stress'. In general terms, green tea contains less caffeine and has more antioxidant potential than black.

Research links both black[28] and green[29] tea consumption with a reduced risk of heart disease. Any benefits here are thought to be, at least in part, due to a polyphenol known as 'epigallocatechin-3-gallate' (EGCG). EGCG has also been found to have a number of cancer-protective actions in the body, including an ability to help in the deactivation of cancer-causing chemicals (carcinogens). This may help to explain why regular consumption of green tea is also associated with a reduced risk of some forms of cancer.[30]

Coffee, like tea, is also rich in polyphenols, and its consumption is consistently linked with a reduced risk of diabetes,[31-33] as well as a reduced risk of stroke in men.[29] All this evidence is epidemiological, but it is strengthened by the knowledge that the polyphenols in coffee and tea have basic health-giving properties.

However, some caution may be prudent because of the presence of caffeine in tea and coffee. The major problem here is that this can cause a seeming boost in energy that can commonly end as a crash some time later. Caffeine can also disrupt sleep (see Chapter 4).

Caffeine is metabolized (broken down) in the liver, and the speed at which this happens appears to vary a lot between individuals. 'Fast metabolizers' clear caffeine quickly from their systems, and therefore tend not to get much of a 'kick' from it. They can also perhaps throw back a double espresso after dinner and still sleep like babies. 'Slow metabolizers' of caffeine, on the other hand, generally feel a distinct 'jolt' from it (particularly strong coffee), and know they need to be careful as to when they consume it if they want to sleep well. Slow metabolizers also tend to find caffeine quite addictive.

These are two extremes, and tolerance of caffeine is a spectrum. However, if you feel you are towards the slow metabolizer end of the range, you might want to consider drinking decaffeinated versions of coffee and tea. However, decaffeination processes can involve chemical solvents that are best avoided. More natural and, I think, preferred forms of decaffeination are those that use water (also known as the 'Swiss' method) or carbon dioxide. Some scrutinizing of labels is required to find appropriate brands. Naturally decaffeinated fruit, herbal and rooibos (redbush) tea are other good options too.

A word of warning, though: abrupt withdrawal of caffeine can precipitate a headache ('caffeine withdrawal' is a common cause of weekend headaches, by the way). The headache normally comes on in the afternoon or evening of the day caffeine is eliminated, and dissipates over the next couple of days or so. Gradual withdrawal may give you an easier ride.

I find that most people who tend to over-consume coffee or tea drink these beverages indiscriminately. If it's wet and warm, they will usually drink it, including from coffee machines and from jugs in meetings that can dispense quite awful bilge.

So, I say, if you like tea and coffee, then have something you really like. Reserving your drinking of tea and coffee to stuff you get genuine enjoyment from will cause the chances of over-consumption to drop like a stone. It might also get you out of the office to a coffee shop or café and therefore provide an opportunity to stretch your legs (see Chapter 6), get out into the light (see Chapter 5) and clear your head.

The Primal Principle: Tea and Coffee

It's difficult to imagine that our early ancestors would sit around campfires chucking back espressos and sipping green tea. However, the main constituent of these drinks is water. And let's not forget that coffee comes from a bean, and tea from a leaf – both of which are naturally occurring. While they look and taste different, tea and coffee are both rich in polyphenols, remember. When these health-promoting substances are infused into some hot water, it's perhaps not too surprising that the resultant beverages might turn out to have some benefits for our health.

Milk

Many of us like to put milk in coffee and tea, and some of us have a penchant for drinks that are predominantly milk, such as cappuccinos and lattes. Unfortunately, the fact that milk is a relative nutritional newcomer to the human diet (along with the process of pasteurization), probably helps explain why it is quite a common cause of 'food sensitivity' (discussed in the last chapter). Just to recap: childhood 'ear, nose and throat' problems such as recurrent sore throats, ear infections, 'glue ear', and near-constant running of the nose can be rooted in an issue with milk sensitivity. Eczema and asthma are other common manifestations (although not everyone with these conditions has a milk sensitivity). In adulthood, milk sensitivity can often cause chronic sinus congestion, a blocked nose and a tendency to snore.

If you suspect you might be milk-sensitive, I suggest taking out all dairy products from your diet for two weeks to see if this helps you. If it does, you're in a better position to judge whether or not it's worth resuming your former intake. Also, you may remember that in the last chapter I shared my observation that while sensitivity to cow's milk and products made from cow's milk are quite common, I find people tolerate goat and sheep products much better.

I don't particularly recommend milk as a drink, and I do think it's worth avoiding cappuccinos and lattes in the main. Better, I think, would be to have an espresso, black coffee and tea without milk or just a splash of milk. If you really feel you cannot live without hot milky drinks, perhaps save them for the weekend to have alongside a nice cooked breakfast or brunch.

Alcohol

Most of us like to drink, and can even relax in the notion that 'moderate drinking' is actually better than not drinking at all. The basis for this belief comes from research linking regular drinking, particularly red wine (see below), with a reduced risk of heart disease.

One problem with this epidemiological research is those pesky confounding factors that can give misleading impressions about the health effects of alcohol. For instance, teetotallers at increased risk of heart disease can be reformed alcoholics (with quite damaged hearts), or may have stopped drinking because they've been diagnosed with heart disease.

Another major flaw of the oft-quoted alcohol research is that it has often only focused on heart disease. Alcohol is associated with adverse effects on health including an increased risk of cancer. It makes sense, therefore, to assess alcohol's relationship not with heart disease alone, but with *overall risk of death*.

When researchers have focused on this, a slightly different picture can emerge. One study found that in men up to the age of thirty-four and women up to the age of fifty-four, the optimal amount of alcohol to drink was none at all.[34] In this study there seemed to be some benefits of alcohol consumption later in life – the optimal intake being about one unit a day for men and three units a week for women. As a sometime drinker myself, I take no satisfaction in imparting the news that the benefits of drinking alcohol have been somewhat overstated.

It should perhaps not be forgotten, either, that alcoholic drinks are generally a source of carbohydrate which, remember, can be a prime driver of weight gain. Perhaps unsurprisingly, studies have found an association between higher alcohol intakes and increased risk of weight gain, specifically around the middle of the body (the type of fat distribution strongly linked with health issues such as heart disease and type 2 diabetes).[35-37] I've lost count of the number of people who have told me: 'If I want to lose weight, I just cut out alcohol.'

I think another significant issue with alcohol is its potential to disrupt sleep (see Chapter 4). When habitual drinkers cut back on alcohol or eliminate it altogether for a period of time, they usually very quickly report feeling as though their sleep has improved and that they feel a damn sight better in the mornings.

I drink (and, occasionally, get drunk) and I'm not in any way puritanical about drinking (or any other dietary habit, come to that). However, I have learned from experience that the less people drink, usually the better.

This does not necessitate us taking the pledge and never allowing alcohol to pass our lips. Personally, I do not promote or support the idea that *everything* we consume need be healthy (there are obviously other factors that might play a part in our dietary choices). However, if we are going to drink, we may at least apply some simple tactics that allow us to do this in a way that does the least damage.

Sour Grapes

Red wine, more than any other form of alcohol, has often been recommended as 'healthy' to drink regularly and in moderation. Much scientific focus has been placed on a constituent of red grapes known as 'resveratrol' (a type of polyphenol), the actions of which in the body would help to explain red wine's proposed benefits for the heart.

However, is red wine actually beneficial to health, or is there another explanation? In the Introduction to this book I specifically mentioned epidemiological studies and how we cannot use them to determine the health effects of lifestyle

↓

factors such as diet. I referred specifically to the research linking red wine with improved heart health there.

Red wine might be beneficial to heart health, but the association might be due to other 'confounding factors' such as better dietary habits in general and lower rates of smoking in red wine drinkers. It turns out that this is precisely what the research shows.[38-40] The evidence suggests that it's not the red wine *per se*, but lifestyle factors associated with red wine drinking that likely account for the supposed 'benefits' of red wine.

Hold Your Drink

For a given amount of alcohol, beer and cider contain much more carbohydrate than wine. Red wine contains, generally speaking, less carbohydrate than white. Is a glass of red wine with your evening meal likely to upset things too much? Probably not. The problem is, many of us can find it quite difficult to limit ourselves to just one glass.

Fortunately, there are tactics we can use to drink less without having to exert conscious control here. Here are my three top tips:

1. Don't be thirsty

It stands to reason that the thirstier we are, the more we will tend to drink (yes, I know it's obvious, but I can't tell you how often people fall foul of this). A busy day, particularly in the summer, where fluid intake may have been just a couple of plastic cups of water and some coffee or tea, can leave us parched and in need of some liquid refreshment. Beer, white wine, vodka-tonics and the like can be extremely appealing in this state (and will usually slip down a treat too).

It makes sense to ensure we're properly hydrated prior to drinking any alcohol. Remember, the aim is to drink enough water to make dark, pungent urine a thing of the past. This tactic alone may well help you reduce the amount you consume quite naturally.

2. Don't be hungry

While the fact that thirst can stimulate drinking is quite obvious, what is less well recognized is that *hunger* can be a major driver here, too. Alcohol can provide ready fuel for the body, and at least some people will find that the hungrier they are, the more they end up drinking. Some individuals can even *crave* alcohol if their blood sugar level drops below normal levels.

One common manifestation of this phenomenon is a tendency to drink a beer, a glass of wine, or a G and T, say, prior to food in the evening. Individuals coming home or entering a restaurant in a very hungry state will often reach for the alcohol before anything else. I've found in practice that when individuals manage their appetite better, they almost always drink less without even thinking about it.

One simple tactic here is to eat something properly satisfying and sustaining such as some nuts at the end of the afternoon or early evening. More about the value of nuts as a snack (as well as why nuts do not appear to be a fattening food) can be found in the next chapter.

3. Match each alcoholic drink with one of water

One trick that usually works wonders to dry up alcohol intake a bit is to match each alcoholic drink (e.g. glass of wine) with a glass of water. This almost inevitably leads to less being drunk, and also 'dilutes' any negative effects the alcohol may have (including a tendency for alcohol to dehydrate the body). Plus, it provides the body with some water (generally a good thing) that would not have been had otherwise. Matching alcohol with water usually leaves people in a much better situation all round.

These tactics tend to work like a charm for most people, though there will be times when they are harder to put into practice than others. If, for example, you spend the day at the rugby or football and beer is the order of the day, good luck matching each pint with one of water (you'll spend a good part of the match in the toilets, for a start). However, for most people, such occasions are just that – very *occasional* – and so are birthdays and weddings. My advice is to enjoy some guilt-free pleasure at these times, and focus more on how you manage your drinking on a day-to-day basis.

That's the Spirit

Of all the alcoholic beverages, spirits such as gin, vodka and whisky probably have the worst of reputations. I actually favour them, mainly on the basis that their sugar content is very low. Of all the spirits, I think vodka is the best. It's generally the purest of all forms of alcohol, and I've noticed it is usually possible for people to get quite drunk on vodka and still feel pretty functional the morning after.

↓

↓

Mixers can be the challenge, though, as we ideally want to avoid sugar and artificial sweeteners. The only real viable option is soda water, though of course we could add some lime juice for flavour (fresh lime is best, but a splash of cordial is not a disaster). For me, vodka, lime and soda is the smart choice if it's going to be a bit of a session.

You may, of course, think that a vodka, lime and soda is just about drinkable, but it doesn't do it for you like the fine wines, mojitos or margaritas that you perhaps love to imbibe. Well, actually, that's one of the reasons you may want to opt for vodka, lime and sodas: they're just *not that nice*. And people find when they drink them they can certainly 'do the trick' but they aren't usually driven to consume them in vast quantities. Particularly when you have to work the next day, this may be no bad thing.

Out and About

One thing that can get in the way of more moderate drinking is evening entertaining. These occasions usually involve alcohol, and are you really going to risk making your dinner date perhaps feel uncomfortable by announcing: 'I'm not drinking, but you go right ahead' (particularly if they're a client).

One tactic worth considering here is not to make any announcements at all, but just order the wine, have it served to you, and then drink hardly any of it. This a bit trickier to do when, say, there are only two of you, but it usually works extremely well in groups.

Some of the wellness programmes I run are residential, and wine is always served in the evenings (yes, we like to emulate what it's like to live in the real world, not the hermetically sealed bubble some people imagine I live in). I'm *working* at these events, of course, and my intention is to be as energized and 'on the ball' as possible at all times. Downing a bottle of wine over dinner, I've found, does not help.

So, I might sneak a vodka, lime and soda at pre-dinner drinks, but once we sit down to the meal the chances are I will drink no more than a few sips of wine. The waiting staff know to serve me the wine, but I just sit with it there in front of me (along with my water), hardly taking any of it. Unless someone has nothing better to do than scrutinize my behaviour, no one would know that over the course of the evening I've hardly drunk a thing. Everyone can relax, even those sitting next to me, and I can get up in the morning in a state where I am able to give my best.

Motivation Matters

There is no doubt that for many of us, drinking alcohol can be pleasurable, relaxing and convivial. However, alcohol has potential downsides too. It commonly impacts on things like wellbeing (at least in part through its likely effects on sleep) and weight.

So, the reality is drinking half a bottle of wine or a couple of beers most nights can lead people to be a stone or two heavier than they'd like to be, or cause them to be a bit slow to start in the morning and lacking in zip for the first half of the day.

If we recognize this, then we may come to realize that the pleasure of drinking is more than outweighed by the 'pain' of the effects it's having on us in other areas. In which case, we may resolve that we'd be better off, say, mainly confining our drinking to the weekend and drinking less in general.

In Chapter 10, we consider the 'pleasure and pain' principle in more depth, and how we may use to it to control unhealthy habits and sustain healthy ones with ease.

'I've Got Over a Thousand Bottles'

I usually allude to our motivations when, after a discussion on alcohol, someone mournfully mentions their love of wine as if it were an adored romantic partner. At the risk of coming across as rather glib, I will commonly retort: 'And I love crack cocaine and crystal meth, but I've decided what I get out of them is more than outweighed by the fact that they make it much harder for me to be healthy and do my job to the best of my ability.'

Some people actually take this comment literally but, to be honest, I'm happy for the occasional person to think of me as a reformed crack-head because, well, it just adds to the mystique.

Even after this exchange some may come back at me with tales of their extensive wine collection or temperature-controlled cellar. To which I usually reply: 'And I live in a crack den, but I'm still resolved to the fact that it's best to keep my class A habit in check.'

The point, as I made earlier, is not necessarily for someone to banish alcohol from their lives, but to contemplate drinking less of it and also choose to drink it in a way where, overall, they get the pleasure from it with little downside.

THE BOTTOM LINE

- Maintaining hydration is key to ensuring optimal levels of energy, particularly mental energy

- Aim to drink enough water to keep your urine pale yellow throughout the course of the day

- Sugary soft drinks pose hazards to the body and should be avoided

- 'Diet' drinks have not been proven to aid weight control, and some evidence suggests that artificial sweeteners may actually promote weight gain and have other adverse effects on health

- Fruit juices and smoothies contain a lot of sugar and are best avoided except in very limited quantities

- Coconut water contains about half the sugar of regular soft drinks, and also contains useful quantities of nutrients such as potassium and magnesium

- Both tea and coffee are linked with health benefits but are best drunk with little or no milk

- The health benefits of alcohol have been overstated

- Alcohol has the capacity to disrupt sleep and often affects performance the following day

- Simple strategies for drinking less include avoiding undue hunger and thirst, as well as matching each alcoholic drink with one of water

- Vodka, lime and soda is the smart option if you want to get drunk but minimize the damage and the risk of a hangover the following day

Chapter 3

Movable Feast

Chapters 1 and 2 will have given you a decent framework around which to build dietary habits that are likely to do wonders for your energy, wellbeing and effectiveness. One last thing that warrants our attention, though, concerns *when* and *how often* we should eat.

As with much dietary information and advice, there can be some mixed messages here. Conventional advice is normally to eat three meals a day, and to eschew eating in between. Others, in contrast, advocate 'grazing' – eating maybe five or six times throughout the day, supposedly to optimize energy and assist weight control. In recent times, though, there has been considerable interest in 'intermittent fasting' – the practice of extending times between meals or having very little to eat at all on certain days.

With all these options on offer, no wonder some of us can be confused about the ideal frequency of feeding. This chapter explores the pros and cons of different patterns of eating and offers practical guidance about finding what's best for you.

Three Square Meals

I'm not sure where the advice to eat 'three square meals' a day comes from, but it's existed for as long as most of us remember. Underpinning this advice is the idea that we need regular food for energy. Breakfast is often said to be 'the most important meal of the day' because, supposedly, it fuels us after an extended overnight fast and sets us up for what's to come.

Another common addition to the 'three meals a day' dictum is the advice to avoid snacking. Eating between meals, we are often warned, will usually up our overall intake and risks putting our daily calorie balance in the black.

The Hunger Games

When individuals veto snacks completely, circumstances mean they can go for long periods of time without eating, particularly between lunch and dinner. As we'll see later, there's nothing wrong with this in principle. But (and it is a big but), if it leads to someone's appetite running out of control, the end result is usually far from satisfactory. While avoiding snacks makes sense on the surface, it can actually lead us down a path to nutritional ruin.

When people get too hungry, this usually drives them to make food choices that simply don't help them achieve their health and performance goals. For example, uncontrolled appetite at lunch can drive people to polish off foot-long baguettes accompanied by a packet of crisps or chocolate bar (maybe with a sugary drink for bad measure).

But worse fates usually await those who get rampantly hungry before dinner. The vast majority of people I work with in workshops and seminars are lucky if they are able to sit down to dinner before 7 p.m., and for a significant number this time can be 8 p.m. or even later. For many, going without food from lunch at, say, 12.30 p.m. to a late dinner will leave them very hungry indeed. Here's how this commonly plays out:

Unhealthy eating

It's all very well knowing what truly healthy eating is, but you try actually doing it when you're hungry enough to eat your own fist. Imagine being faced with a piece of fish and some vegetables at dinner time when you're starving hungry. Most people know this is 'not going to touch the sides', and will look for something such as bread, pasta or rice to fill the void. Once we get very hungry, it becomes much harder to control *what* we eat, and *how much* we eat of it.

Many people may even start to run into problems here even *before* dinner: although a full meal is imminent, some will find themselves working through industrial quantities of cheese and crackers or hummus and pitta bread.

Also, this hunger may mean that your first priority on crossing the threshold is not your partner or family, but the *fridge*. Someone might be looking to communicate with you about something important or be seeking some comfort and affection, but all they can see is the back of your head as you rummage around looking for the Marks and Spencer dips.

Even in a restaurant there can be demons in the form of the warm, fragrant, freshly baked bread delivered under your nose just as your perusal of the menu and an apéritif are sending your appetite into overdrive.

Alcoholic excess

Most alcoholic drinks can pick up blood sugar levels pretty quickly, and some people unwittingly use alcohol as a substitute food when they get hungry. Sometimes, this manifests itself as reaching for a vodka tonic, wine or beer as soon as they walk in through the door. But even if this does not happen, generally the hungrier someone is, the more alcohol they'll pack away over the course of the evening.

We touched on this in the last chapter, where we also explored the likely effects of alcohol on health and wellbeing. I also offered three simple strategies for reducing alcohol consumption without sacrifice or deprivation; you may remember that one of these was the importance of keeping our appetite in check.

Mood issues

When people get hungry, and particularly when blood sugar levels dip too low, the brain tends to malfunction. In the first chapter I mentioned how this can turn on the stress response and ramp up the production of the 'excitatory' substance glutamate in the brain. This is not ideal for those about to re-engage with the people at home.

I've heard countless stories from people who tell me that, despite the fact that they were looking forward to coming home, they somehow magically transform into the very worst versions of themselves in response to something quite trivial.

If this sounds at all like you, imagine the impact this might have on those around you. They may not have seen you all day and are looking forward to your return. You, on the other hand, may cause upset in those around you in a few nanoseconds with your stern, over-controlling ways that have been given life simply because you've allowed yourself to get too hungry.

My experience with countless business professionals is that getting too hungry at the end of the day is one of the most common problems of all. I also know that it's something well worth avoiding if you are looking to keep your mood buoyant and your relationships as harmonious as possible.

There are other pitfalls to allowing ourselves to get too hungry that we would do well to sidestep. These include issues relating to weight, work and willpower:

Weight Issues

Some of us get a pay-off from being hungry because, consciously or unconsciously, we believe this is a clear indication we're in calorie deficit, and the pounds must be 'dropping off us'. Some maths reveals, though, that we are almost certainly deluding ourselves.

Let's say we burn 2,500 calories in a day. For each hour we go hungry the body, technically, will have a deficit of around 100 calories. Each gram of fat contains about 9 calories. This means that a 100-calorie deficit equates to about 11 g of fat (a little more than a third of an ounce). Not exactly melting away, is it?

But the real problems are likely to come later. Remember, allowing ourselves to get very hungry before meals is what can drive us to eat quantities of food that cause sugar levels to skyrocket. Insulin will then be secreted in response, driving fat storage. And, if blood sugar levels come plummeting down two or three hours later, we may get an urge to eat again, and usually something that will dash any weight-loss aspirations we had.

So, in summary, while going hungry may have led to you shedding an ounce or so of fat, it may have also possibly driven you to eat a tonne of fat-forming food. It's perhaps easy to see how going hungry might be counterproductive to any desire we may have to attain and maintain a healthy weight.

How Hungry?

I don't advocate eating when not hungry (if we're not hungry when we eat, then we're just eating out of habit or boredom, usually). But I most certainly don't suggest eating when too hungry either. Here's a little guide to help you:

Imagine hunger is measured on a scale of 0 to 10 where 0 is 'I can't eat another thing' and 10 is 'I'm so hungry I could eat my office chair'. I generally recommend that people aim to eat meals when they're about a 6 or a 7 on this scale.

What I find overwhelmingly true is that when individuals effectively manage their appetite, it makes eating healthily and in appropriate amounts *easy* (and life does not need to be difficult).

As we discussed above, some people imagine that hunger is just part of the pain one has to go through to lose weight. In reality, generally the reverse is true: the less hungry people are, the easier it is for them to eat the right foods, and the more weight they tend to lose. The absence of undue hunger also makes maintaining weight loss much, much easier. For a more thorough discussion of this and other keys to successful weight control, see my book *Escape the Diet Trap*.

Work Issues

Hunger, we know, can do strange things to the brain. Even if it does not lead to the ogre in you making an unwelcome appearance, it's very likely to get you thinking about food. The problem is, it's harder to concentrate on work when your mind keeps being dragged to the interior of the local sandwich shop as you fantasize about the damage you're going to do there later.

While we can try to put thoughts about food out of our minds, getting hungry is usually distracting. The cure? Don't allow yourself to get into this state if you can possibly help it.

Willpower Issues

In Chapter 10, we're going to be looking at some mental strategies we can use to embed healthy behaviours into our lives so that they are automatic and can be sustained with ease. A lot of us rely on willpower to maintain healthy habits and maybe keep unhealthy ones in check. However, research shows that willpower is a very finite resource indeed. Basically, it's a bit like a muscle: when 'exercised' it becomes weaker for some time after. This is a major reason why people ultimately fail to keep up with their good intentions (they can weaken in the end), and why I advocate approaches that do not rely much on willpower and self-control in the long term.

However, willpower is something that you, ideally, should be able to rely on in times of need. You can use it, say, to maintain your focus on a piece of work when faced with a tight deadline, or to keep your lip buttoned when part of you would like to tell a client where they can shove their unreasonable and ridiculous requests. Depleted will can impact negatively on all sorts of behaviours including attentiveness, emotional control and our ability to cope with stress, as well as impulsivity and aggression.

What's all this got to do with eating, you may ask? Well, evidence shows that our 'willpower muscle' is actually weakened by hunger. When blood sugar levels are lowered, willpower ebbs away.[1]

And it gets worse because, in addition to hunger's ability to sap the willpower, there is also evidence that exerting willpower can lower blood sugar levels.[2] This perfect storm of disordered physiology and neurochemistry can culminate in anything from a needlessly tetchy or sarcastic comment directed at a valued colleague or client, to aggression or anger triggered by something that is quite insignificant in the grand scheme of things.

Research has found that if individuals are given a sugary drink between two tests of self-control, they do better on the second one. This strengthening effect does not occur if the drink is artificially-sweetened, demonstrating that sugar feeds the willpower 'muscle' and strengthens the resolve. Sugary drinks are not ideal foodstuffs for achieving this effect, though, but eating in a way that keeps hunger at bay and blood sugar levels stable is (Chapter 1 provides all the details, if you haven't read it already).

Appetite Control

My experience with thousands of individuals has led me to conclude that many of us run into problems with hunger on an almost daily basis, and benefit massively simply by adjusting their food intake to counter this. The most common danger time, as we touched on earlier, is the evening, but some people struggle before lunch too.

Many people benefit from eating a snack in the late morning and/or the late afternoon. Fruit is usually recommended as the snack of choice, but I don't rate it all that highly. Here's why …

If we're eating a snack, we should be reasonably peckish, and our aim should therefore be to *sate our appetite properly* and ensure we get to the next meal without being too hungry. The question is, though, does fruit do a great job of sating the appetite? I've asked this question hundreds of times of my patients and in presentations and workshops, and almost without exception the answer I get back is a resigned 'no'. Most people find that if they get hungry, eating an apple or half a bunch of grapes will leave them about as hungry (if not hungrier) about ten minutes later. This is obviously a problem if the main point of eating the fruit was to fill a hole.

If you're looking for a practical and effective alternative, I suggest nuts. Their relatively protein-rich and blood sugar-stabilizing qualities should, in theory, give nuts superior appetite-sating properties, and I can vouch for this in practice. Time and again, I've witnessed how, for the vast majority of people, a handful or two of nuts can keep the wolf from the door for two to three hours or even longer. This allows people to get on with their work without the distraction of food fantasies and also makes it easier to eat (and drink) more healthily later on. Nuts may not be the cheapest of foods, but they offer a fantastic return on investment.

Fatty But Not Fattening

Nuts are fatty and pack a lot of calories into a small space. For this reason, many health professionals advise against their consumption in anything but micro-portions. Yet, when researchers have reviewed the impact of nut-eating on weight, they've found no evidence for fattening potential. If anything, the reverse is true.[3] In general, the evidence shows:

1. Those who eat nuts generally weigh less than those who don't

2. When people are fed nuts, they usually don't gain weight

3. Several studies show that when individuals increase their nut consumption, they actually lose weight

Can we explain these observations using what we learned in Chapter 1?

Nuts are generally low in carbohydrate, have low glycaemic indices (see Chapter 1, for more about the significance of this), and will generally not cause much in the way of insulin secretion. These fundamental facts are likely to be reflected in limited fattening potential.

Also, when we eat, it's a bit like putting fuel on a fire; it causes the 'fire' (our metabolism) to burn a little brighter (this is known as the 'thermogenic effect of food'). Nuts have considerable capacity to induce this effect.[4]

↓

↓

Of course, another thing nuts have going for them is their ability to satisfy the appetite, which can put a natural ceiling on how much we eat of them, as well as how much we eat of other foods later on.

Some people worry a bit about nuts, because they can find themselves polishing off a big bag over the course of an afternoon. Although nuts are generally healthy, it is possible to overeat them, and I suggest some tactics that can help ensure this is a non-issue.

First of all, if you find it difficult to stop eating a food after starting it, the chances are it is tasty and 'moreish' for you. In some people, certain foods can cause parts of the brain known as 'reward centres' to light up like a Christmas tree, which can drive continuing consumption. We mentioned this in the last chapter, in relation to sweet foods. For some, specific savoury foods, including some varieties of nuts, can be similarly rewarding.

While some rewarding food from time to time is not necessarily a bad thing, it's probably wise to keep away from this stuff on a day-to-day basis. So, if you find hickory smoked and salted almonds difficult to leave alone, then perhaps save these for pre-dinner drinks at the weekend, and the rest of the time opt for, say, some raw almonds (not many people will knock themselves out over these, to be honest). Other nuts that people generally enjoy (but not too much) in their raw form include cashews, walnuts and pecans. Roasted nuts are OK, and even salted nuts are not an issue as long as you do not have problems with high blood pressure

↓

↓

and the saltiness does not make the nuts too difficult to leave alone.

Another potential factor in overeating relates to the *visibility* of snacks. Accessibility is important because, well, otherwise we can't eat them. On the other hand, if the nuts or other snack are visible, we can end up with a constant visual reminder of their presence that can drive some 'mindless eating'.

So, in short, snacks such as nuts should be *available*, but *not visible*. You should know they're there should you need them, but ideally they should not be sitting on your desk or the arm of your sofa. Ideal storage places include a desk drawer, briefcase or laptop bag, or a kitchen cupboard. Now, if we get peckish, you're at liberty to take some nuts and eat them. I recommend tipping a few into the palm of the hand and returning the bag whence it came. If, after a while you're still genuinely peckish, you are at liberty to go back and take some more.

So, How Often Should I Eat?

If I were to summarize my advice on the frequency of eating, I'd say: eat regularly enough of the right foods to ensure you never get very hungry.

This converts to a frequency of eating that can vary quite a lot between people, and even from day-to-day.

I've come across many people who, as a rule, do best with quite regular feeding (say, three to five times a day). I have also, however, seen a significant number of people who eat quite errat-ically (and eat well when they do eat) and maintain high energy and performance. Some of these people will go the whole day eating little or nothing, but just don't get that hungry or feel weak or under-fuelled, and neither do they spin out of control food-wise in the evening. This way of eating most certainly does not suit everyone, but it can be right for some.

On the surface, it does not seem to make sense that these people are apparently getting by on so little fuel. But the question is, are these people really making do with *nothing*? All of us carry some fat, and a primary function of that is as a fuel store. If the truth be told, we really should be able to mobilize and utilize that fat in times of need (remember, that's what it's there for). Going back to the evolutionary argument for a moment (from Chapter 1), we should be able to cope with some irregularity in our eating schedule.

In the first chapter, we looked at some of the reasons why a diet lower in carbohydrate and richer in protein and fat than is traditionally advised may be effective for controlling the appe-tite. The relatively protein-rich nature of this sort of eating regime and its ability to stabilize blood sugar levels will likely have some role here. But, as we discussed in that chapter, such a diet will also help to temper insulin levels which will allow more ready release of fat from the fat cells, which can then go on to fuel the body (just like a hibernating bear).

Intermittent Fasting

Recent times have seen considerable interest in 'intermittent fasting' – essentially the practice of going for extended periods of time with little or no food. One type of intermittent fasting is known as '5:2', where individuals eat very restricted amounts of food on two days each week, but eat normally on the remaining days. Another form of intermittent fasting is known as 'alternate day fasting' (days of unrestricted eating which alternate with those during which very little is eaten). Yet another approach is to contract the 'window' available for eating each day. Typically, in intermittent fasting, eating windows last from four to eight hours each day.

The concept of intermittent fasting is relatively new, and consequently the research in the area is scant. However, what little science we have on intermittent fasting is generally positive.

In one study, for instance, overweight women undertook continuous or intermittent calorie restriction over a six-month period.[5] Half the women limited food intake to 1,500 calories a day. Those on the 'intermittent fasting' regime, on the other hand, ate 650 calories on each of two days in each week (the rest of the time they were free to eat as much as they liked). Both groups of women effectively restricted calories to the same degree (about 25 per cent of total calories normally consumed).

Both groups lost weight, and also saw improvements in measures such as blood pressure and inflammation. Insulin levels fell and insulin sensitivity rose, but it did so more in the intermittent fasters. Improved insulin sensitivity is a good thing that should translate into improved weight loss and reduced risk of type 2 diabetes over time. Intermittent fasting has also been linked with preservations of muscle during weight loss compared to daily calorie restriction.[6]

Not for Everyone

Intermittent fasting has merit, I think, but it's not for everyone. First of all, even if you're in a good state of health, I'd advise not even attempting this way of eating unless you have first ensured that your appetite and blood sugar balance are well controlled. Being able to delay a meal without undue hunger, having no food cravings and feeling that your energy levels are high and sustained throughout the day are all good signs in this respect. A few weeks of eating this way may also allow your body time to become better 'fat adapted', meaning that it can better subsist on fat stores and is less reliant on food for energy.

Those who should avoid intermittent fasting include individuals with a history of eating disorder (bulimia nervosa or anorexia nervosa) and type 1 diabetics. Even type 2 diabetics need to be careful here, as some adjustment of medication is likely to be required, and this should be done with the support and advice of a doctor.

Other individuals who should be wary of intermittent fasting include those who are generally very 'stressed' and suffer from persistent fatigue. Stress can weaken organs known as the adrenal glands (that sit on top of the kidneys) that have a role to play in blood sugar balance and metabolism. In the long term, compromised adrenal function can lead to fatigue and chronic fatigue (and even burnout). Intermittent fasting puts further stress on the adrenal glands, and is best avoided by those who are chronically stressed and have persistent issues with fatigue.

Individuals who are seeking to optimize their sporting performance should approach intermittent fasting with care, particularly if they are in an active phase of building muscle and strength. Working with a fitness professional with experience of intermittent fasting is advised.

What To Do?

If you decide to give intermittent fasting a go, you may wish to try a 5:2-type regime described above, and there are books devoted to this approach. However, these books can seemingly give individuals liberty to eat whatever they like on non-fasting days. That is something I would counsel against: if you're going to take this or any other intermittent fasting approach, for best results it helps for it to be in the context of a fundamentally healthy diet.

Another approach is simply to extend times between eating. This will help bring down insulin levels, of course, which can help things like fat loss and reduce the risk of insulin resistance (see Chapter 1). Bearing in mind that insulin levels are usually low during the night, one approach might be to capitalize on this by delaying eating in the morning. Another tactic might be to avoid eating beyond, say, 6 or 7 p.m.

If you're generally hungry in the morning and find your appetite tails off at the end of the day, then I recommend contemplating skipping supper. If you usually have little appetite in the morning, then missing breakfast would probably be a better bet for you. In general terms, I think individuals find it easier, socially, to skip or delay breakfast. Many of us live in a culture where breakfast is not so commonly a family or social event as dinner.

There's no reason to be rigid with intermittent fasting, either. If you tend to skip breakfast, but find yourself uncharacteristically hungry one morning, my advice is to eat something. On the other hand, if you normally eat dinner, but are simply not hungry one evening, this might be a good opportunity to forgo a late meal that day.

My Intermittent Fasting Experiment

I have personally experimented with intermittent fasting. I had been hearing good things about it from some of my clients, so decided to engage in a bit of self-experimentation. I also had been discussing intermittent fasting with a female client who had read my book *Waist Disposal: The Ultimate Fat Loss Manual For Men*. Not put off by the male-oriented title, she had applied the dietary principles in the book and lost about 100 lb. She had plateaued, though, and was looking for something to get her going again. I suggested intermittent fasting, and even volunteered to try it myself at the same time.

Although I had rarely skipped breakfast for many years, I am generally less hungry in the morning than in the evening. I therefore opted to skip breakfast, but resolved to do this gradually by slowly increasing the time in the morning before I ate anything. I generally get up quite early (6–6.30 a.m.), and after a week or two, I found myself being able to get to 1 p.m. or later before I felt I needed lunch.

To be clear, I was not consciously resisting food before this time – I just wasn't hungry. I felt no decrease in energy

↓

either. If anything, my energy levels improved, particularly my mental energy, focus and clarity (quite a lot of people report this, I've since found).

My fellow 'intermittent faster' found her weight loss kick-started again. I lost weight too. Within about a month I'd lost 5–6 lb and about an inch off my waist, which is significant seeing as I tend to never be very far from my 'fighting weight'. Even to this day, I typically eat breakfast about twice a week, and only if I'm hungry.

THE BOTTOM LINE

- Going too long without eating can cause us to get too hungry which can make it very difficult to eat healthily

- Hunger can drive us to drink more alcohol in the evening

- Many people can turn into not very attractive versions of themselves if they get too hungry

- Hunger is not a prerequisite for weight loss and, in fact, generally the less hungry people are, the easier it is for them to control their weight

- Hunger saps willpower, which can make life harder on a number of levels

- There is no one ideal pattern of eating

- As a rule, aim to eat the right foods regularly enough to ensure you never get very hungry

Chapter 4

Dream Ticket

This book is primarily written for people who would like to be more effective and productive. In this context, sleep can sometimes look like a bit of a waste of time: after all, while we slumber we are barred from doing 'useful' things like writing emails and performing billable work. It can seem, on the face of it, that 'if we snooze, we lose'.

Yet, at the same time, we are somehow programmed to devote about a third of our lives to sleep, and this does suggest it performs vital roles for us. This chapter will explore what contribution sleep makes to our wellbeing and health, and the issues that can befall us if we don't get enough of it.

The chapter will also give you an opportunity to gauge whether your current sleep patterns are meeting your needs. Finally, you'll be offered a range of simple strategies that will help ensure you get the quantity and quality of sleep required to leave you feeling refreshed and raring to go each morning.

A Sleep Primer

It might seem as though not much is going on when we sleep, but in reality the body and brain can be awhirl with activity. At certain times, this can be reflected in a state known as 'rapid eye movement' sleep (REM sleep). REM sleep is relatively shallow sleep, during which we are usually dreaming and the brain is surprisingly active. In REM sleep, brainwaves have a frequency of about 8–12 cycles per second (hertz) – about the same as when someone is awake but in a relaxed state (more about the brain-wave frequencies can be found in Chapter 7). This type of sleep appears to be important for optimizing certain brain functions including memory.

At other times, sleep is deeper and brainwave frequencies are slower (often 4–7 hertz, but sometimes even slower than this). This state of sleep is usually referred to as 'non-REM sleep' (or 'slow wave sleep'). The brain is relatively quiet during non-REM sleep, but there can still be a lot going on in other departments. For example, it's during non-REM sleep that the body secretes 'growth hormone' from the pituitary gland at the base of the brain.[1] As its name suggests, this hormone drives growth during childhood and adolescence. But, once we've reached our full height, growth hormone still has plenty to do for us. Some of the functions of growth hormone include:

- Maintaining the size and strength of our muscles

- Stimulation of the release of fat from fat cells ('lipolysis')

- Maintaining bone strength

- Supporting the immune system

Also, during non-REM sleep, secretion of the stress hormone 'cortisol' is suppressed. We need cortisol, in particular for driving energy production in the body and helping us cope with and adapt to whatever challenges we face in life. But we don't want too much cortisol either, as this can have adverse effects as well including fat accumulation around the midriff and muscle wasting. Excesses of cortisol can also impair the functioning of the hormone insulin ('insulin resistance'), which can ultimately lead us down the road towards type 2 diabetes (see Chapter 1 for more on this). Deep sleep's ability to suppress cortisol secretion is no bad thing at all.

Typically, the early part of the night is spent in predominantly non-REM sleep. As the night progresses, though, and particularly as we get into the small hours of the morning, we get progressively more REM sleep (see figure for a typical sleep profile).

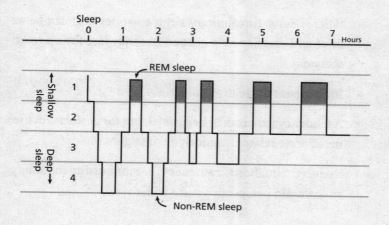

So, what happens when sleep is curtailed? Short sleep has been shown to affect key physiological and biochemical processes (see below). It also can have wide-ranging effects on the brain. These include:

- Increased effort required to complete a task

- Increased errors in tasks that are time-pressured

- Slowed mental performance in tasks that are not time-pressured

- Impairment of short-term memory

- Impairment of 'working memory' (important for things like comprehension and reasoning)

- Increased tendency to persevere with ineffective solutions to problems

- Reduced reaction time

- Reduced performance on tasks that require attention, leading to an increase in omissions and errors

- 'Microsleeps' (involuntary sleep episodes that can be as brief as a fraction of a second but may last for up to 30 seconds)

- Impairment of creative thinking

- A tendency for a task to begin well, but for performance to deteriorate relatively quickly as time goes on

- Reduced 'situational awareness', compromising the ability to maintain perspective and a wider view

Lack of sleep over the long term has the potential to have an impact on mood, too. In animals, sleep restriction has been found to alter the neurological and hormonal responses to stress in a way that predisposes to depression.[3]

All the mental deficits sleep loss can cause are things most of us could well do without. My experience is that these issues are common, but that many individuals are 'blind' to them. This may be because when we are deprived of sleep, brain-related issues tend to manifest themselves before more obvious symptoms such as fatigue. The risk here is that someone can have significant mental deficits that they won't necessarily connect with sleep deprivation because, on the whole, they don't feel particularly low on energy. I'd say lack of awareness about the impact sleep loss is having on functioning is one of the most pervasive wellness issues I come across in business professionals.

There appears to be considerable variation in sleep requirements (see 'Are You Getting Enough?' below). However, my experience is that even those with relatively low needs can 'push it a bit' and suffer as a result. Very few people actively volunteer to me that they feel sleep is an issue. However, when we start talking about sleep and how sleep debt can affect us, it often quickly dawns on individuals that they are running chronically short of sleep. Later on in the chapter, you'll be able to gauge how well your sleep needs are being met.

It May Be Written All Over Your Face

One thing sometimes worth considering is the effect sleep debt might be having not just on you, but the people around you. If you're running short on sleep, you may be radiating negative signals to colleagues and clients alike. I recently met a friend for dinner and when he turned up, he looked as though he'd been dug up, to be frank. When I asked him if he was OK, he said he just hadn't been sleeping well lately. He looked shocking, and this was not the result of long boozy evenings or a newly developed drug habit – just not enough sleep.

↓

↓

We may think we can compensate for our flagging energy with double espressos and cans of Red Bull, but there is evidence that the people we interact with will be able to tell, nonetheless. In one study, individuals were photographed after eight hours' sleep, and then again after being up for thirty-one hours without sleep. Observers then assessed the 'tiredness' of people just from these photographs (they did not know anything about the sleep conditions of the study subjects).[4] Observers rated individuals in a sleep-deprived state as looking more tired, less healthy and even less attractive. A follow-up study found that, when short on sleep, individuals appeared to have redder, more swollen eyes, as well as having darker circles under the eyes.[5] In addition, they were rated as looking sadder too.

These two studies' research suggests that some of the effects of not getting enough sleep can be all too obvious to others.

Some people give off even more obvious signals of sleep debt. I've spoken to many individuals, usually at senior levels within organizations, who have been running short of sleep for years and experience microsleeps at inopportune moments. However good someone is at what they do, literally falling asleep on the job is unlikely to send the right messages to those around them.

Most people prefer working around and doing business with people who appear energized, fit and fresh. Could it be that the 'sleep debt' signs leaking out of you might therefore have a considerable indirect impact on your career and the business because of the perception individuals have of you?

Sleep and Health

We know that sleep loss can sap our mental powers, but might it also have implications for our general health, too? One way to assess the effect of sleep deprivation is to induce this in people in 'sleep labs', and see what effect this has on their physiology and markers of disease. There are plenty of such studies now, and together they show sleep debt can have some serious consequences for our health and wellness. Some of the things shortened sleep has been found to provoke include:

- An increase in levels of inflammation in the body.[6] The pathological process of inflammation is thought to be a key underlying factor in chronic (long-term) diseases, including heart disease and type 2 diabetes

- Reduced effectiveness of the hormone insulin. In one study, just one night of only about four hours' sleep was enough to impair insulin functioning[7]

- Raised levels of the hormone 'ghrelin' (an appetite-stimulating and metabolism-slowing hormone)[8]

- Lowered levels of the hormone 'leptin' (an appetite-suppressing and metabolism-boosting hormone)[9]

- Increased hunger. In one study, stopping men sleeping for a single night led to them eating significantly more the following day[10]

- Increased levels of the stress hormone cortisol[11] (short sleep represents another stress for the body)

- Reduced metabolism of fat. In one study, disrupting men's sleep with an alarm clock and allowing them only an average of six and a half hours' sleep, compared to no alarm clock and eight hours' sleep, caused their metabolism of fat to fall by two-thirds[12]

- Unhealthy changes in body composition. In one study on the impact of sleep on weight loss, shortened sleep was found to reduce fat loss but increase muscle loss.[13] This effect may have something to do with the ability of sleep deprivation to increase levels of cortisol, as this hormone predisposes to fat gain and muscle loss

Some researchers have suggested that changing sleep patterns over recent decades is an important but under-recognized factor in the burgeoning rates of obesity and chronic disease.[14]

Time for Bed

In some research, investigators have attempted to assess the relationship between 'short' and 'long' sleep times and health. This research is quite varied in terms of how researchers defined 'short' and 'long' sleep. But, overall, research links shorter sleep with increased risk of conditions such as heart disease and type 2 diabetes, as well as overall risk of death.[15]

This epidemiological evidence does not tell us for sure that short sleep increases the risk of disease and death. However, we know that when individuals are made sleep-deprived, biochemical and physiological changes occur that would predispose us to these problems. Taken as a whole, the research points quite strongly to a lack of sleep being a genuine health hazard, I think.

Also, though, *long* sleep times are associated with poorer health outcomes and increased risk of death.[15] It may be that sleeping too much is genuinely bad for us. But it might be that those with generally poorer health have greater sleep needs and tend to get more sleep as a result. We actually don't know.

The varied nature of the evidence and the fact that it is epidemiological in nature makes it hard to draw any firm conclusions about what might be an optimal amount of sleep. Besides, as we discussed above, our needs for sleep are quite individual: whatever the science says about the optimal amount of sleep for people in general may have little or no relevance to *you*. How can you judge if you are getting enough sleep to meet your needs?

Are You Getting Enough?

In Chapter 2, we discussed how our needs for fluid are highly individual, and depend on variables like body size, levels of activity and temperature. Sleep's a bit like this. There may be people who need nine hours a night to function well, but others may require only seven hours or even less. Also, our need for sleep can vary from time to time. For instance, immediately after our sleep is particularly disturbed or constrained due to a busy or stressful period at work, we may need to catch up on sleep a bit to get us back to optimal functioning. Our sleep requirements are likely to be lower, though, after a fortnight's holiday.

Here are some questions you might ask yourself to get a better idea of whether the amount of sleep you're getting is doing the job:

1. Are you regularly woken by an alarm clock?

The use of alarm clocks to wake us up in the morning is common and part of life. If, however, we're having to forcibly awaken ourselves from sleep, the suggestion is we may well be getting sub-optimal amounts of sleep (otherwise we would wake naturally in a well-rested state).

2. Are you tired when you wake up?

When you wake in the morning, are you brimming with energy and raring to go, or is the first thought that goes through your head an expletive? Do you often struggle to get out of bed and wish you had more time to sleep? If these scenarios ring true for you, then 'sleep debt' is likely.

3. Do you use the snooze button?

A sign of not being immediately refreshed by sleep is the use (and abuse) of the snooze button. Some people use their alarm time and snooze function tactically: they set the time of their alarm earlier than the time they know they need to get up, because they know it's going to take two or three presses of the snooze button before they feel human enough to get up.

When I talk about this particular phenomenon with groups, I find up to half of the people in the room will be nodding away because they recognize that this is precisely what they do. If you're nodding away too, then the chances are high that you are running chronically short on sleep.

4. Do you need caffeine in the morning?

Do you feel you need a major shot of caffeine to get you going in the morning? If you do, this may also be pointing to sleep debt.

5. Do you have difficulty staying awake when you should be energized and alert?

Do you find waves of fatigue and a desire to sleep come over you in meetings sometimes? Can you find yourself drifting in and out of consciousness in the cinema or theatre? Do you find yourself falling asleep on trains and planes?

I've heard lots of people tell me how they regularly fall asleep in these settings, even at times when you would think it would be virtually impossible to sleep. For example, many people who do a lot of business air travel confess to sleeping through take-off. Think of the G-force, noise and vibration as the plane accelerates down the runway, and there they are, fast asleep, dribbling onto their lapel. If you drool in public, you probably need more shut-eye.

6. Do you catch up on sleep?

Do you catch up on sleep when you can, such as at the weekend or on holiday? Over the years, I've discovered the majority of people do this, and I've even met people who confess that their number one aim when on holiday is to catch up on sleep. If you recognise that you try and get more sleep when you can, then sleep debt during the working week is likely.

7. Do you think you're getting optimal amounts of sleep?

Think of the length of sleep you think you need for optimal energy and functioning. Now compare this to the average amount of sleep time you get in the week. I've done this exercise with hundreds of clients and the vast majority of responders quote a second figure that is about an hour less than the first. If this applies to you, then suspect sleep debt.

If you've gone through those questions and found a fair few of the scenarios resonate with you, then there's a good chance you will benefit significantly from getting more or better quality sleep. The following tips should help a lot:

Sleep Easy

1. Value sleep

As we discussed above, when questioned directly, many people confess to getting about an hour less sleep each night than they feel they need to function optimally. Some of this may be genuinely due to time constraints and workload. However, even if we worked for ten solid hours each day and had six hours for eating, commuting, relaxation and other activities, that still leaves eight hours for sleep.

One major reason for scrimping on sleep is that, as mentioned before, many of us view it as *unproductive* time. It is not. It prepares the body physiologically and psychologically for the day ahead and helps us be more productive. Getting enough sleep may well have a positive impact on your overall health too. One could argue that an additional hour of sleep each night, say, has the potential to pay us back handsomely in terms of how we feel and function, and may even help stave off conditions such as heart disease and type 2 diabetes. When individuals look at sleep in this light, they very often relax about the idea of getting more of it.

2. Consider going to bed earlier

There's an old adage: an hour of sleep before midnight is worth two after. There is some basis for this dictum in that the natural time for the secretion of growth hormone (see above) is before midnight. If we're not asleep at this time, growth hormone secretion can be impaired and we can miss out on some of the benefits it has to offer.

Some resistance to going to bed earlier can come from the idea that the evening is someone's only opportunity for 'me time', and I totally understand this. If 'me time' means doing something genuinely relaxing and rewarding such as playing or listening to music, reading a good book or watching a television programme that provides genuine enjoyment, then it might well be worth preserving.

However, I find that 'me time' for many can mean drifting in and out of consciousness in front of Newsnight, or 'pottering around' doing things that could be done at other times (such as the weekend). Some of us can find ourselves sitting glassy-eyed in front of our laptop or tablet device in bed, doing some mindless internet surfing.

This used to happen to me, by the way. Once too often I found myself watching a series of internet clips of people falling off their skateboards or blowing themselves up with fireworks. The cure? I gave my iPad to my parents who are now using it, among other things, to send me funny and heart-warming emails that take mere moments to read and leave me a lot more enriched than trips down the YouTube rabbit-hole.

So, if you feel perhaps the evening can sometimes be filled with non-essential 'stuff and nonsense', you may resolve that you'd be better off going to bed a bit earlier and getting the benefit of some more precious sleep.

Going to bed earlier generally allows people to get more sleep and feel better rested in the morning. Some individuals will find that they are able to wake up earlier than before, and have curiously *more* energy. Most people find that an extra hour or two in the morning can be useful for endeavours such as clearing some emails, putting the finishing touches to a pitch or presentation, or taking some exercise.

Compare these activities with, perhaps, the time you may have 'stolen' from the late evening the day before. Because, to be frank, if this were spent dozing in front of the telly or watching clips of people doing themselves serious injury, then you've probably not missed out on much.

Some of the strategies that may help you get your head down a bit earlier include:

- Set a time for when the TV gets turned off or, better still, don't turn it on in the first place

- Set a time for closing down your computer or tablet device

- Set a time after which there will be no checking of email on your smartphone

- If you have a partner, discuss your intentions around getting earlier nights and, if appropriate, enlist their support

- If possible, arrange work-related dinners to start a bit earlier. Is 6.30 p.m. out of the question? Often, others are secretly delighted by the suggestion as they appreciate they're going to get home at a reasonable hour

3. Do a 'brain dump'

Some people can have difficulty relaxing in the evening or getting to sleep at night because of all of the thoughts 'running through their head'. A lot of people find that getting these out of their head and 'down on paper' allows them the freedom to forget about them once they've retired to bed.

One practical application of this is to write a 'to-do' list in the evening for the following day. It's generally best to restrict this to a small number of tasks that you *need* to get done the next day. Referring to this list and executing the tasks on it on a regular basis during the day can give us confidence that what goes on the list gets done (and therefore doesn't have to be ruminated on at other times, like when we're trying to get to sleep).

4. Go easy on the caffeine

Caffeine is a stimulant and too much of it can keep us up at night. What constitutes 'too much' varies a lot from individual to individual, though. In Chapter 2 we discussed how caffeine is metabolized in the liver, and how there's considerable range in our capacity here. Some of us are slow metabolizers of caffeine, and can have it disrupt our sleep relatively easily. If this is you, then you may need to be quite wary about how much caffeine you consume, and when. Some individuals are so sensitive that they need complete or almost complete elimination of caffeine to optimize their sleep. Decaffeinated tea and coffee along with herbal and fruit teas are alternatives. See Chapter 2 for more information.

5. Go easy on the alcohol

Most individuals are well aware that coffee and tea can impair sleep, but there's much less recognition of the fact that another favoured beverage that can cause problems here is *alcohol*.

Some of the reasons for this general lack of awareness, I think, relates to the fact that many people find alcohol can 'anaesthetize' them and aid their ability to get to sleep. This is true, I believe, and there's even evidence for it.[16] However, the research also shows that alcohol tends to disrupt sleep in the second half of the night. It has, for example, been shown to suppress REM sleep, which may impact on mental functioning.

Alcohol can impair the quality of sleep through other mechanisms, too. It is known, for instance, to alter the functioning of what is known as the 'autonomic nervous system'. This is the part of the nervous system that regulates processes not ordinarily under our conscious control, such as our breathing, heart rate, the stress response and sleep. The autonomic nervous system has two main parts: the 'sympathetic' and 'parasympathetic' nervous systems. In general terms, the sympathetic part is activated when we are alert and stressed. The parasympathetic part, on the other hand, is more dominant when we are relaxed and at rest.

When we sleep, it's important for the parasympathetic nervous system to be 'dominant'. The problem is, alcohol has been found to disrupt parasympathetic nervous system activity.[17]

Another reason alcohol can disrupt sleep, I think, has to do with the fact that it is generally disruptive to blood sugar levels. The fundamental problem here is that any peak in blood sugar caused by alcohol can lead to a trough in the middle of the night. You may remember from Chapter 1 that, in this situation, the body will want to correct low blood sugar levels by secreting hormones such as adrenaline and cortisol that stimulate the release of sugar from the liver. These are also our major stress hormones, though, and the last things we want coursing through our system if deep, restorative sleep is our aim.

As a result of this mechanism, some people find that even though they had nothing particular on their mind when they went to bed, they can still find themselves awake and alert at three or four o'clock in the morning, at which point they will almost certainly find something to worry about (after all, who has nothing that might concern them?)

Often individuals will not sleep well subsequently, only to finally drop off about half an hour before the alarm goes off (at which point they usually feel dreadful).

One thing I have found almost universally true is that when individuals who habitually drink alcohol in the evening cut this back substantially or stop altogether for a period of time, they report better sleep and feel much more energized in the morning.

Of course, ideally we should be able to reduce alcohol consumption without feelings of sacrifice or deprivation or a sense we are 'missing out'. Tips on this can be found in Chapter 2. Also, in Chapter 10, we explore how realizing what impact alcohol can have on us in the working week can lead us to view drinking less as a bit of a 'no-brainer'.

6. Eat a primal diet

Eating the right sort of diet is key to stabilizing blood sugar levels and ensuring deep sleep. Here's how not to do this: get starving hungry before you come home, eat some crisps or cheese and crackers followed by a pile of pasta, topped off with some ice cream or a slab of chocolate. Eat along these lines, and you are almost certainly heading for a blood sugar low in the middle of the night, even in the absence of alcohol.

For the best blood sugar stability (and sleep), an evening meal should be made up of some meat, fish or perhaps an omelette, coupled with some salad and/or vegetables. Not coming home or walking into a restaurant too hungry is key to doing this successfully (more detail about this can be found in Chapter 3). If you haven't already, read Chapter 1 for advice about the best foods to eat to ensure blood sugar stability.

7. Get light exposure during the day

Our sleep-wake cycle is, to a large degree, regulated by the secretion of a hormone called 'melatonin' (secreted by the 'pineal' gland in the brain). Melatonin is actually made from the brain chemical 'serotonin'. Serotonin's manufacture is, at least in part, stimulated by light exposure.[18] Once evening comes, serotonin can be converted into melatonin to induce sleep.

Lack of sunlight exposure during the day can, therefore, cause us to run low on serotonin in the day and lack sufficient melatonin at night. More about the positive impact of light exposure and how to make sure you get enough can be found in the next chapter.

8. Avoid bright light exposure in the evening

Light exposure in the day promotes better sleep, but it may have the reverse effect late in the evening. In one study, light exposure from room lighting was found to delay melatonin secretion by about ninety minutes, and reduced the overall amount of melatonin secreted, too.[19] Turning room lighting down or perhaps off altogether (and using dimly lit lamps) in the evening may help sleep.

But light can also come from other sources too, including TVs, laptops and tablet devices, and this can suppress melatonin secretion too.[20] The tendency to be affected by this sort of light exposure will vary from person to person. However, for those who sense that they don't sleep terribly well, it's probably a good idea to be mindful of the potential impact of evening light on sleep. Some things worth thinking about include:

- Avoiding the use of TV, laptops and tablets within two hours of bedtime

- Dimming the display brightness. There exists a free piece of software that filters out blue light from computer screens at dusk. I use this and find it useful, as do many others I've recommended it to. You can read more about it and download it from www.stereopsis.com/flux/

- Having no TV in the bedroom

- Getting a pair of blue-light-blocking (orange) sunglasses. Orange-tinted lenses filter out blue light and, theoretically, should help sleep. In one study, the use of orange-tinted glasses three hours prior to sleep improved both the quality of sleep and subsequent mood.[21] Wearing orange-tinted specs are certainly worth a shot for people who struggle with sleep and can't necessarily control light exposure in the evenings (as long as they don't mind looking like Bono)

9. Eyeshades

Ideally, our bedrooms should be as dark as possible to ensure the best sleep. This can be difficult to achieve for many of us, particularly when we travel and may not have much control over our environment. Sometimes, eyeshades can come in handy. The problem is, many are uncomfortable. Some, for instance, can cause sweating or press uncomfortably on the eyes. I'm no engineer, but I see these things as serious design flaws.

I find people get on well with a make of eyeshades called 'Pure Comfort'. These are made of a soft, absorbent material and have a padded strip at the bottom that lifts the shades off the eyes. The eyeshades handed out in first class on British Airways flights are also very good. However, as someone once remarked to me, the Pure Comfort eyeshades are probably cheaper.

10. Earplugs

Noise is a common cause of disturbed sleep. Even within our own homes we can be bothered by extraneous sounds from kids, pets or a snoring partner. When we travel, we sometimes have to run the gamut of TV noise from adjacent bedrooms, traffic and aircraft noise, buzzing fridges and whirring air-conditioning units. Once, while staying at a hotel in Athens, I was woken at 7 a.m. by the sound of music that was being automatically piped into my room.

Many people find that life is made infinitely easier by simply inserting some earplugs. The problem is, as with eyeshades, these can be quite uncomfortable. Over the years, I've found the best make are foam earplugs made by the company Quies. When scrunched up they stay that way for quite a few seconds, which means they can be properly inserted into the ear canal. They're also comfortable, and don't tend to cause the ear irritation other makes often do.

I never travel without these earplugs myself. I wear them at night as a matter of course, but often use them during the day, too, say on trains and planes. No longer do I need to put up with the deafening drone of aircraft engines, or listen to someone speaking overly loud on their mobile phone to 'Roger in accounts'. My earplugs have saved me losing sleep (and maybe even my sanity) on countless occasions.

11. Sleep apps

There are some good 'sleep apps' available that use a combination of voice, music and sounds to help us drop off to sleep. One of the most popular is known as 'Pzizz', which also makes use of a technology known as 'binaural beats' (more about this in Chapter 7). Pzizz comes in two versions: one is for general sleep, while the other is designed to help individuals revive themselves through napping. And while we're on the subject of napping …

Grabbing Forty Winks

When conducting training sessions and workshops, I get a lot of questions about napping. I've discovered that's because many people avail themselves of the opportunity to nap (usually at the weekend), and they wonder whether they should. The majority of habitual nappers say they feel much better for it, but in their heads have put this habit in the category of 'guilty pleasures'.

For what it's worth, the seeming ability of napping to restore energy and improve performance is supported in the scientific literature. In one study, half of a group of medical students were instructed to take a short nap at midday, while the other half were not.[22] Average nap time was just eight and a half minutes. Compared to those who did not nap, those who did saw an improvement in brain function and attention in the afternoon.

A short nap does seem to have the capacity to restore our mental energies and revive us, but it seems the operative word here is 'short'. Sleeping for about fifteen to twenty minutes does seem to offer significant benefits, but if this is extended to thirty minutes or more there is a risk of feeling extremely groggy on waking.[23] This phenomenon appears to be due to the fact that taking longer naps risks us dropping into *deep* sleep, from which waking can feel a bit like coming round from a coma.

In the UK, napping is not really part of work culture (though in other countries – notably Japan – it can be not just tolerated but positively advocated). Nevertheless, even in the UK I have met a few people who manage to sneak a nap into their weekday schedule.

I once met a partner at a professional services company who told me that each afternoon he would take himself off to some rarely frequented toilets. He'd sit on the lid of a toilet in a cubicle with his elbows on his knees and his head resting on his hands. He would go to sleep very readily, and come round again quite naturally about ten minutes later.

Snoozing in a toilet cubicle does not sound like the most romantic of experiences, but the reality is it always left him totally revived. He told me, after his nap, he would churn through copious quantities of high-quality work until the end of the working day. He was rather sheepish about his napping habit, as if it were maybe something he shouldn't be doing. Actually, as I told him, I felt he had found a fantastic strategy that required relatively minimal time investment, but paid him back massively in terms of improved productivity.

Sleep Technology

Some people find that tracking their sleep objectively helps ensure they do not run chronically short on it. There are several devices available now that can monitor and measure sleep. These include wearable technology such as Jawbone's 'Up', and Fitbit's 'Flex' and 'One'. All these devices monitor sleep through body movement (they all track activity in the day too – see Chapter 6 for more about this). The Flex and One come with the added bonus of alarm functions that use vibration to wake up the wearer (but nobody else).

Non-wearable technology is available too, such as the 'Renew' sleep monitor. This is a device into which an iPhone or iPad is docked. After downloading an app to the iPhone, the device uses low-power radio waves to monitor sleep through our movement and breathing patterns. One clever

$\downarrow$

feature of this system is that it allows you to set a range of alarm times (e.g. 6.30–7 a.m.) and the device will activate the alarm at the optimal point in this range (when sleep is at its shallowest). Another option is the app 'Sleep Cycle', which does a similar job but monitors sleep via a smartphone kept on the bed (e.g. under your pillow).

Taking the Lag Out of Jet Lag

Jet lag can result from travelling across time zones and ending up in a place where the time showing on the clock on the wall is not the time our body 'thinks' it is. As a result, we can be asking our body to do things that it resists, such as staying awake (when the body would rather be asleep) or sleeping (when the body would rather be awake).

There are a number of factors that affect how badly someone will be affected by jet lag, including the number of time zones crossed (more time zones generally means more trouble) and the direction of travel (travelling to the east is usually worse than travelling to the west).

We're going to look at how we can mitigate the effects of jet lag now. But before we do, it's worth bearing in mind that the people who tend to be most affected by jet lag are those who may not have the best sleep habits, generally speaking, and are exhibiting symptoms of sleep debt. In other words, acting on some of the general advice in this chapter will likely leave you less susceptible to jet lag and the energy-sapping rigours of long-haul travel.

Flight times

Sometimes we can feel hostage to flight schedules, but then again we don't necessarily help ourselves by opting for flights that cut into our sleep at either end of the journey. Taking a very early flight from our point of departure, or arriving very late at our destination are sometimes better avoided. What we appear to lose in terms of 'working time' can sometimes be repaid in terms of improved efficiency when we are working.

Getting sleep on a red-eye

Getting sleep on red-eye flights is important if, again, we are not going to graft sleep deprivation onto jet lag. A useful tactic here is sometimes to think of red-eye flights as an opportunity to sleep (and nothing else). This means no work, reading or in-flight entertainment.

If you are committed to this I suggest eating *before* the flight. As soon as the seatbelt light goes out, my advice would be to flatten your seat, put a blanket over you and the seatbelt over that, put an eye-mask on and earplugs in, and find as comfortable a position as possible. Neck pillows can help a lot if you're travelling in economy.

Food and drink

The guidelines about maintaining energy and vitality through smart food and drink choices don't suddenly become null and void at 40,000 feet. The problem is, long-haul flying can mean a nutritional free-for-all that can cause our vitality to plummet.

Temptation is made that much greater by being hungry and thirsty, so I suggest avoiding these states by making sure you drink water and satisfy your appetite (perhaps with some nuts) prior to and during the flight if need be. See Chapters 1–3 for more detail on how to manage your diet to optimize your energy and vitality.

Light exposure and avoidance

Earlier in this chapter we introduced the idea that light affects the sleep-wake cycle, and this can be helped by getting light in the day but avoiding it close to bedtime. Tactical use of light also has the capacity to help reset the body clock and mitigate the effects of jet lag.

When travelling to the west, what this means is seeking bright light in the evening hours but avoiding it immediately before sleeping. When travelling to the east, seeking bright light in the morning is the preferred strategy.[24] There is a very handy (and free) light exposure calculator available on the British Airways website here: http://www.britishairways.com/travel/drsleep/public/en_gb

Melatonin

Remember, melatonin is the hormone that initiates and maintains sleep. It also plays a fundamental role in the regulation of the sleep-wake cycle. Taking melatonin as a supplement can help reset the 'body clock' and help us to adjust to time zone changes. In one major review of ten individual studies, melatonin use roughly halved jet-lag symptoms.[25] My experience with melatonin is that it tends to work well for about half the people who try it, but for the other half it does little or nothing.

How easy melatonin is to obtain depends on where in the world you are. It is, for example, available over the counter in the US, but requires a prescription in the UK. Doses of 0.5–5.0 mg appear to be effective. I generally recommend long-acting melatonin for individuals travelling to the west (to help people stay asleep) and short-acting melatonin for individuals travelling to the east (to help individuals get to sleep).

THE BOTTOM LINE

- Sleep is important for psychological and physical functioning and performance

- Lack of sleep can lead to a wide range of mental deficits

- Lack of sleep can predispose to chronic health issues including weight gain and type 2 diabetes

- Symptoms of 'sleep debt' include not feeling refreshed on waking, use of the snooze button, the need for caffeine in the morning and the need to catch up on sleep at the weekend or when on holiday

- Going to bed earlier is one simple strategy that often helps to ensure we get optimal amounts of sleep

- Performing a 'brain dump' and constructing a to-do list in the evening can often help clear the head and help sleep

- Both caffeine and alcohol have the capacity to disrupt sleep

- For the best sleep, it's best to avoid bright light exposure from room lighting or devices in the evening

- Eyeshades and earplugs can sometimes be very helpful for ensuring deep, restful sleep

- Ensuring blood sugar stability generally helps to improve sleep quality and prevent episodes of waking in the night

- Napping (ideally, ten to twenty minutes) often really helps to improve energy and brain function

- Jet lag can be combated using a combination of strategies including basic good sleep habits, flight time choices, seeking and avoiding bright light and supplementing with melatonin

- Sleep tracking devices can be useful for monitoring sleep

Chapter 5

Light Relief

Most of us prefer a sunny day to a dull one, and lack of sunlight can leave some people distinctly below par and lacking in vitality. Some people are so sensitive to low light levels that, for them, every winter is one of discontent.

In this chapter we're going to be exploring how light can affect our *mental functioning* and *mood*, and what practical steps we can take to make sure we get enough of this natural resource.

Later on, we'll be looking at the role of sunlight in physical health too. While we are generally warned against unprotected sun exposure, sunlight can actually boost wellbeing and general health, primarily through the production of vitamin D in the skin. This chapter will also discuss how we may maintain optimal levels of this critically important nutrient.

In the Bleak Midwinter

In the preceding chapter, I mentioned how light has the ability to stimulate the production of 'serotonin' in the brain. This 'neurotransmitter' has broadly mood-enhancing effects so, in theory at least, light might help maintain a cheerful outlook and buoyant disposition. The fact that light boosts serotonin is believed by some to explain why some people are prone to depression in the darker months known as 'seasonal affective disorder' or 'SAD'.[1]

Those who live in the northern hemisphere and a long way from the equator can be prone to a dipping of serotonin levels in the winter.[2] This may not always cause full-blown SAD, but for many people may still compromise their mood and functioning in a way that impairs their sense of contentment and effectiveness. Sometimes, this less acute form of SAD is referred to as 'subsyndromal SAD'.

If you find you do not look forward at all to the shortening of the days at the end of the year and are relieved when the days start to lengthen again, then there's a good chance that you're taking an annual trip to the dark side.

Lighten Up Your Mood

'Bright light therapy' is a first-line treatment for individuals suffering from SAD, but it seems not just any light will do. The research shows that it's actually the blue part of the visual spectrum that is most effective for combating seasonal mood-related issues.[3,4]

Bright light therapy does not just help those with SAD, but also those with subsyndromal SAD too. In one study, individuals with SAD and subsyndromal SAD were treated with bright light therapy for ten days.[5] Mood, fatigue and wellbeing were rated before the light therapy, immediately after the ten-day treatment period, and then a month later. Individuals in both groups (those with SAD and subsyndromal SAD) saw improvements in symptoms such as fatigue and daytime sleepiness, as well as seeing a boost in 'health-related quality of life'. What is more, the benefits were still apparent a month after the treatment had stopped.

In another study, light therapy was administered to office workers, some of whom had symptoms of SAD, and others who did not.[6] Light therapy was found to improve SAD symptoms but it also benefited non-sufferers too, who enjoyed improvements in their sense of vitality and mood.

The effect of blue-enriched light has also been tested in the office environment. In one study, blue-enriched light exposure (compared to light without blue-enrichment) improved workers' ability to concentrate.[7] In another study, blue-enriched light exposure for four weeks improved a range of measures including those of performance, alertness, end-of-day fatigue, irritability, difficulty focusing and concentration.[8]

Into the Light

My experience is that many people benefit from being mindful of the need for sunlight each day, particularly during the darker months. The remedy may be no more sophisticated than getting out of the office for twenty minutes or so at lunchtime. In the winter, you may wonder what the point is of doing this as you peer out of the window to see an overcast sky and no hint of direct sunlight. However, even on a dull day, the light intensity is generally much greater outside an office than it is inside.

I have even checked this out myself with a light meter. Outside in the winter, light is usually at least several thousand lux (lux is a measure of light intensity), even on a dull day. In offices, though, I get readings of about a few hundred lux, with noticeably lower readings the further away one gets from a window.

Sometimes, the weather makes getting outside difficult. However, even if you take shelter from the elements and have your face in the light for fifteen or twenty minutes, this may well be much better than staying hunched over your desk in a dimly lit office (all compounded by munching on a sandwich, I might add – see Chapter 1).

Another option is to invest in a light therapy device. Small, portable units are now available that can deliver a useful dose of concentrated light in as little as twenty minutes or less. The device I personally use is the Philips GoLite, though alternatives do exist, including those made by the company Lumie.

If you are going to try one of these devices, my advice would be to 'get in quick' and start using it as soon as the days get noticeably shorter. In the UK, this would be some time in September. Studies suggest it does not matter much *when* in the day individuals get their light exposure: morning, midday and evening exposure appear to be equally effective.[9] I would suggest avoiding bright light exposure within about three hours of bedtime, though, as this runs the risk of making the brain more alert and suppressing melatonin, which could disrupt sleep (see Chapter 4).

When using a light device, you do not have to look directly into it – it just needs to be shining on your face. You could, for example, have the light on while eating breakfast, reading or working at a desk.

Good Morning

Another application of 'light therapy' is 'dawn simulation' –
the use of gradually increasing light intensity to wake us up
in the morning. Dawn simulation has been found to help
people suffering from SAD,[10-12] and in particular seems to
help people get up in the morning.[13] This could be of
particular use in the winter, as many find getting out of bed
on dark mornings quite a struggle. Other research has found
that dawn simulation can improve energy on waking, as well
as mood, productivity and quality of sleep.[14] Dawn simulation
alarm clocks are available from manufacturers such as
Philips and Lumie.

A Place in the Sun

In addition to its role in brain function and mood maintenance,
sunlight also has the potential to influence physical aspects of
health, too. When the sun is close enough to the earth, the sun's
rays have the power to stimulate the production of vitamin D in
the skin. Evidence suggests that maintaining good levels of this
nutrient in the body helps to maintain good health and contrib-
utes to our sustainability.

Vitamin D has traditionally been recognized as critical to the
absorption and utilization of calcium in the body. However, in
recent years, sunlight and vitamin D have been linked with relative protection from myriad health issues including heart disease,
multiple sclerosis and many different forms of cancer (see
below). Sometimes, this evidence can get lost in the rash of

stories that normally emerge each summer urging us to take care in the sun, lest we give ourselves skin cancer.

The remainder of this chapter will explore the role sunlight and vitamin D have in our wellbeing, and how we might make use of these natural commodities to enhance our health and sustainability. Before we get on to the benefits, let's explore the alleged hazards of sunlight.

Are We Really 'Dying for a Tan'?

Much of the negative press directed at the sun concerns its supposed ability to cause skin cancer. There are three principal forms of skin cancer: 'malignant melanoma', 'squamous cell cancer' and 'basal cell cancer'.

These latter two cancers are not so well known outside medical circles, despite the fact that they are actually much more frequent than malignant melanomas. Although relatively commonplace, risk of death from squamous and basal cell cancers is low. This is partly due to the fact that these cancers are usually quite slow-growing and not very 'aggressive'. Also, these particular skin cancers tend to occur in sun-exposed parts of the body, like the face and the back of the hand. This means they are very often spotted (and dealt with) before they are advanced enough to pose a threat to life.

The fact that squamous and basal cell cancers tend to occur in sun-exposed parts of the body is consistent with the idea they are primarily caused by sunlight, as is the fact that individuals who have the longest cumulative sunlight exposure over the course of their lives have the highest risk of these cancers.[15]

Malignant melanoma, on the other hand, is an altogether different disease. It's much less common than squamous and basal cell cancers but, once it has developed, is much more likely to prove deadly. Part of the reason for this is that the cancer is generally aggressive and prone to spread.

Also, though, melanomas tend to be spotted later because, in contrast to other skin cancers, many of them occur in regions of the body that are not commonly exposed to light and are therefore more easily missed. Actually, a full three-quarters of malignant melanomas occur in parts of the body that are not habitually exposed to the sun,[16] including the soles of the feet and between the toes. This fact casts some doubt on the idea that sunlight causes melanoma, and weight is added to this by the presence of many studies that link *higher* levels of sun exposure with *lower* melanoma risk.[17-26]

Even if we assume that sunlight is a major factor in the development of melanoma, though, it's important to balance this with any other evidence we have regarding the relationship between sunlight exposure and other forms of cancer and aspects of health. There exists a wealth of research linking sunlight exposure with relative protection from several different forms of cancer. A review of the evidence found greater exposure to the sun to be strongly associated with a reduced risk of fifteen different types of cancer including those of the breast and colon.[27] This epidemiological evidence does not prove that sunlight protects against these cancers (only that sunlight is associated with reduced risk). However, sunlight can stimulate the production of vitamin D, and this nutrient is known to have several different anti-cancer effects in the body.

But the potential role of vitamin D as a cancer-protective is only the tip of the iceberg. Vitamin D is also known to have natural anti-inflammatory actions in the body. This has relevance because inflammation has emerged as an important underlying mechanism in atherosclerosis (the 'gumming-up' process on the inside of the arteries which can lead to heart attacks and strokes). In one study published in the *Archives of Internal Medicine*, men with low levels of vitamin D were more than twice as likely to suffer a heart attack compared to those with higher levels.[28]

Other research links sunlight exposure and heightened vitamin D levels with relative protection from so-called 'auto-immune' diseases – conditions in which the body's immune system reacts against its own tissues. One example of this is the neurological condition multiple sclerosis, the incidence of which is close to zero in equatorial regions, but increases steadily the nearer one gets towards the poles.

Vitamin D also plays a role in warding off infection. It increases the production of what are known as 'anti-microbial peptides' that help protect against foreign organisms.[29,30] This effect helps to explain the observation that higher vitamin D levels are associated with a reduced susceptibility to infections such as colds and flu. In one study, infections lasted for an average of two days in those with high levels of vitamin D, compared to an average of nine days in those with lower levels. Again, this is epidemiological evidence and does not prove that vitamin D protects against infection. However, the idea that vitamin D has direct protective roles here is supported by its known ability to enhance levels of anti-microbial peptides.

There is also some research that suggests that vitamin D influences *body composition*. In one study, vitamin D was given to a group of seventy-seven overweight and obese women.[32] Half of the women were treated with 1,000 international units (IU) of vitamin D each day for twelve weeks, while the other half took a placebo. Body weight was static over the course of the study in both groups. However, the women taking vitamin D lost an average of 2.7 kg of fat and gained 1.8 kg of muscle at the same time. In those taking the placebo, though, there was no significant change in their levels of muscle or fat.

Testing Times

Because of its fundamental role in health and wellbeing, it can be useful to know what one's levels of vitamin D are, and to increase these if appropriate. Vitamin D levels are measured in the blood, and can be expressed either as ng/ml (nanograms per millilitre of blood) or nmol/l (nanomols per litre of blood). Their relationship is that 1.0 ng/ml = 2.5 nmol/l (e.g. 30 ng/ml = 75 nmol/l).

Toxicity does not appear to occur at levels less than 200 ng/ml. My preference is for levels to be around 40–50 ng/ml (100–125 nmol/l). Yet evidence shows that in the UK, almost 90 per cent of forty-five-year-olds will have levels lower than 30 ng/ml in the winter, though in the summer and autumn (when vitamin D levels are naturally higher), still about 60 per cent fall into this category.[33]

The research on vitamin D levels quoted above was conducted in Caucasians, and the relevance of this is that, for a given amount of sunlight, fairer skins generally make more vitamin D than darker ones. What this means is that vitamin D deficiency is likely to be even more prevalent in those of Asian and Afro-Caribbean descent.

Those living at more northerly latitudes are also at increased risk of vitamin D deficiency, as are those whose exposure to sunlight is limited (such as the elderly). There is increasing recognition that levels of vitamin D are much lower than they should be, overall, and increasing numbers of people are at risk of severe deficiency.

Testing of vitamin D levels can be done via a doctor, though home-testing kits (which use just a few drops of blood sent to a lab on a piece of blotting paper) are also available (see http://www.vitamindtest.org.uk for such a service which is convenient and economical).

Vitamin D levels can be improved with sunlight exposure, but will only be made when the sun is high enough in the sky. This means that in the UK, vitamin D is only made from March through to September, and only in the middle portion of the day. A good rule of thumb is that the sun is strong enough to generate vitamin D when one's shadow is shorter than one's height. While it is important not to allow the skin to burn, even ten or twenty minutes of daily sun exposure (without sunscreen) to bare legs, arms and torso can do much to boost and maintain vitamin D levels.

Although fair individuals can generally make a lot of vitamin D quite quickly, evidence shows they are actually quite prone to vitamin D deficiency. This is perhaps because they are particularly wary of burning and therefore avoid the sun and protect their skin with sunscreens (which block vitamin D production) when they are in it. Again, while it is important to prevent burning, short bursts of unprotected sun exposure may help to optimize vitamin D in these individuals, too.

Internal Affairs

Another way to enhance vitamin D status is to consume more of it. Yet while this nutrient is found in foods such as oily fish and eggs, the amounts here generally pale into insignificance compared to the amount we make from sun exposure. Vitamin D supplementation represents a practical option for some people, though the dosages required to optimize vitamin D levels are usually in the order of several thousand international units (IU) per day.[34-36] In practice, I've found that about 1,000 IU (25 micrograms) of daily supplementation with vitamin D3 (the preferred form of vitamin D for supplementation) usually raises blood levels by about 10 ng/ml (25 nmol/l) over time.

The Dark Side of Sunscreens

Sunscreens are vigorously promoted for their supposed ability to protect against sunburn and skin cancer. While it's clear these products can help us extend our time in the sun without burning, there is evidence that relying on them for the prevention of skin cancer may be misguided.

In 2000 the International Agency for Research on Cancer in France held a meeting to discuss the role of sunscreens in skin cancer prevention. A report of the meeting's findings was subsequently published.[37] The agency concluded that there was evidence that sunscreens could reduce the risk of squamous cell cancer but only if individuals did not use sunscreens to extend their time in the sun. Although in fact a lot of people use sunscreens in precisely this way. When people coat themselves in sunscreen on the beach or by the pool, the usual intention is to allow them to stay longer in the sun without burning.

But what of the role of sunscreens in melanoma prevention? A press release generated from the meeting stated that:

> Several relevant epidemiological studies have shown significantly higher risks for melanoma in users of sunscreens than in non-users. This paradoxical observation could in part be due to the fact that users of sunscreens deliberately spend

more time in the sun than they would otherwise. Thus, the protective effect of sunscreens can be outweighed by overexposure based on the false assumption that sunscreens completely abolish the adverse effects of [ultraviolet] light. In light of these findings, [we] concluded that sunscreens prevent sunburns and may reduce the risk of squamous cell carcinoma, but only if they do not mislead people to extend their exposure to sunlight.

In another review of the role of sunscreens in skin cancer prevention it was concluded that: 'no melanoma study has shown convincingly that sunscreen use reduces the risk of melanoma.'[38] The authors put forward several theories for why this might be, including the fact that sunscreens may protect against burning by blocking ultraviolet B (UVB) rays but may allow longer exposure to potentially damaging rays from other parts of the spectrum (such as UVA). The vitamin D-blocking effects of sunscreens are also cited, along with the potentially carcinogenic nature of certain chemicals used in sunscreens including avobenzone and ecamsule.

The article goes on to refer to the fact that 'interests that are not scientifically based seem to be driving the heavy reliance on sunscreens as the first line of prevention against skin cancer', adding: 'The fervor with which companies promote sunscreen can perhaps be traced to the profit that sunscreen sales bring.' Further cause for concern comes from research linking sunscreen use with not just malignant melanoma, but basal cell carcinoma too.[39]

Personally, I don't advocate the widespread use of sunscreens, and have not used them myself for more than twenty years.

Safe Tanning

While I'm no fan of sunscreens, sunburn is still something that should be avoided if at all possible. My advice here is to employ *physical* (rather than chemical) protection. This means wearing appropriate clothing and seeking the shade when necessary.

Around water it's especially important to protect the skin when the sun is baking hot. The use of specialized clothing for wearing in water is a very good idea, here, I think. Being in water is one situation where there is an argument for sunscreen on parts of the body that are at risk of burning that cannot easily be protected with clothing, such as the face and ears.

THE BOTTOM LINE

- Light is important for brain function and mood maintenance, and lack of sunlight can have an impact on how we feel and function

- Getting some natural light exposure each day is a good idea throughout the year, especially in the winter

- The use of a bright light device may help those who are prone to mood or general wellbeing issues in the winter and find it difficult to get natural light exposure

- There is evidence that suggests sunlight is not an important cause of malignant melanoma, though it does appear to cause other more common but less problematic forms of skin cancer

- Sunlight and vitamin D are associated with protection from several other forms of cancer and other benefits for health

- Vitamin D is linked with a wide range of benefits for body and brain

- Vitamin D levels can be tested in the blood, and taking steps to optimize levels may enhance health and sustainability

- Sunscreens do not appear to protect against malignant melanoma and may, in fact, increase risk

- Getting sun exposure is important, but so is avoiding burning

- For the most part, burning is best avoided using physical (rather than chemical) means

Chapter 6

Fit for Business

Pretty much everyone appreciates the value of regular physical activity for health, but for some people the challenge is finding the time to 'fit it in'. I find many individuals in the corporate environment have enjoyed previously active lives and have often excelled at sport. However, as their career has progressed, they can find themselves with less and less time for exercise. Some retain exercise in their lives, but can still find they have extended periods of relative inactivity as a result of work pressures. For others, being sedentary has become their new norm.

This chapter provides real-world strategies for staying fit and healthy in as practical and time-efficient a way as possible. The chapter focuses on the virtues of regular walking, but also offers a brief but highly effective home-based exercise regime for maintaining our strength and functionality. Finally, for those keen for the 'advanced class', the chapter discusses 'high-intensity intermittent exercise' and how this can help us achieve our health and fitness goals with minimal time investment.

'Exercise' is a word that covers a wide range of activities, all of which fall into one or more of three broad categories:

1. Cardiovascular exercise

Cardiovascular exercise includes forms of activity that can be prolonged and provide a good workout for the heart and circulatory system (hence the name). Examples include walking, running, cycling, swimming and rowing.

These forms of exercise are generally good for improving fitness, stamina and endurance. Also, individuals who take this form of exercise on a regular basis are generally at lower risk of a range of health issues including heart disease and type 2 diabetes. Risk of death measured over a finite period of time is also lower in those who take regular cardiovascular exercise.

This sort of epidemiological evidence does not prove exercise reduces disease risk and extends life, as such – just that these things are associated with each other. However, when individuals are enrolled into exercise programmes and the effects measured, generally there have been improvements in disease markers such as blood pressure and blood sugar control that would be expected to translate into a reduced risk of chronic disease and death.

We are often encouraged to take cardiovascular exercise to help us control our weight. Actually, the evidence does not particularly support this, and later on in this chapter we'll be exploring the mechanisms that appear to explain this paradoxical finding.

Also, many cardiovascular exercises such as walking and running do little or nothing to maintain the strength of our muscles and functionality, particularly those in the upper body. For this, we need to turn to 'resistance exercise'.

2. Resistance exercise

As its name suggests, this form of exercise involves moving parts of the body against resistance provided by our own body weight (such as a press-up) or a piece of equipment (such as an elastic exercise band, dumb-bell or weight-training machine).

This sort of exercise is particularly good for improving the strength, tone, definition and (sometimes) the size of our muscles. Resistance exercise generally improves body composition and aesthetics, but is also vital for maintaining functionality as we age, thereby reducing the risk of frailty and injury.

3. High-intensity intermittent exercise (HIIE)

This form of activity involves brief periods of intense exercise (e.g. sprinting, 'spinning' or rowing), interspersed with periods of rest. In recent years, some focus has been placed on HIIE as a way of improving fitness and other aspects of health in a more time-efficient way than, say, cardiovascular exercise.

This type of exercise has value for people who are already fit and are looking to 'step things up a bit'.

Be Active

If you regularly engage in cycling, swimming, jogging, running or aerobic-type classes in a gym, then you will almost certainly be getting more than a useful 'dose' of aerobic exercise on a weekly basis. However, for those of us for whom these pursuits are unrealistic or just do not appeal, the risk is we can retreat into a life of inactivity that can jeopardize our health, wellbeing and quality of life.

In the first chapter, we introduced the idea of eating broadly in accordance with the diet of our evolutionary ancestors. If we were to take the same approach with exercise, then our go-to activity would be *walking*.

Just like the 'diet industry', the health and fitness arena is prone to fads and fashions. We are often bombarded with news of the latest craze be it aerobics, spinning, 'body pump', 'boxercise', or Zumba. With all this 'noise', walking can easily get forgotten or be labelled in our minds as something that somehow doesn't count as exercise. It does.

Walking has been shown to improve health in a number of areas, including:

Fitness

Several studies demonstrate that regular walking can significantly improve fitness.[1-4] Walking at a rate where very slight breathlessness is induced, but not so much that it makes it difficult to conduct a conversation will almost certainly return significant fitness benefits over time.

General health and disease protection

Epidemiological evidence suggests that, broadly speaking, walking offers similar health benefits to running. In one study, thousands of walkers and runners were followed over a six-year period, during which their health and disease markers such as blood pressure and blood sugar control were monitored.[5] For a given distance travelled, running and walking were associated with similar benefits. In other words, whether someone walked a mile or ran it, the benefits appeared to be about the same.

The act of walking, say, a couple of miles takes longer than running them. However, bear in mind that this is offset by the fact that no time needs to be spent getting changed (twice) or showering. For many, walking can also be more sustainable than other types of exercise such as cycling or rowing because it can usually be more easily slipped into the day. Risk of injury is generally very low too compared to, say, running.

Brain function

Another aspect of health that walking appears to benefit is brain function. In one study, a group of sedentary middle-aged and elderly individuals had their brain function assessed and were then randomized to one of two exercise regimes: walking (at one's own pace for forty minutes, three times a week), or regular stretching and toning.[6]

Twelve months later, compared to those who had been stretching and toning, those on the walking regime saw improvements in cognitive test results, especially those relating to what are known as 'executive control tasks' (e.g. planning, scheduling and multi-tasking). It is these mental skills, by the way, that tend to take a bit of a hit as we age.

Back pain

Back pain is a common problem and a major cause of absenteeism. Some research suggests, though, that something as simple as regular walking can keep back pain at bay.[7] In this research, individuals with back pain either engaged in back muscle-strengthening exercises using specialized equipment, or bouts of walking lasting twenty to forty minutes. In both groups, individuals exercised two to three times a week, and the whole programme lasted for six weeks.

Individuals were assessed in a number of ways before and after the interventions, including a test of how far individuals were able to walk in six minutes, back and abdominal muscle endurance tests, and measures of disability and back pain. All these measures improved significantly in both groups, and there was no difference between the groups. This means, in essence, that walking has the potential to help back issues, but without the need for any specialized exercises or equipment.

Is It OK to Split Exercise Up?

Some people imagine that exercise should ideally be continuous and extended for it to provide real benefit. But is this really so, or are there benefits to be had from shorter, more frequent periods of activity?

In one study, men exercised for thirty continuous minutes, or for three, ten-minute sessions each day. Disease markers (blood pressure and levels of blood fats known as triglycerides) improved to the same extent with both regimes.[8] In a similar study, women exercised for a total of thirty minutes each day, several times each week. For some women, the thirty minutes were made up of one continuous session; for others they were made up of two fifteen-minute sessions over the course of the day. For still others, the exercise was divided into three ten-minute sessions. All three groups saw improvements in measures of fitness that were essentially the same irrespective of exercise timing.[9]

The evidence suggests that we can derive considerable benefits from activity and exercise, even when it's split up into time periods that are quite brief.

Step Up Your Walking With a Pedometer

Pedometers are small, relatively inexpensive devices that count steps. There is evidence that using a pedometer encourages higher levels of activity,[10] and I've certainly found that to be true in my own life (see below) and in those I've worked with.

The technology in this area has developed massively in recent years, and now several devices are available that accurately track metrics such as the number of steps taken, distance covered and floors climbed. Examples include Jawbone's Up, and Fitbit's Flex, Zip, and One. The first two of these devices are wristbands, and the latter two can be clipped to clothing or simply carried in a pocket. All the devices can sync with smartphone apps and on-line interfaces that keep a convenient record of activity over time.

I've experienced the benefits of owning one of these devices in my own life. Walking is a core activity for me, but I can get caught out too. On a 'writing day' based at home, it is not impossible for me to be so absorbed in my work that, if I'm not careful, I get practically no activity at all in a day. Having a tracker makes this significantly less likely to happen.

Even at home, I wear the device visibly clipped to my pocket. Regularly, I catch a glimpse of it and it serves as a reminder of just how active (or inactive) I've been that day. When, say, in the early evening I press the display and am informed I've taken just 337 steps the whole day, this is a strong message to me that I need to get out more.

Many people find that using an activity-monitoring device is particularly helpful when coupled with a daily stepping target. For instance, I strive to walk at least 5,000 steps (about two to two and a half miles) on days where I am busy or the opportunity to walk is maybe limited. However, on days where I feel I have more freedom, particularly at the weekend, I adjust that target upwards to at least 10,000 steps.

These devices also allow people to engage in 'competitions' with family, friends and colleagues. One delegate from a US-based firm told me his company had an internal competition utilizing step-tracking technology. Teams of people were competing against each other to be the first to walk a distance equivalent to the Route 66 highway in California.

A Matter of Time

If you're still stuck on the idea that walking or some other physical activity is too time-consuming, here are a few ideas that might help:

- Even if you work for a solid ten hours in a day (that's 8 a.m. to 6 p.m. without a break) and sleep for eight, there are still six hours left over. Could at least some of that time be given over to activity or exercise?

- Keep in your mind that activity is natural to the body and something that helps optimize your health, performance and sustainability (it's not 'unproductive time')

- Do you ever find you can lose half an hour or more engaged in often fruitless pastimes such as reading on-line newspapers, watching rubbish TV, or spending time on Facebook? Could that time be better spent, say, walking before or after work, at lunchtime or maybe between meetings?

- If you walk outside, you may get other benefits from being in sunlight (see Chapter 5 for more about this)

- You can make and take calls when you walk, so work does not need to stop dead while you're moving. Some people also conduct one-on-one meetings while walking

- Getting out of the office and a change of environment may help revitalize and stimulate your thinking. I've met lots of people who have experienced flashes of inspiration while out walking that they may well not have had staring at the wall in their office. The structure and main content points of this book were not conceptualized in front of my laptop, by the way – they came during the regular walks I take

- Walking is a perfect opportunity to listen to some music or even learn something. In Chapter 7 we will explore how music can help boost our mood and functioning. However, while walking you might instead choose to listen to some educational recordings relating to, say, personal development, or learning a new language

Even if you prefer more formal exercise such as cycling or working out in a gym, you may still consider incorporating more walking into your life. Many people find that when they are pushed at work, trips to the gym and other formal exercise endeavours easily fall by the wayside. Rather than dropping to nothing, it can help to look to walking as a way to keep activity levels 'ticking over'.

Action Planning

It's much easier to miss out on activity or exercise if we don't plan ahead. A day can easily get consumed with work, calls, meetings and interruptions. One trick to combat this is to *schedule* activity, and either put it in your diary or have it at least planned out in your head.

I engage in three main forms of exercise: walking, swimming and home-based resistance exercise (see below for more on this). The resistance circuit is actually the easiest to perform because it's brief and I can do it more or less wherever I am, even when travelling.

However, the swimming takes a little more planning. I aim to swim three to four times a week, and at the start of each week I will look at my schedule and nominate the times where I know I can get to my local pool. These sessions are now sacrosanct unless something really urgent and important springs up.

I tend to plan my walking on a day-by-day basis. I live in London, and if travelling into the centre of the city, I will normally get off the bus or Tube about a fifteen-minute walk from my destination. I'll do this on my way home too. I will usually do the same in the evening if I go out. I don't think: I don't have time for this, because it's scheduled into my journey. And all the while, I have the satisfaction of seeing another chunk of steps taken out of my target on my activity-tracking device.

Diminishing Returns

Regular exercise is good for a lot of things, but is weight loss one of them? While exercise is commonly advocated for shedding fat and weight maintenance, the research does not actually support this.

The largest review to date amassed evidence from forty-three individual studies.[11] These studies assessed a variety of factors, including weight loss in individuals who are enrolled in an exercise programme, compared to those who remain sedentary. The average weight loss enjoyed from regular exercise over a three- to twelve-month period was found to be just 2 kg.

The review also looked at what happens when exercise is *added* to dietary change. Say, for example, individuals are put on a 'diet' and lose 10 kg in weight on average over six months. If regular exercise is added to the dietary change, the average additional weight loss is now a mere 0.6 kg. The authors of this review concluded that: 'exercise resulted in small weight losses across studies.'

The idea that exercise is generally ineffective for the purposes of weight loss may be counterintuitive. However, there are several potential explanations for this phenomenon:

1. Exercise doesn't burn that many calories

Depending on factors such as body weight and intensity, jogging for thirty minutes will burn about 300 calories. However, sitting at a desk for thirty minutes will burn about 50 calories, so the additional calorie burn for half an hour's jogging is about 250 calories. The fact is, it takes quite a lot of time and effort to burn significant quantities of calories.

And how do these calories compare to those found in fat? One pound of fat contains 3,500 calories. So, theoretically, to lose a pound of fat one would have to do fourteen of those thirty-minute jogs. This is not looking like a fantastic return on investment. It also assumes that we're not going to end up eating a bit more as a result of the exercise. But, as many of us know ...

2. Exercise can lead to us eating more

Have you ever heard the expression 'working up an appetite'? Another barrier to losing weight through aerobic exercise is the hunger it can bring on.[12] Also, some people reward themselves with food after exercise, either because they feel they deserve it, or because they rationalize they can because, well, they've just burned some calories during exercise. The problem is, it doesn't take much additional intake to undo the calorie deficit induced by, say, a thirty-minute jog.

3. Exercise can cause people to be more sedentary at other times

One other phenomenon that helps explain the lack of effectiveness of exercise for weight loss concerns the fact that when individuals take more formal exercise, there's a tendency for activity levels to decline at other times.[13–16]

4. Exercise can suppress the metabolism

There's no doubt that, generally speaking, exercise burns more calories than when we are sitting at a desk or slouched in front of the TV. Some claim that additional calories are burned for quite a long time after exercise, too. There is some truth in this idea, but the effect is relatively small, and unlikely to lead to any meaningful weight loss. For moderate-intensity activity lasting up to an hour in length, fat metabolism over the next twenty-four hours is essentially the same as when no exercise is taken.[17]

However, it seems the overall impact of exercise on the metabolism varies from person to person, and *overweight* individuals (who perhaps are most likely to be using exercise for weight loss) might be at a general disadvantage here. In four well-conducted studies, individuals who exercised for the equivalent of 300–600 calories a day for weeks at a time saw significant reductions in their resting metabolic rate.[18–21] When overweight individuals do more than one hour of endurance exercise each day, resting metabolism declines by about 10 per cent on average.

This reduction in metabolic rate will not affect everyone and won't necessarily completely negate the effects of the additional calorie burn achieved during exercise. It will, however, tend to put a dent in the expected weight loss from exercise.

The idea that the body would down-regulate the metabolism in response to exercise makes, I think, intuitive sense. We know, for example, that when people consciously cut calories to lose weight, it very often puts a considerable brake on the metabolism. This reflects an inbuilt survival mechanism: the body reduces the metabolism to eke out its fuel stores in response to reduced food intake. It's perhaps no surprise that the body may sometimes do the same thing when activity is increased.

Could Poor Weight-loss Results from Exercise Be Down to Muscle Gain?

One explanation for the failure of exercise to induce weight loss could be this: exercise builds muscle, which offsets the weight that is lost due to the shedding of fat. However, the aerobic exercises deployed in these don't build significant quantities of muscle, so this is unlikely to be the explanation.

We have some evidence of this too. One six-month study assessed the impact of aerobic exercise (aerobics and spinning classes) on weight and body composition. There was no reduction in weight nor body fatness as a result of the exercise,[22] demonstrating that the fact that weight did not change was not the result of muscle being gained as fat was lost.

The truth about the impact of exercise on weight loss is not particularly motivating, so why bother to share it with you here? I've found that, for the most part, understanding this makes it more, not less, likely that someone will persist with regular activity.

Many of us believe, even at the back of our minds, that regular exercise will deliver on its weight-loss promise (because it's logical that it should), but can easily become demotivated when this theory does not appear to translate into reality and then just jack the whole thing in. On the other hand, those who are not expecting exercise to cause their pounds to melt away are less likely to be disappointed, and can then be satisfied with the other benefits exercise brings.

In addition to not being a particularly effective aid to weight loss, cardiovascular exercises such as walking and running are limited in their capacity to strengthen our muscles, particularly those in the upper body. This is where resistance exercise comes into its own.

Offer Some Resistance

As part of the natural ageing process, muscle is lost. Without anything to mitigate this, we can end up weak, infirm and prone to injury. In practice, I see many individuals whose activity is based exclusively on cardiovascular endeavours such as walking, running or cycling. None of these exercises does much for the upper body though, and walking or even running may not even contribute much to strength (as opposed to speed and endurance) in the legs. Fortunately, some simple resistance exercises can come to the rescue.

What follows is a brief resistance exercise 'circuit' that can do much to increase the strength and tone of the upper body, though it includes lower body exercises too. If you already do regular resistance exercise, you won't need this. However, you may pull it out of the bag when you are pushed for time.

One of the advantages of this circuit is that it can be done at home or in a hotel room, and requires very little time. If you don't currently do any resistance exercise, this regime is likely to help you a lot in terms of your strength and functionality over time.

A Complete Workout in 12 Minutes

This 12-minute resistance-exercise-based regime is made up of two 6-minute sections. The first 6 minutes focuses on resistance exercises for the upper body, while the second 6 minutes works the legs with a mix of resistance exercise (squats) and cardiovascular activity (running on the spot).

Special Equipment

There are really only two pieces of equipment you need consider purchasing:

1. Elastic exercise band

Elastic exercise bands come in a variety of forms but are usually essentially giant, wide elastic bands (e.g. Dyna-Band) or tubular affairs with handles on the end. These come in a range of thicknesses and 'resistances' to suit different people's strengths.

One of the great things about these exercise aids is that they are small and light, and therefore perfect for people who travel or are on the road a lot and want to maintain their exercise regime, wherever they are.

2. Dumb-bells

A set of dumb-bells is an alternative to an elastic exercise band. Go for a set where the amount of weight can be varied, because you may want to increase this as you get stronger over time. These are obviously not ideal for packing in your hand luggage, but can be useful if you're exercising at home.

The First 6 Minutes

The first 6 minutes of the session is divided into 1-minute blocks, each of which is designed to work a major muscle group. The ultimate aim with these exercises is to do each of them continuously for a minute. If you are new to resistance exercise then start with relatively low loads and go slowly. Focus on completing each 1-minute exercise with good form throughout.

As your fitness and strength improve you will find yourself being able to complete more repetitions within the allotted minute. You may also increase the load of some of the exercises in time by, for instance, increasing the weight of the dumb-bells or progressing to an elastic exercise band of higher resistance.

The six parts of the body each exercise is designed to work are:

1. Chest

2. Back

3. Shoulders

4. Biceps

5. Triceps

6. Abdominals

1. Chest

Press-ups

Press-ups exercise and strengthen several muscles including the pectoral muscles (chest), the deltoids (around the shoulders) and triceps (at the back of the upper arm). They also work muscles at the side of the chest wall and in the back.

There's a choice of three sorts of press-up, of varying degrees of difficulty. Full press-ups are the most challenging, and box press-ups the least. Start with the type you can comfortably do and work up if relevant.

Full press-up

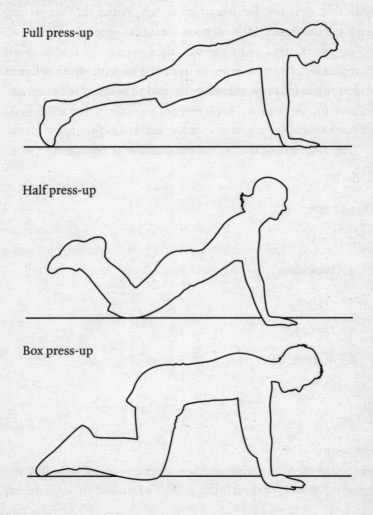

Half press-up

Box press-up

- Full press-up: keep your hips and knees straight. Your hands should be directly under your shoulders. Lower your body by bending your elbows until your chest is about 10 cm from the floor. Push up again in a controlled fashion

- In addition to exercising the muscles listed above, full press-ups count as a 'core stability' exercise, meaning that it helps strengthen muscles in and around the abdomen, lower back and pelvis

- Half press-up: similar to full press-ups, but the knees are on the ground set back behind the hips

- Box press-up: similar to half press-ups, but with the knees placed directly under the hips

2. Back

One-armed rows

These exercise the muscles in the upper arm and back, principally the 'latissimus dorsi' (found in the flanks) and the rhomboids (which run from the inner shoulder blade to the spine).

To perform a one-armed row, stand left side-on to a sofa or bed and put your left knee on the sofa/bed. Lean forward and put your left hand on the sofa/bed. Keep your right foot on the floor. Take a dumb-bell in your right hand with your arm extended down towards the floor. Pull the dumb-bell up to your armpit, pause for a moment, and lower the dumb-bell again in a controlled fashion. Repeat for 30 seconds, and then reverse your position to do another 30 seconds with your left arm.

This exercise can be performed with an elastic exercise band, in which case it should be trapped under whatever foot you have on the floor.

3. Shoulders

Shoulder Press
The shoulder press principally works the deltoid muscle, which is the major muscle in the shoulder at the top of the arm.

Sit comfortably in a steady chair with your back straight. Take dumb-bells in both hands and hold in front of your chest with

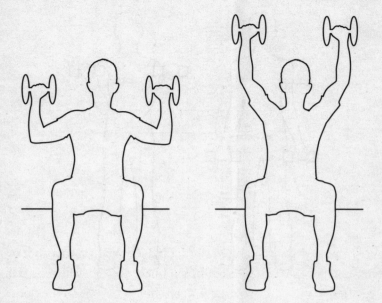

your palms facing forward. Steadily lift the dumb-bells above your head, pause briefly, and return the dumb-bells in a controlled fashion to the front of your chest.

This exercise can be performed using an elastic exercise band. Sit on the band and take the ends in each hand. Alternatively you can perform the exercise while standing with the elastic exercise band trapped under both feet (you may need to tie two elastic exercise bands together to make it long enough).

4. Biceps

Biceps Curls

The biceps is the major muscle at the front of the upper arm.

To perform biceps curls, stand with a dumb-bell in each hand and let your arms hang, palms facing forward. Lift both dumb-

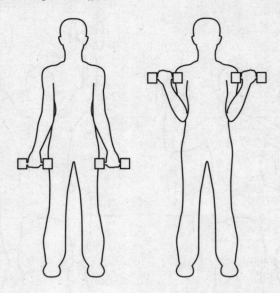

bells to your shoulders, pause briefly and lower again in a controlled fashion.

This exercise can be performed using an elastic exercise band by trapping it under both feet.

5. Triceps

Triceps Dips

The triceps is the muscle at the back of the upper arm.

You will need a chair for this exercise. Place the front of the chair behind you. Put your palms on the seat of the chair with your fingers pointing forward. Bend your knees and keep your feet flat on the floor. Take your weight on your arms and slowly bend your elbows to 90 degrees, lowering your hips towards the floor. Push back up again. Keep your back straight and close to the chair throughout this exercise.

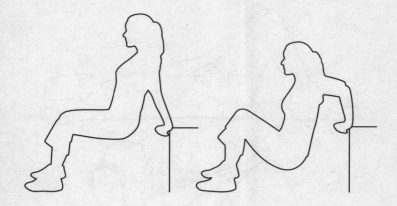

This exercise can be made harder or easier depending on how bent you keep your knees (the more the legs are extended, the harder the exercise).

If, on occasion, you do not have access to a chair or something similar and are unable to perform this exercise, don't worry – press-ups (see above) will give your triceps a decent workout too.

6. Abdominals

Sit-ups

Lie with your back flat on the floor, knees bent and feet flat. Place your right hand on your right thigh and place your left hand behind your neck. Lift your left shoulder off the floor by squeezing your abdominal muscles. Curl your upper torso as you move forward towards your knees. Slide your hand along your thigh until your wrist touches your knee. Hold briefly, and then lower yourself back to the ground slowly and in a controlled fashion. Keep your lower back in contact with the floor throughout this

exercise, and do not pull your neck or head with the supporting hand.

Complete 30 seconds and repeat for 30 seconds on the other side (extending your left arm and with your right hand behind your head).

Once you've finished these upper-body exercises, it's time to work your legs.

The Second 6 Minutes

The second 6 minutes are a combination of jogging on the spot (aerobic exercise) with resistance exercise for the legs in the form of 'squats'.

1. Jogging on the spot

The aim here is not to leap away, but to take relatively small steps, lifting your feet about 10 cm off the floor.

Jogging on the spot may be too intense an exercise to maintain for six minutes for some, particularly if you have not exercised for some time. An alternative would be to march on the spot, in which case the legs should be raised about 30 cm off the floor. As you get fitter you may want to introduce jogging on the spot gradually into the regime until, ultimately, you're able to jog on the spot throughout.

2. Squats

Place your feet a little more than shoulder-width apart, toes pointed out slightly. Sit back until your thighs are roughly parallel

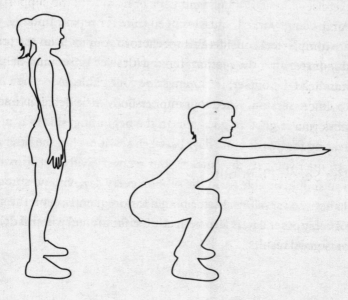

with the floor (the hips should end up higher than the knees). Keep your knees over your ankles and swing your arms forward as you sit back, to keep your balance. Return to standing and repeat.

Start the second 6-minute session by running on the spot for 75 (one count equals one step on one side). After this, immediately perform 10 squats. Repeat this sequence until 6 minutes have elapsed.

This whole regime is relatively brief but is quite intense so it can feel like it's taken a lot out of you, especially in the beginning. It delivers a good all-round workout and crucial resistance exercises for both the upper and lower body in a time-efficient and convenient form.

How Often Should I Do This?

After being worked, muscles need time for repair. Initially, you are likely to feel considerable soreness in your muscles starting a day or two after the session (termed 'delayed onset muscle soreness'). At the outset, let soreness be your guide as to when next to do the session. Once your muscles have little detectable soreness, you're good to go again. In the beginning, this may mean resting for two or more days between sessions. But the fitter and stronger you get, the quicker your recovery will be. Ultimately, you should be able to do the session every day, with no soreness in between sessions. Performing it less frequently, say an average of every other day, is also perfectly legitimate and will still deliver very good results.

Burning Issue

Many individuals who take regular exercise, particularly endurance exercise, will be familiar with the idea of 'carbohydrate loading'. The idea here is that during extended periods of exercise we can eat into our carbohydrate reserves (in the form of what is known as 'glycogen' in the muscles and liver). This can impact on performance, and if we run out of glycogen completely we can 'hit the wall' or 'bonk' (experienced as extreme and sudden loss of performance). I used to do a lot of long-distance running, and I know what this feels like and it's not pretty. But is loading up on carbohydrate before the event the solution?

Habitually eating a lot of carbohydrate attunes the body to utilizing glucose as fuel by inducing specific enzymes involved in this process. The problem is, glycogen is relatively finite in supply. Could an alternative approach be to 'train' the body to run better on fat, which even in lean individuals provides far more energy and could get us much further than glycogen ever can?

It's known that relatively low-carbohydrate diets push the body's metabolism towards 'fat burning' (technically termed 'keto-adaptation'), and this can be a legitimate strategy for endurance athletes. This concept, and the evidence that supports it, is detailed in the book *The Art and Science of Low-Carbohydrate Performance* by researchers Dr Jeff Volek and Dr Stephen Phinney.

I've found that this approach can work well for people engaged in extended periods of exercise that may go on for

↓

↓

two hours or more, say. However, for shorter duration
activity, and for sports like football and rugby, it generally
helps to have a little more carbohydrate on board. I'd avoid
grains, though, and suggest finding this carbohydrate in
foods such as fruit, potato and sweet potato. These are
concentrated sources of carbohydrate, but much less
troublesome from a food sensitivity and toxin perspective
compared to grains.

For most individuals, a combination of regular walking (or other
aerobic activity) and the 12-minute resistance-based regime
covered earlier will meet their activity and exercise needs very
nicely. However, some like to 'push it a bit', and may get additional benefits from progressing to high-intensity intermittent
exercise.

High-Intensity Intermittent Exercise

In recent years, there has been growing interest in high-intensity intermittent exercise (HIIE) as a novel and time-efficient
way of deriving health and fitness benefits. As we touched on
earlier, HIIE entails periods of relatively brief, intense exercise
(usually, at 90–100 per cent of maximum effort), interspersed
with periods of relative rest. One typical regime uses 30-second
'sprints' on a stationary bicycle, interspersed with 'rest' periods
of 3–4 minutes. Usually 4–6 of these individual cycles will be
completed per session. Total session time will be about 20
minutes.

Thirty seconds of high-intensity sprinting is hard work for even highly trained individuals. Also, such intensity of exercise is not to be recommended for individuals who are relatively unfit or who have medical concerns that preclude hard exercise. An alternative is to reduce both the sprint and recovery times. One common protocol employs 8-second sprints, interspersed with 12-second rests, for a total of 20 minutes.

In addition to stationary cycling, other forms of exercise that are amenable to HIIE include rowing (on a machine) and running. I give some examples of regimes at the end of this chapter.

HIIE has been subjected to studies to assess its impact on a variety of health markers.[23] One consistent finding is HIIE's ability to improve fitness, even in two weeks. Another consistent finding is one of improved functioning of the hormone insulin (enhanced 'insulin sensitivity') – something that is taken as a sign of improved health and a reduced risk of developing type 2 diabetes.

HIIE has also been found to stimulate the metabolism of fat and fat loss, particularly in those with weight to lose. There is also evidence that HIIE might offer fat-loss advantages compared to extended, aerobic exercise.

In one study, women engaged in either HIIE (spinning) or 'steady state' cycling for fifteen weeks. The steady state exercise involved 40 minutes of continuous exercise. The HIIE came in the form of 8-second sprints interspersed with 12-second rest periods, for a total of 20 minutes. Exercise sessions were performed three times a week.[24] Over the course of the study, individuals engaging in HIIE lost a total of 2.5 kg of fat. In contrast, those who engaged in steady state exercise lost no weight at all.

In another study, overweight men were randomly divided into two groups: one group engaged in an HIIE regime over twelve weeks while the other did not.[25] Each HIIE session was made up of the following exercises:

1. Five minutes warm-up on a stationary bicycle

2. Twenty repetitions of 8 seconds sprinting followed by 12 seconds of easy pedalling

3. Five minutes warm-down on the bicycle

The sessions were performed three times a week. The men saw a range of benefits, including:

- An average fat loss of 2 kg

- A reduction in 'visceral' fat (fat found in and around the organs that is particularly strongly linked with chronic diseases such as heart disease and type 2 diabetes)

- A reduction in waist circumference

- Increased fitness

- Increased power output

- Increased fat metabolism (average increase of 13 per cent)

How to Do It

Because HIIE can be very challenging, it is generally better to work up to it gradually. This helps ensure the intensity of HIIE is not too much of a shock to the system and reduces the risk of injury. HIIE is not for everyone: individuals with a history of cardiovascular or lung disease or any other major illness should proceed with some caution, and only attempt HIIE once given the go-ahead by a health professional.

If you're not used to exercise, even if you are generally healthy, it makes sense to establish a base level of fitness first. Regular cardiovascular exercise at moderate intensity over two or more months will help provide the necessary base level of fitness.

High-intensity intermittent exercise is hard work, and in the beginning it is unlikely that you'll be able to sustain the sprints for much more than 10 seconds. The length of the sprints can be built up over time, but at the outset, here are some examples of what a HIIE workout may look like.

Running

Warm up with some gentle jogging for 2 minutes.

Sprint for 10 seconds at about 80–90 per cent maximum intensity.

Jog very gently for 30 seconds.

Repeat this cycle for a total of 6–10 sprints.

Warm down with some gentle jogging for a total of 2 minutes.

Cycling

On a stationary bike, warm up for 2 minutes.

Sprint at about 80–90 per cent intensity for 12–15 seconds.

Cycle slowly for 45–48 seconds (so that the sprint plus 'rest' make up a total of 1 minute).

Repeat this sprint and rest for total of six to ten times.

Warm down with gentle cycling for 2 minutes.

Rowing

> Warm up for 2 minutes with gentle rowing.
>
> Row hard for 10 strokes.
>
> Row gently for 20 strokes.
>
> Repeat this cycle six to ten times.
>
> Warm down with gentle rowing for 2 minutes.

Perhaps start with one of these sessions a week, though as your fitness improves you may think about doubling this frequency. As you progress, you can also make the sessions more challenging. Different parameters can be altered to achieve this, including the total number of sprints, the length of the sprints, and the rest times between sprints.

Aim for gradual progression over weeks and months. Whatever efforts you make here are likely to bring you handsome returns in terms of your fitness and general health.

THE BOTTOM LINE

- Cardiovascular exercises such as walking, jogging, cycling and swimming have benefits for general health

- Walking has been shown to benefit many aspects of health, including fitness, brain functioning and back health

- Using an activity-tracking device, along with daily stepping targets, can help ensure we get good levels of general activity

- Putting activity in the diary reduces the risk of it getting squeezed out of our schedules

- Resistance exercise is good for muscle strength and tone, and is important for maintaining functionality and preventing frailty in later life

- Resistance exercise can be done in the gym, but home-based circuits requiring very little equipment are perfectly adequate too

- For those who are already fit, high-intensity intermittent exercise represents a time-efficient way of achieving improved health and fitness

Chapter 7

Sound Effects

This book is geared towards providing you with a range of tips, tricks and tools you can use to enhance how you feel and function in the work setting and beyond. Some of the approaches will reap huge dividends, but do require at least some effort. Others, in contrast, require practically no effort at all, but can still give us an edge and make life better. Listening to music is one such strategy.

In this chapter we're going to explore how music can affect our mood and physiological functioning for the better. Science has also revealed that sounds of specific frequencies have the power to alter brainwave patterns and induce states such as relaxation or focus. This emerging technology – known as 'binaural beats' – will be discussed at the end of the chapter.

Mood Music

Have you ever heard a song on the radio that was upbeat and melodic and perhaps took you back to a happy time in your life, maybe your youth? If so, then you have probably experienced the almost-instant boost music can give our mood and outlook. On the other hand, if you've ever sat through a 'sad song' or the dirge of a funeral march, you'll also be aware of how music can 'bring us down'. Different types of music clearly can have different effects on our mental state, and there's even some science in the area.

In one study, individuals were exposed to fifteen-minute bursts of four types of music: grunge rock, 'New Age', classical and 'designer' (synthesizer music designed to be uplifting).[1] Psychological testing was performed before and immediately after each musical exposure. The response to different types of music varied considerably.

For example, grunge rock increased feelings of hostility, sadness, tension and fatigue, while reducing positive attributes such as relaxation, mental clarity and sense of vitality. Classical music was found to reduce tension, sadness and fatigue, while the New Age music reduced negative experiences but also increased positive ones such as clarity, sense of vitality and feelings of relaxation. The 'designer' music was the stand-out winner, though: it reduced all the measured negative feelings and boosted all the positive ones.

This research demonstrates that different types of music can have different effects on our mood and sense of wellbeing (which we knew already). But, of course, there is likely to be considerable individual variation here. There may be people, for instance, who like nothing more than to kick back and relax to some of Kenny G's 'smooth jazz'. Maybe like a lot of people, I'd rather stick pins in my eyes (apologies if you are a Kenny G fan). On the other hand, I know many who would find it hard to sit through even a few bars of 80s music from the likes of Duran Duran and Spandau Ballet. But for me, songs from this era can evoke the same feelings of excitement and elation I would get when I was a teenager complete with my New Romantic hair and ruffly shirts.

This personalized nature of our response to music has come out in the research. One review of more than twenty studies found that music has genuine ability to calm the stress response.[2] Interestingly, the extent of the benefit was dependent on several factors including the subjects' musical preferences.

Get Ahead with Headphones

Most people who listen to music during the daily commute or while out for a short walk will use headphones for this, and 'ear-bud' types work just fine for the most part. However, more conspicuous headphones that cover the ears have another role: they give off a signal that the wearer is 'otherwise engaged'. This makes unwelcome disturbances in the office less likely, and is a major boon for sociopaths who want to cut down on the chances of someone attempting to strike up a conversation on a train or plane, for instance.

Noise-cancelling headphones are particularly worthy of consideration, I think, as their ability to block out a lot of extraneous noise helps keep us in a protective 'bubble' that can aid focus and output.

Music on the Brain

Music can affect our sense of wellbeing and mental state, but evidence suggests it may affect basic brain functioning too. Research in both humans and animals shows that music has the capacity to induce measurable changes in mental processes including 'synaptic plasticity' (communication between nerve cells).[3]

In one study, individuals were exposed to classical music (Vivaldi's *Four Seasons*), white noise (essentially, a hissing sound) or no sound at all, at different times. The classical music, compared to the other conditions, enhanced what is known as 'working memory' (the ability to hold multiple pieces of information in the mind in the short term, and important for skills such as reasoning and comprehension).[4]

The effects of music have also been tested on individuals' abilities to complete work-related tasks. In one study, surgeons were exposed to music of their choosing, some other music, or no music at all, while performing a laboratory-based task.[5] Surgeons exposed to music of their choosing showed lower objective signs of stress and performed better too. I recall from my days as a junior doctor that there was often music playing in the background during surgical sessions in operating theatres. I thought this was perhaps a reflection of the idiosyncratic and eccentric nature of many of the surgeons (which I liked, by the way). Maybe, though, the music was also helping them do a better job.

Scientific research reveals that music even has the capacity to improve our *physiological* state, including the functioning of the immune system. In one study, the effect of rock music, New Age music and 'designer' music (see above) on the antibody levels in the saliva was assessed (higher antibody levels are a sign of better immune function).[6] While rock music and New Age music did nothing, here, listening to 'designer' music led to a boost in antibody levels of more than 50 per cent. If, at the same time, listeners focused on creating a feeling of appreciation (see Chapter 9 for more on the relevance of this), antibody levels rose by an average of more than 140 per cent.

Let's Get Physical

Some of us swear that listening to music helps our motivation and performance while exercising. Research suggests that this impression is not necessarily all in our mind.[7] In one study, listening to music (compared to no music) during treadmill walking to exhaustion boosted endurance by 15 per cent.[8]

The fact that gyms tend to have music blaring in the background is probably no coincidence. In Chapter 6, we discussed the attributes of walking. The simple act of listening to some of your favourite music as you do this might make it an altogether better and more enjoyable experience.

The Beat is On

Some of the benefits of music may come through the associations we may have with specific songs or just through the sheer enjoyment of the sounds we are hearing. However, research suggests that enjoyment *per se* is not necessary for sound to elicit a response in the brain. Just playing *specific frequencies* of sound into the ears has the potential to do this. This branch of acoustics, known as 'binaural beats' (or 'binaural sound') has some ability to induce specific mental states 'to order'.

Different mental states have different brainwave frequencies associated with them. Brainwaves 'cycle' at a frequency of anything up to 40 hertz (cycles per second). Generally speaking, the higher the frequency, the higher the brain's activity. There are four main 'bands' of brainwave frequency (see box).

The Brainwave Bands

Beta: 13–40 hertz. This is the predominant frequency when we are applying our mind to tasks, thinking about things, and also when we are anxious. The chances are, you'll spend extended periods of the day in this state when at work.

Alpha: 8–12 hertz. This is the predominant pattern when we are relaxed, just about to fall asleep, just waking up, and when we are in relatively shallow sleep ('REM sleep', as discussed in Chapter 4).

Theta: 4–7 hertz. This is the predominant frequency when we are in deeper sleep. Some individuals can also achieve this state during meditation.

Delta: less than 4 hertz. This is the predominant frequency when we are in the very deepest sleep (also known as 'slow wave sleep' – see Chapter 4).

Binaural beat technology is based on the concept that certain frequencies of sound can 'coax' the brain in brainwave patterns of a specific, desired frequency. This might be useful, say, to reduce brainwave frequency before sleep. Or it could help to increase brainwave activity if we were looking to elevate ourselves from a mental low and increase our concentration and focus. The idea of inducing a specific frequency in brainwaves using sound is sometimes referred to as 'entrainment'.

Eliciting particular states in the brain is not as simple as listening to a tone of the same brainwave frequency we're seeking to achieve. The reason that this technology is referred to as 'binaural' is because *two frequencies* are required, each one played into a different ear.

Imagine, for example, playing a tone of 300 hertz into the left ear, and a tone of 290 hertz into the right one. What this can do, in effect, is evoke a frequency within the brain that represents the *difference between the two frequencies* – in this case, 10 hertz. This particular frequency corresponds to a relaxed, alpha state.

However, if the two tones were 300 and 270 hertz, the difference would be 30 hertz. This may induce a beta state that might be desirable if we're looking to give the brain a bit of oomph so we can crack on with some work.

While binaural beat technology has not been studied extensively, there is at least some positive evidence to be found. For example, in one study, individuals due for surgery were randomly assigned to one of three pre-surgery conditions, and the effects on anxiety levels were measured. The three conditions were:

- Music listening

- Music listening with embedded binaural beats

- No music listening

Compared to no music at all, listening to music did not significantly reduce anxiety, but listening to music embedded with binaural beats *did*.[9] In fact, in this group, anxiety was reduced by more than a quarter.

In another study, individuals performed a task requiring vigilance three times under different conditions.[10] On one occasion, they were exposed to 'pink noise' (similar to white noise, and heard as a hissing sound). On another occasion, the pink noise had binaural beats in the beta frequency added. On one further occasion, the pink noise had binaural beats of lower frequency (theta/delta) added. The subjects did not know what types of sound they were listening to.

The beta frequency binaural beats led to an improvement in a test of vigilance task, and improved mood too, leading the study authors to conclude that: '[Binaural beat] technology may have applications for the control of attention and arousal and the enhancement of human performance.'

Resources

Binaural beat technology is available as smartphone apps, CDs and downloadable mp3s. The Immrama Institute in the US produces binaural-beat-embedded soundtracks in CD and mp3 form at relatively low cost. They have two signature products: 'Insight' (for inducing a relaxing, meditative state) and 'Focus' (for inducing a focused and productive state). For more details, see http://www.immramainstitute.com

THE BOTTOM LINE

- Music can improve our mood and mental state

- Music has been shown to have a positive impact on our physiological state too (including immunity)

- Listening to upbeat, enjoyable music can put us in a more resourceful state prior to or during, say, a task or exercise session

- Binaural beat technology may help induce specific states in the brain such as relaxation and mental focus

Chapter 8

Breath of Life

Most of us know that the act of breathing is essential for providing us with the oxygen we require for survival, but will usually not give it much more thought than this. However, as this chapter will explore, many of us can be prone to inefficient patterns of breathing that can drain our energy levels and even disrupt our mental state.

This chapter will provide you with a quick and accurate way to assess your own breathing, and describe some simple and practical exercises that can optimize your wellbeing and help you perform at your best.

Every Breath You Take

When we breathe in, oxygen in the air is absorbed through the lungs into the bloodstream, which then transports it to our tissues. The metabolic reactions that utilize oxygen give off carbon dioxide, which makes its way into the bloodstream to be transported to the lungs, where it can be released into the air we breathe out.

The act of breathing in (inhalation) is an active process, and there are fundamentally two mechanisms involved here. One primarily involves the contraction of the muscles found between the ribs (the 'intercostal' muscles), causing the chest to rise up and widen. This expands the volume of the chest, which naturally draws air into the lungs. The other major breathing mechanism involves a dome of muscle at the base of the chest known as the 'diaphragm'. Contraction of the diaphragm flattens it, thereby drawing air into the lungs.

The act of breathing out (exhalation) is essentially a passive process, the result of relaxation of the intercostal muscles and diaphragm.

Blood Borne

Most of the oxygen in the blood is transported attached to protein known as 'haemoglobin' (contained in the red blood cells). It is haemoglobin that 'picks up' oxygen in the lungs and delivers it to our organs and tissues including our brain and muscles.

Oxygenation of the body can be thought of as a two-stage process: absorption of oxygen from the air, followed by the delivery to our tissues (via haemoglobin). Ideally, both processes should work efficiently. In reality, though, there can be problems with one or both of them that can leave us devitalized and defocused.

Get it Off Your Chest

You'll remember that air can be drawn into the lungs through the action of either expansion of the ribcage or contraction of the diaphragm – often referred to as 'chest breathing' and 'diaphragmatic breathing' respectively.

Chest breathing will generally not allow full expansion of the larger, lower reaches of the lungs, and this may compromise optimal oxygen absorption from the air into the bloodstream. 'Diaphragmatic' breathing, on the other hand, may improve oxygenation of the blood by allowing more complete inflation of the lungs.

Chest breathing can be problematic in another way in that it can be relatively *rapid* in nature – sometimes referred to as 'over-breathing'. This pattern of breathing can lead to excessive 'blowing off' of carbon dioxide.

This may not sound like much of an issue because carbon dioxide is generally viewed as a waste product. However, the reality is that carbon dioxide is critical to the healthy functioning of the body, and low levels of this gas can actually 'starve' us of oxygen.

Issues here have to do with the fact that carbon dioxide is *acidic* in nature, which means low levels of this gas in the bloodstream tends to make it more alkaline. The problem is, due to a physiological phenomenon known as the 'Bohr effect', as the blood becomes more alkaline, *less* oxygen is released from haemoglobin to be available to the tissues.

Basically, when we over-breathe our tissues (including our brain) can become starved of oxygen (even if there is plenty of oxygen in the bloodstream). Low levels of carbon dioxide (technically termed 'hypocapnia') can cause constriction of blood vessels too, further compromising oxygen delivery to our tissues and organs.

I remember learning the perils of over-breathing as a thirteen-year-old in a biology lesson. Our teacher, Mr Luck, got us to demonstrate this phenomenon by having us breathe in and out very quickly. Before long, I and my classmates were feeling 'spacy' and I recall Micky Noble even falling off his stool. Luckily for Mr Luck, this was in the days before Ofsted inspections.

Low carbon dioxide levels can upset the body's chemical balance in another way too: they lower calcium levels in the blood. Calcium is important for normal functioning of the nerves and muscles, and low calcium can lead to symptoms such as pins and needles and possibly 'cramping' in the hands and feet. These symptoms are common during episodes of 'hyperventilation' ('panic attacks'). Incidentally, the emergency medical treatment for hyperventilation is to breathe in and out of a paper bag held tightly around the nose and mouth. This increases carbon dioxide levels in the blood, which helps restore normal physiology and calm to the system.

Classical hyperventilation is quite an extreme state of affairs, but between this and an optimal breathing pattern is a spectrum. Some people may not suffer from full-blown panic attacks but may still experience symptoms that are unpleasant and drag performance down including dizziness, breathlessness, chest tightness and anxiety.[1] None of this, of course, helps individuals to get the best out of themselves whether at work or not.

I've seen quite a few people over the years with these symptoms who have 'done the rounds' of a number of medical specialists seeking an explanation for their symptoms. Because breathing patterns get relatively little focus in medicine (even by doctors specializing in 'chest medicine'), a fundamental problem with over-breathing is easily missed.

In short, maintaining a healthy breathing pattern can do a surprising amount to keep us energized and productive. Key to getting these benefits is cultivating the art of slower, diaphragmatic breathing.

Breath Test

This simple exercise will enable you to get a good idea about whether, at any moment in time, you are breathing predominantly from your chest or your diaphragm.

Put your left hand on the middle or your chest and your right hand over your navel. Breathe normally. Look at your hands and observe which, if any, hand moves more than the other. If your right hand is moving more than your left, it is likely that your breathing is diaphragmatic in nature at this time. If your left hand is moving more than your right, though, it is a sign that you are chest breathing and may benefit from some remedial action.

Belly Up

Let's say you repeat the exercise above from time to time and find, on the whole, that you tend to breathe from your chest. It is possible to retrain breathing, though this generally requires some practice. One simple strategy here is to focus on breathing into your belly from time to time.

In a private moment, put your hands on your chest and belly as before, and this time make a conscious effort to breathe in a way that causes the hand over your belly to move more than the one over your chest. It may take a little getting used to, but with time you're likely to find yourself able to 'belly breathe' to order.

Another key aspect of efficient breathing relates to the *frequency* of breaths. Usually, it helps for people to slow down their breathing. Generally speaking, cycles of about ten seconds (six breaths per minute) are usually manageable and work well. In fact, some evidence shows that just slowing down breathing to this frequency has the capacity to lower both subjective and objective measures of anxiety.[2] You may want to gradually slow your breathing to this rate during a session rather than try to force it quickly from the start.

Usually only a minute or two of slower, diaphragmatic breathing is all that is required to have a tangible effect on someone's state – generally experienced as a greater sense of calm and focus. This is obviously useful in many situations, including deciding on which bit of work to tackle next, or before an important meeting or presentation.

Best Practice

Practice makes perfect, as they say, so spending a few minutes twice or more each day practising slower, diaphragmatic breathing can help make it second nature to you. Many individuals find that regular practice means that they rarely have to consciously focus on maintaining an optimal breathing pattern because, well, they're doing it quite naturally and automatically.

One technique you may want to add is to phase breathing so that there is a pause after exhalation. This might help raise to carbon dioxide levels a bit which, remember, will help oxygen delivery as well as blood flow. A ten-second cycle may therefore be split up this way:

Inhalation – 2 seconds
Exhalation – 4 seconds
Pause – 4 seconds

You may need to work up to this over time, but once you have, you'll likely have better breathing patterns overall. You'll also have a simple technique that can be highly valuable to you when, say, you are feeling overwhelmed or in need of some focus.

Breath for Health

The short-term benefits of diaphragmatic breathing on wellbeing are often immediately apparent to those who practise it. However, research suggests that healthy breathing patterns can have a very positive impact on our long-term health too.

In one study, regular diaphragmatic breathing was added to the normal care of diabetics. After three months, compared to just usual care, the breathing exercises brought a number of improvements including reduced body weight and improved short- and long-term blood sugar control.[3]

In another study, the effect of diaphragmatic breathing on a biochemical process known as 'oxidative stress' was assessed.[4] Oxidative stress (also known as 'free radical damage') is disease-promoting and ageing, and can be induced by several factors including spikes in blood sugar. In this research, diaphragmatic breathing was found to dampen oxidative stress after individuals ate a high-carbohydrate meal. In addition, diaphragmatic breathing was found to lower the heart rate and improve blood sugar control.

Another time when oxidative stress is increased is during exercise. In one study, the impact of diaphragmatic breathing after a cycle training session was assessed.[5] Compared to just sitting quietly, diaphragmatic breathing was found to increase 'antioxidant' status (antioxidants counteract oxidative stress) and also lowered levels of the stress hormone cortisol in the body. The authors of the study concluded that diaphragmatic breathing could help protect athletes from the long-term adverse effects of oxidative stress.

In short, the simple act of breathing more slowly into the belly has the power to enhance our mental state and feeling of wellbeing in the short term, as well as our overall health in the long term. This technique is also completely free and can be practised anywhere to breathe new life into you.

THE BOTTOM LINE

- Breathing allows absorption of oxygen into the blood so that it can be delivered to the tissues

- Breathing also transports carbon dioxide to the lungs where it can be 'blown off'

- Some people are prone to over-breathing and low levels of carbon dioxide in the bloodstream, which can reduce oxygen delivery to the tissues

- Over-breathing can cause symptoms such as dizziness, breathlessness, chest tightness and anxiety

- Slower breathing, particularly into the diaphragm, can help to ensure proper chemical balance in the blood and oxygen delivery to the tissues

- Slower, diaphragmatic breathing has been shown to improve markers of disease including blood sugar levels and oxidative stress

Chapter 9

Mind Control

Even when our physiology and energy production are running efficiently, our performance can still get scuppered by a bit of 'negative thinking'. Life's problems and challenges can sometimes cause us to be despondent or become anxious. Occasionally, we may just feel overwhelmed and wonder how we're ever going to cope with the demands of the job.

What can help is to cultivate simple strategies for getting into a resourceful mental state – a zone where we can be highly productive though without a perceived need to drive ourselves on. This state is sometimes described as being 'in the flow', and most people will know what it feels like. The trick is being able to recreate it at will.

In this chapter, we're going to explore the physiological basis for this state, as well as how to reproduce it to order. This is often less about altering how we *think*, and more about making positive shifts in what we *feel*. The key, then, is not necessarily to focus on the brain, but another organ entirely – the *heart*.

Your Beating Heart

A major function of the heart is to pump blood around the body, but recent evidence suggests there's much more to this organ than that. While the heart's beating is controlled by nerves that travel from the brain to the heart, there are in fact more nerves travelling in the opposite direction. Basically, our 'heart and mind' are constantly 'talking to each other', and thus have the ability to influence each other too. If we perceive a threat in our head, then this can be reflected in a more rapid heart rate. But evidence shows it works the other way round, too: what we 'feel in our heart' can influence our emotional response and how we think.

Our language is actually peppered with expressions that suggest the heart is the seat of our emotions and can influence how we think and act. Examples include: 'it warmed my heart', 'my heart sank', 'cry your heart out' and 'take it to heart'.

Not only is there two-way communication between the heart and the brain but, as this chapter will reveal, there is evidence that the quality of this communication can have an important bearing on our internal experience and how we then perform. When the heart and the brain are 'out of sync' we can feel anxious, defocused, scattered in our thinking and stressed. When the heart and brain are harmonized, though, we have the potential to feel peaceful, energized, focused and full of bright ideas.

Understanding the physiology behind these effects requires a knowledge of the heart rhythm, and what is known as 'heart rate variability'.

Heart Rate Variability

Imagine a heart is pumping at a rate of sixty beats per minute. Most people would imagine that this means each heartbeat is separated from the next by one second, as illustrated below.

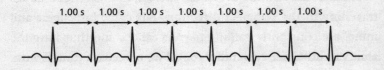

Actually, though, the length of time between heartbeats varies from beat to beat. The interval between beats may be one second between some beats, but between others it may be a little longer or shorter. This variation in the pauses between beats is what is meant by the term 'heart rate variability'.

Sometimes, the difference between the pauses between heart rates is relatively small, such as in the example below.

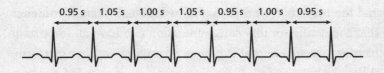

This is an example of *low* heart rate variability. But, at other times or in another person, the amount of time between heartbeats can vary more, such as here:

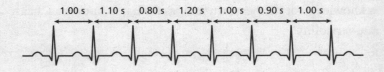

This would be termed *high* heart rate variability. These differences in heart rate variability are not just academic: heart rate variability is believed to be a marker for the body's ability to adapt to changing circumstances. In theory, then, the higher the heart rate variability, the better our overall wellness may be.

There is indeed some evidence for this, in the form of studies that find that higher heart rate variability is associated with improved health outcomes. For example, in one study, higher heart rate variability in middle-aged men was associated with less than half the risk of dying (over a finite period of time) compared to men with lower heart rate variability.[1]

One might imagine that reduced survival in those of lower heart rate variability might be the result of heightened risk of heart-related conditions such as sudden death (often caused by a serious heart rhythm disturbance) or heart disease. Actually, lower heart rate variability turned out to be associated with increased death rates due to 'non-cardiac' (as well as cardiac) conditions, including cancer. The authors of this study concluded that low heart rate variability is a marker for 'compromised health' in broad terms.

Boosting Heart Rate Variability

Is heart rate variability somehow hard-wired into the system, or is it modifiable and something we can boost for our benefit? Research shows that, fortunately, it's the latter. Three of the lifestyle factors that are covered elsewhere in this book have the capacity to enhance heart rate variability: proper sleep,[2] exercise[3] and diaphragmatic breathing.[4] See Chapters 4, 6 and 8 respectively for more about these factors and how to incorporate them into your own life.

Heart rate variability is a marker for better long-term health, but it is also connected with our physiological and emotional state in the moment. This relates to the synchronization that can exist between the heart and the brain we touched on earlier.

Be Coherent

Have you ever produced a substantial piece of work of high quality and in good time, and felt somehow that all this happened with relative ease? Do you know what it's like to think creatively and conjure up solutions to problems as though it's the easiest thing in the world? Have you ever engaged in some task or hobby, felt absorbed and focused, subsequently to feel as though time has flown by?

These experiences are examples of a focused and resourceful state where the communication between the heart and the brain is synchronized and harmonious. Some researchers describe this state as 'physiological coherence' or simply 'coherence'. Coherence can actually be measured and tracked, and it's closely tied with heart rate variability.

Remember, heart rate variability is the beat-to-beat variation in the heart rate. For illustrative purposes, imagine someone with a heart rate of 60 beats per minute where the time between beats varies from 0.8 to 1.2 seconds. The heart rate at the moment when the pause between beats is 0.8 seconds is 60 divided by 0.8 = 75 bpm (beats per minute). When the gap is 1.2 seconds, the heart rate is 50 bpm. If we were to plot a graph of heart rate against time for this person, it might look something like this:

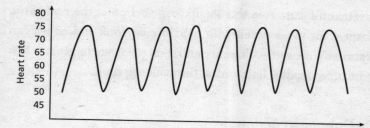

Notice here how the heart rate's variability rises and falls in a smooth and consistent manner. This is what 'coherence' looks like.

On the other hand, someone with the same heart rate variability might look like this:

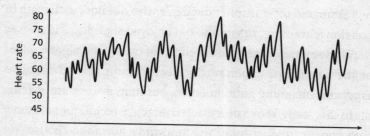

You'll see that the heart rate still varies between about 50 and 75, but that the changes in heart rate variability are volatile and erratic.

This is incoherence, and just as with a misfiring engine, it's a state in which our performance and 'fuel efficiency' can be severely compromised. In real life, this can be experienced as having to put more effort in to whatever we do, only to get inferior results. You know those days when you seem to flit from project to project or find yourself distractible and frustrated by your lack of productivity? That's you in an incoherent state.

Technology allows us to know whether we are coherent or not, and can also help us develop the art of recreating this resourceful state (see the 'Resources' section at the end of the chapter for more details). But, before we look at how we can objectively measure coherence and train ourselves to get into this state more readily, let's look at the evidence for it.

Coherence in Action

Studies show that getting into a coherent state improves how we feel and helps balance our physiological functioning and response to stress. In one study conducted in the workplace, individuals were trained in coherence-boosting techniques. These were then practised consistently for one month.[5]

Compared to 'control' individuals who did not participate in coherence training, those who did enjoyed significant increases in positive emotions such as feelings of caring and vigour, while at the same time experiencing decreases in several negative emotions including guilt, hostility, burnout, anxiety and stress.

In this study, those practising coherence techniques also saw a 23 per cent reduction in the key stress hormone cortisol on average. They also saw increases in levels of the hormone 'dihydroepiandrosterone' (DHEA), which is associated with better overall health and vitality. The authors of this study concluded that: 'individuals may have greater control over their minds, bodies and health than previously suspected.'

In another study conducted in the workplace, coherence-directed training led to meaningful reductions in blood pressure and significantly lowered symptoms of stress, depression and psychological distress.[6] Peacefulness and positive outlook also improved for participants.

Coherence training has been shown to have the capacity to help children, too. In one study of US high school students, coherence training reduced test anxiety and improved results.[7] In a UK study, coherence training improved a range of symptoms in children diagnosed with attention-deficit hyperactivity disorder (ADHD).[8]

Change of Heart

What does it take to get into a more balanced, coherent state? In the previous chapter we learned that what is known as 'diaphragmatic' or 'belly breathing' has the ability to improve heart rate variability. Evidence shows that this simple strategy can enhance coherence too.[9] See Chapter 8 for more about this form of breathing and the simple exercises that will allow you to cultivate it.

The Feel-Good Factor

Beyond breathing, much of the research into coherence has focused on how we can create this state using specific mental techniques and attitudes of mind.[10] What is clear from the research is that when we feel negative emotions such as frustration, stress, anxiety and hostility, this is reflected in an incoherent heart-brain pattern. In this state, it's sometimes difficult to make any meaningful progress and it sure does not feel too good either. On the other hand, positive emotions have been shown to induce coherence – a state where mountains can sometimes be moved with relative ease.

The US-based company HeartMath has been a pioneer in this field, and has conducted a lot of research into coherence and how to practise it. The evidence shows that a key here is simply to focus our attention on the heart and evoke any *positive emotion*.

The challenge for some of us is that life can throw a lot at us quite quickly, and it is sometimes easy for us to be rather 'reactionary'. Many of us can feel our state is determined by the events and situations we find ourselves in, and that we are often 'hostages to our emotions'. Sometimes, the best thing we can do is to stop for just a moment, and consciously work towards a state that serves us (and probably everyone around us) better. What follows are three strategies that can induce coherence, and can improve our personal power if made consistent parts of our day, both in and out of the workplace.

The attitude of gratitude

Many of us are driven and ambitious, and strive to achieve 'success' which we may define in all sorts of ways including our status, income and wealth. The problem is, even when we achieve our goals, feelings of satisfaction and contentment can be fleeting. Some of us reflect only momentarily before moving on to the next thing.

Sometimes, it can help to reflect on our achievements and other things to be grateful for. Studies show that simply evoking a feeling of gratitude induces a coherent state.

Take a few moments now to think about just one thing in your life that you appreciate and are grateful for. It could be a significant, loving relationship, say, with a partner, parent, friend or child. It might be another sort of relationship, like a healthy, functional, respectful relationship you have with a colleague. Or perhaps put your attention on something inanimate that you appreciate, such as your home or a place you like to visit. Focus on whatever it is for a moment, putting your attention on what you like and are grateful for about it, and note how this makes you feel.

Chances are you'll find that you are calmer or less anxious or more mentally energized (or possibly all three) than you were before. That's the power of the attitude of gratitude right there.

You can use this technique whenever you like to centre and ground you, but it can help to formalize this strategy. Perform any mental process regularly enough, and it can actually start to pervade how we feel and behave on a daily basis.

How about starting each day with this exercise? You may even do it while still lying in bed before getting up. Or maybe while preparing your breakfast or drinking your first coffee or tea of the day. I do this. I usually get up earlier than my other half. While she sleeps, I'll often fix myself a coffee and spend just a few moments reflecting on what is good about my life before I start the day. This simple mental exercise usually puts me in a state where I can make best use of my time. My perception is that in this better frame of mind I encounter far fewer 'challenges', and am also better able to deal with those that do surface.

As you get more and more used to this exercise, your perception of things that you are grateful for might expand. How about keeping a note of them? In challenging times, even the briefest of references to that list may do wonders to return you to a state in which you can respond positively and creatively.

Back to the future

When we have problems and unwelcome experiences in our lives, many of us have a natural tendency to focus our attention on them. If we're in a highly resourceful state when we do this, then it might make perfect sense to do so. The problem is, if we are 'not in a good place' when we attempt to resolve issues, we may end up struggling for solutions as a result. This will usually compound any feelings we have of being out of control and somewhat helpless.

It can sometimes help to step away from the issue at hand, and direct our attention onto things that help us feel more positive and productive. One way to do this is to reflect on *what's gone well*.

For example, let's say someone has recently pitched for a couple of contracts, neither of which they have won. This may be perceived as a 'problem', and may also put them in a somewhat despondent state where they may feel stressed about whether they are on some sort of perpetual losing streak.

However, a more productive response may come from focusing on what went well in those pitches (maybe they just lost out on price), as well as remembering other pitches that proved successful. The positive attributes that now become the centre of our attention do not need to relate to pitching or sales – they could relate to anything. All we're doing here is using any positive event or outcome as a focal point so that we can shift our state into one that feels better, and also allows us to make best use of our internal resources.

As with the attitude of gratitude, it can be helpful to 'hardwire' this way of thinking into our neurology, and the best way to do this is to practise it regularly.

So, perhaps at the start and end of each day, just take a few moments to reflect on what's gone well. Some of the easiest events to focus on will be ones from the preceding day or two. It could be a useful conversation with a colleague or a piece of feedback from a client or customer. If nothing springs readily to mind, then by all means go to another point in your life, even some time back, which you identify with 'things going well' and success.

This exercise helps send powerful positive messages to yourself, such as: 'I can do this' or 'I am good at this' or 'I can succeed at this'. This elicits a far more resourceful state than one in which you are asking yourself how you're ever going to get yourself out of a situation or turn things around.

Random acts of kindness

Have you ever offered someone your seat on a train whom you felt was more in need of it than you and been thanked for it? What about dropping some coins into a busker's guitar case or giving money to charity? Many of us will get a positive feeling from such acts that put us in a good mood. When we perform such acts, we usually get a lot more out of them than we put in.

I first started thinking about random acts of kindness as a sort of 'lifestyle choice' after an experience I had on the London Underground shortly before Christmas some years back. While changing platforms at one station, I was walking up some steps separated in the middle by a railing. I and hordes of others were walking slowly up on the right-hand side. The left-hand side of the stairs (for people coming down) was pretty much empty.

Up in front of me I noticed a young man vaulting the railing in the middle of the stairway. Once over the railing, he began running up the stairs. At first, I thought he had jumped the railing to ease his passage. Actually, he was making his way to a woman who was near the top of the stairway and was attempting to negotiate a buggy (complete with toddler) down the stairs. He lifted the front of the buggy, allowing the woman to make her way down the stairs much more easily.

On one level, one could argue this was a relatively small gesture. But just witnessing this event had a positive effect on me. I suspect the lady being helped was touched by the gesture, but my guess is the good Samaritan got a kick out of it too. I resolved to make random acts of kindness my New Year's resolution that year. Since then, I have carried out at least one random act of kindness, however small, each day.

My random acts of kindness since that time have come in a wide variety of forms including text messages to old friends or calling someone out of the blue, pushing cars stuck in the snow and giving lifts to hitchhikers. I have, also, carried more push-chairs and bags up and down flights of stairs on the Tube than I care to mention.

Most of us work in competitive arenas where the focus can be what we can get out of any situation. But many of us will also know that what we get out of life can be a reflection of what we put in. And random acts of kindness, I think, are a perfect example of this.

Organizations I have worked directly with vary enormously in terms of culture, but I'd say most are quite pressurized environments where random acts of kindness generally don't feature much. Could you perhaps buck the trend? For instance, after a potentially difficult meeting is skilfully negotiated by a colleague, could you later tell them: 'I thought you handled that really well'? If you've found something that has helped in your work and life in general (perhaps something you have learned in the pages of this book), could you just share that spontaneously with others you feel may benefit?

The corporate environment actually offers me personally considerable potential for random acts of kindness. For example, I may get asked a question at the end of a presentation and ask the person to stay behind so I can give them some individualized advice. I regularly give copies of my books away to people who I feel would get value from them.

Small acts like these are inspired by a desire to help and support others. But there's no denying that I get something out of them too. I know I do my best work when I am in a state of generosity, and you may too.

Resources

HeartMath has not just done a lot of the research into coherence, but has also developed technology to measure and help us cultivate this resourceful state. One convenient piece of kit they make is called the emWave2. It's small, handheld device that monitors heart rate via a thumb-pad (or sensor that attaches to the earlobe and plugs into the device).

The emWave2 has two light displays. One coaches the user into a slow, steady breathing pattern. The other lights give visual indication of the level of our coherence: red for incoherence, green for coherence, and blue for somewhere in between. This device can be highly useful for helping us learn how to get into a coherent state at will.

HeartMath also has an app for smartphones called 'Inner Balance' that essentially does the same thing as the emWave2 but requires the use of a heart rate monitor worn around the chest.

THE BOTTOM LINE

- The beat-to-beat variation in heart rate – known as 'heart rate variability' – is a marker for health

- Healthy sleep habits, regular activity and diaphragmatic breathing can all help to improve heart rate variability

- There is an important connection between heart and brain that can influence our state and effectiveness

- Harmonized body–brain communication – referred to as 'coherence' – induces a more resourceful state and helps optimise our effectiveness and performance

- Eliciting positive emotions through, say, practising appreciation, reflecting on what's gone well, and practising random acts of kindness, can increase coherence and resourcefulness

Chapter 10

Habit Forming

Have you ever resolved to make healthy changes that seemed like a very good idea at the time, only to find your newfound habits slipping by the wayside within a few weeks (or even sooner)? Do you know what it's like to make New Year's resolutions that didn't even make it into February? Do you find yourself going in and out of 'healthy' phases over time?

If I've learned one thing from my own life and my experience of others, it's that *starting* a positive habit or behaviour does not normally present much of a challenge for people, but *sustaining it* often does. Also, most people can nix a bad habit reasonably easily initially, but can then find themselves somehow irresistibly drawn back to it in time. This chapter is about how to make good habits and break bad ones – for good.

You might be wondering whether this chapter is going to be a chapter about self-discipline and willpower. It's not. As we discussed in Chapter 3, willpower is like a muscle: once 'exercised' it is weaker for some time later. If we keep having to activate our 'willpower muscle' we can eventually weaken it to the extent that self-control just drains away.

The key to making and breaking habits is not to rely on willpower, but to make these things *easy* to do so that self-restraint and gritted-teeth determination are not required. This is what this chapter is about.

Habits Versus Choices

There are books written about behaviour change, and here we'll usually find a lot of talk about how much of our actions are very *unconscious* in nature. From how we do up our shoelaces and how we dry ourselves after a shower, to what we eat for breakfast and the time we usually go to bed, the bulk of what we do is done without much contemplation – we just do it.

Some of us eat rubbishy breakfast cereal (see Chapter 1) in the morning and resist going to bed for no other reason than that we're in the *habit* of doing these things. However, one could argue that once we're aware of a habit and the impact it's likely to be having on us (good or bad), then it ceases to be a habit, and now becomes a *choice*.

So, taking breakfast as an example, perhaps before reading the first chapter of this book (you did read it, didn't you?) you never gave much consideration to your bowl of breakfast cereal or what else you might eat. However, upon reading that most cereals are more fodder than food, you may subsequently have considered your options.

Whether you make an altogether better breakfast choice will be, ultimately, down to whether you are *motivated* to do so. In fact, motivation is ultimately at the heart of all the things we do (and don't do). Understanding what motivates us is the key to making positive change easy and permanent.

The Motivating Factor

Imagine you're at home getting ready for work in the summer, and it's already quite a warm and sunny day outside. At some point before walking out of the door you'll likely choose some clothes and get dressed. Here's a question: why bother with the whole clothes thing? Why not set off to work naked? Partly, it's habit, right? But, at its root, the habit of getting dressed is a choice that has specific motivations. Let's think about what these might be for a moment. Here are some ideas:

- Actually, I quite like dressing smartly for work

- I think I look better with clothes on than clothes off, to be honest

- Everyone else does it, and I like to fit in

- I don't think I'd feel right sitting on the train with only *The Times* to cover my embarrassment

- I think my colleagues and clients quite like my sense of individuality, but would view nudity at work as a step too far

- Isn't public nudity illegal?

All these are valid reasons in their own way and the list could be far longer. But whatever someone's specific motivation, the desire to leave the house dressed (rather than naked) is all connected with pleasure and pain.

Basically, we are instantly and *automatically motivated* to do things that we perceive bring us *more pleasure* (e.g. from dressing well and looking good) or less pain (e.g. fear of arrest or feeling quite self-conscious when sitting on the train in the nude). By the same token, we are instantly demotivated to do things that we perceive will bring us less pleasure and more pain.

Getting dressed in the morning is an obvious example because, for most of us at least, it's a 'no-brainer'. However, what about when decisions are a bit more in the balance?

I'm going to use myself as an example here because over the last twenty-five or so years there have been many healthy habits I have taken up and persisted with, as well as a few unwholesome ones I have broken with relative ease.

Given what I do for a living, it's perhaps natural to imagine I have always enjoyed a life of self-restraint and purity. Actually, nothing could be further from the truth. I have, at certain periods of my life, been spectacularly unhealthy. I mentioned my studenty eating and drinking habits in the Introduction. I also, for many years, was a heavy and committed smoker. How I finally came to stop, I realize now, is a study in using motivations to make change easy and sustainable. Before that, though, a little background …

I started smoking when I was thirteen, and by the time I stopped I was getting through about thirty cigarettes a day. Smoking a cigarette was, quite literally, the last thing I would do before going to sleep and the first thing I would do once I woke, and I would never be without cigarettes on my person. I had over the course of my smoking history tried and failed to stop smoking several times. I saw myself as seriously addicted, and had some vain hope that I would wake up one day and just not want to smoke any more.

My Smoking Habit Goes Up in a Puff of Smoke

One Easter holiday while at medical school, exams were looming and I was trying to get down to some revision. As was often the way in those days, the work was not going that well, and I was easily distracted. One morning, a brown package came in the post. I recognized the writing on its outside as my brother Joe's. Inside was a copy of a book entitled *The Easy Way to Stop Smoking* by author Allen Carr.

I thought this an ideal distraction from my studies, of course, and as I started to read the book I had no intention of stopping smoking (and was sceptical about the claim that this could be 'easy'). One of the early instructions in the book is that the reader should continue smoking until the book is finished. I was liking this book already, safe in the knowledge that I could relax, read on and continue puffing away.

As I read, it occurred to me that Allen Carr's main point was that smoking addiction is more a *psychological* issue than a physical one. He also made the point that having the correct attitude of mind is imperative if one is to stand a decent chance of stopping, and staying stopped.

Too many people, he wrote, fail because when they attempt to kick the habit, they focus almost exclusively on what they feel they're missing out on. The trick, he claimed, was to focus on all the benefits we perceive of not smoking. Put another way, our focus should be, not on the 'pain' of not smoking, but the pleasure we can derive from it.

This made sense to me, so I began thinking of all the advantages of not smoking as I saw them. I still remember my mental list. Here it is:

- Not perpetually smelling like an ashtray

- Not coughing up things that should probably have been sent to a microbiology lab for analysis

- Not having to be mindful of having cigarettes with me at all times, even in the bath (see below)

- Having more money to spend on other things

- Having more self-esteem because I had finally conquered something I feared I never would

These thoughts actually worked wonders because now I felt motivated – dare I say *inspired* – to stop. I finished the book while taking a bath that evening. I threw the book onto the bathroom floor, took one last smoky drag from my 'ceremonial cigarette', and then put it out in my bath water (yes, classy, I know). I have never smoked since.

Now, in the early days, I have to admit I did have the occasional wobble. But even here, getting my mind focused on the positives helped a lot. One weak moment I recall was two weeks to the day after I smoked my last cigarette. I was in the pub celebrating my birthday with a group of friends and the conviviality of the event, combined with a skinful of lager and gin and tonic and the smoky atmosphere, triggered quite a considerable urge for a cigarette. I slurred to my friend Smithy to 'get me a cigarette'.

Smithy, however, had my best interests at heart, and here's my recollection of what he said in response: 'If you have a cigarette now, you may well end up smoking for the rest of your life. If you don't have it, though, you may well never smoke again.'

While he may not have known it at the time, what Smithy said in that moment had the effect of making me realize that there might be a big price to pay for the 'pleasure' of having that cigarette. But also, there may be much pleasure (and far less pain) to be had from resisting it. I can still remember how Smithy's prophetic words caused the desire for a cigarette to drain away from me. I don't think I kissed him, but I recall blurting out: 'I bladdy love you, Smizzly'.

Other Unhealthy Habits Go by the Wayside

I make no secret of the fact that inside me there is quite a chubby fella ready and willing to show himself without much encouragement. I can gain weight quickly when I throw all caution to the wind. For example, in the middle of writing this book I went away for a walking holiday with some friends on the north Cornish coast. We were away for three and a half days, and we did a lot of quite hard walking on coastal paths each day. However, we're all food lovers too, so we partook of all that was on offer, including things I would not normally eat in a month of Sundays including Cornish pasties, bread and scones. I also drank a fair bit.

Apart from feeling like Vesuvius was erupting in my upper digestive tract, the other undesirable side effect of all this relative hedonism was an increase in my body weight – to the tune of seven pounds. Of course, that would not have all been fat, but the rate of weight gain was disconcerting nonetheless.

So, while the weekend was a whole lot of fun and I would do it all again in a heartbeat, I just wouldn't do it *too soon*. If I ate and drank like that on even a semi-regular basis I'd run the serious risk of ending up visibly overweight. I'm genuinely not at all 'fattist' about other people but, if the truth be told, I am about myself.

Not only do I not like being overweight, in my head I'm convinced it's a major 'occupational hazard' for me. Just imagine me talking to a room full of delegates about healthy eating, all the while pacing around at the front with a pot belly hanging over my belt. Consider the impact looking seriously out of shape might have on some of my patients. Over the years, I've actually heard many individuals express how they have mentally shut off to health practitioners with remarks like: 'My doctor smokes, so I'm not inclined to take any lectures from him about healthy living' or 'The dietician they sent me to was substantially fatter than me.'

Basically, if I don't eat healthily the majority of the time, then not only does it affect my energy and wellbeing, it even compromises my ability to be effective in my work. This is a big motivator for me. It's a chief reason why I've lost my attachment not just to obviously unhealthy foodstuffs such as KFC and pints of Kronenbourg 1664, but also to those that are perceived as healthy that actually aren't including wholemeal bread and breakfast cereals. Any 'pleasure' I might get from eating this stuff on a regular basis pales into insignificance compared to the 'pain' I would have to subsequently endure. To me, eating healthily is simply a no-brainer because it's heavily pegged to the advantages and benefits I attach to it.

That's not to say I don't indulge myself from time to time – my carefree Cornish weekend is a case in point. I just do it rarely enough to ensure it doesn't lead to persistent problems with my energy and effectiveness, or the shape I'm in.

How About You?

Let's see how this sort of mental approach may work in practice with an issue that I see commonly in my patients and clients: sandwich-eating at lunch. If you've read Chapter 1, you'll know that this 'habit' can cause problems with energy and effectiveness in the afternoon. This does not affect everyone, but it commonly causes people to 'lose' a couple of hours that could have been used so much more productively.

We're going to explore what might entrench someone in their sandwich-munching ways, and the sorts of changes in thinking that might motivate them to reach for something better.

Let's start with the 'pain' associated with not having a sandwich and think of ways we can reduce that. I'm going to write a list of barriers to change I've heard from people over the years, followed by ways in which we may look at things differently to remove them.

'That won't fill me up'

People who need 'filling up' at lunchtime (or any meal) have generally allowed themselves to get too hungry. I've found that if people approach lunch in a 'ready to eat but not-too-hungry' state (a 6 or 7 out of 10 on the hunger scale mentioned in Chapter 3), then they will generally happily forgo sandwiches. Once someone is famished by lunchtime, bread-based options become almost irresistible. The solution can be as simple as a handful or two of nuts in the mid to late morning.

'There's nothing else to eat'

I hear this a lot, including from people who regularly go to places where there are plenty of foods other than sandwiches to eat including decent salads and substantial soups. Some people just need to walk a few paces to the left or right.

'I like sandwiches'

Yes, and I like crack cocaine and crystal meth. And if that comment means nothing to you, please read the section on alcohol in Chapter 2.

'It's more expensive'

Granted, this can be true from my experience. However, how about thinking of lunch as an *investment*? So, let's imagine you spend a couple of quid more on a better lunch, but what do you get back?

Likely returns on investment include sustained energy through the afternoon and the satisfaction of finishing the day with a greater sense of having 'got the job done'. Maybe, in the process, you've impressed your colleagues and clients just a bit more through your liveliness and productivity. Now ask yourself this: Is this worth two quid?

'It takes too long'

Again, it generally takes longer to eat a salad or soup compared to a sandwich, but is that a bad thing? Sometimes we can be really pushed for time, but in the grand scheme of things, will another ten minutes make much difference? Actually, a bit more time to clear your head may be paid back several times over in terms of improved productivity in the afternoon. And if you're into numbers and data and stuff, that additional ten minutes represents 0.7 per cent of a twenty-four-hour day.

For most people who learn they suffer from the after-effects of sandwiches almost every day, these changes in thinking will be enough to knock down any barriers to opting for altogether better lunch options. However, for those who need more incentives, there are other, longer-term motivations that might be worth considering.

In Chapter 1, we explored how gluts of carbs in the diet can cause us to have surges of insulin that promote fat deposition. So, if you're a lithe little thing, then you can ponder the fact that dispensing with sandwiches may help keep you that way. If, however, you feel you're carrying body baggage you'd prefer to be rid of, then another likely benefit of eating less bread will be reduced weight and a shrinking waistline, and without any need for hunger or unrealistic exercise regimes.

Let's see how we can use the 'pleasure and pain' principle to address another common issue that I see in practice: the habit of drinking a bit too much alcohol. In Chapter 2 I made the point that while many of us like to drink, it's not as good for us as we have been led to believe, and often disrupts sleep and our performance the following day. It's not just me saying this, by the way: in seminars, workshops and one-to-one sessions individuals very commonly state that while they don't feel they have a 'drink problem', they nonetheless believe they have a 'problem with drink'.

So, let's say someone resolves that they would benefit from drinking less. What barriers might there be to this? As we explored in Chapters 2 and 3, sometimes people are 'driven to drink' not because they need alcohol, but because they are *hungry*. That's one of the reasons I suggest not coming home or sitting in a bar or restaurant in a very hungry state. A few nuts at the end of the afternoon or early evening can take this driver out of the equation. On a similar note, the chances of us drinking more are increased by getting thirsty, so that's another condition we can easily remedy to make reducing our alcohol intake automatic and easy.

Not being unduly hungry or thirsty make it easier to drink less, basically, and therefore reduce the 'pain' of drinking less. Now, what can we mentally stack on the 'pleasure' side?

Let's say you get pleasure from drinking half a bottle of full-bodied red. But what if that leads to you being a bit thick-headed and slow to start in the morning? Put another way, could drinking less pay off the next day in terms of improved energy and performance?

Could it allow you, say, to fire off a couple of cogent, pithy emails that you may have delayed or perhaps not even have sent at all if you hadn't felt so energized? Could your clearer head allow you to conjure up a brilliant (even though you say so yourself) solution to a client issue? Might you resolve finally to act on something that you've been procrastinating about, simply because you have the energy to do so and feel the day has started so well? Now ask yourself this: is all this worth forgoing the wine for?

Swapping something healthy for sandwiches and drinking less are examples, but the principle is the important point here: thinking about what is to be gained from any change (and the pain that might be avoided) is what provides the necessary motivation to *act*. This approach can be applied to any 'bad' habit you want to be rid of, and any 'good' habit you'd like to embed.

Habit-Forming Tips, Tricks and Tools

Motivation is a major key to sustaining behaviours, but other tricks and tools can help. These include:

1. Get Support

When delivering presentations and seminars, one of the most common comments I hear is: 'I wish my wife/husband/partner could hear this.' For most people, this remark is partly motivated by their sense that their other half may benefit from the information and advice contained in the session. But, also, many realize that enlisting the support and advice of their partner might be critical to how successfully they apply and sustain positive change.

It's often worthwhile someone having a conversation with their significant other regarding the changes they'd like to make to enlist their support. If you decide you want to drink less and go to bed earlier in the week, for instance, then your chances of success are likely to improve if your partner is happy to do the same.

However, a word of warning about sharing what you've learned in this book: I know from experience that it is often the case that partners can give good health advice, which has nonetheless been studiously ignored or resisted for years. It can be highly irritating for your partner if you finally act on their advice and encouragement as a result of

↓

↓

'reading it in a book'. I suggest treading gently where relevant, and giving credit to your partner for the wisdom of their advice.

You may seek support outside the home too, of course. An example might be to ask a colleague or your assistant to alert you to the absence of water on your desk. If you do not manage your own diary, maybe instruct the person who does to block out time each lunchtime so that you can get out of the office and eat something half-decent.

2. Be Realistic

When change is contemplated, it can sometimes help not to set the bar too high. So, for example, if you were planning on adopting a new exercise regime, then setting a goal of going to the gym five times a week may be unrealistic. A better approach might be to commit to the 12-minute resistance regime (described in Chapter 6) five times a week. This is much more 'doable' and less likely to end in 'failure'. Any trips to the gym can then be regarded as a bonus.

3. Avoid Looking Too Long-term to Begin With

Much of this book is about sustaining habits in the long term. However, looking too far into the future can be daunting. It's sometimes better to set yourself a goal of sticking with something for, say, one to two months; this is often long enough for a new habit to bed in or for a bad habit to be broken.

↓

4. Don't Be Hungry

This chapter is mainly about how to adopt healthy habits and scotch bad ones without needing to exert much in the way of willpower. A key, here, is the avoidance of undue hunger. In Chapter 3, we saw how hunger can sap willpower, which makes any positive changes we make harder and less sustainable. See that chapter for more on the importance of keeping appetite under control and how to do this.

5. Put Things You Want to Do in Your Diary

Many people find that habits they would like to persist with are much more likely to happen if they go in the diary (just like work appointments). This could be activity or exercise sessions, or social things such 'date nights', music lessons and trips to the cinema or theatre.

6. Keep an Activity Diary

For some people, there's something nice about being able to look over a diary peppered with entries of past activities, be they trips to the gym or pool, football or tennis matches, or home resistance exercise sessions. Also, the 'pain' at the thought of leaving blank spaces in the diary can help drive people to be consistent in their exercise endeavours.

7. Remind Yourself

From time to time, motivation can wane. It can be useful to remind yourself why you are doing something (or not doing something). Focusing, even for a brief moment, on the pleasure we'll get and the pain we're avoiding from whatever changes we have made can really help to keep us resolved, focused and on-track.

8. Check In With Yourself from Time to Time

An extension of the previous tactic is to keep track of your progress. Before making any changes, you might make a note of the main issues you'd like to manage. As you apply change, you might like to review how you feel you are doing in terms of sustaining these and the positive effect they are having on you. At the outset, you may do this at a set time each week, such as when you're on the way home on a Friday night.

Change of Life

Given all that's gone before in this book, what new habits might you want to develop? Here are some ideas:

- An emphasis on eating a 'primal' diet, based on natural, unprocessed foods

- No or very few bread-based lunches

- A commitment to avoiding getting too hungry

- Having nuts or some other snack food to hand to help keep your appetite in check, particularly between lunch and your evening meal

- Drinking enough water to keep your urine pale yellow throughout the day

- Getting into bed an hour or so earlier when possible

- Avoiding bright light exposure in the evening

- Doing a 'brain dump' and constructing a to-do list for the following day before going to bed

- Seeking natural sunlight each day for at least twenty minutes, particularly in the winter

- Incorporating a brief, brisk walk at the start and end of the day, and possibly at lunchtime too

- Performing a brief home-based resistance exercise session on most days

- Practising slower, diaphragmatic breathing for five minutes, twice a day

- Listening to some uplifting music on the way into work, and those Spanish lessons you've been putting off on the way home

- Spending a couple of minutes, twice a day, practising the attitude of gratitude

- Reflecting at the start and end of each day on what went well

- Executing one random act of kindness, however small, each day

All Together, Now?

I've had the pleasure of speaking to and coaching a large number of very successful and determined individuals. These people did not get that way by not acting. So, if someone sees the sense of the advice I'm giving them, I've learned there's a very good chance they will take immediate steps to improve their condition. For instance, even during that same day they will often ensure they are better hydrated and snack on a few nuts to ensure they do not get too hungry before returning home. Usually, the benefits of moving in a positive direction are felt right away.

Adopting healthy habits and liberating ourselves from unhealthy ones is a bit like juggling: it can help to become proficient with three or four balls before we attempt to master six or eight. I've found that people usually benefit from focusing on one or two key areas to begin with, and once these feel embedded and second nature, to add other strategies over time. While I'm enthusiastic about the idea of you feeling inspired to act on a lot of the advice contained in A Great Day at the Office, it's sometimes best to make changes *gradually*.

Someone might, for example, first focus on sorting out their diet (Chapters 1, 2 and 3), and adding regular walking if they are currently sedentary. Later on, they may add the brief resistance exercise regime presented in Chapter 6, and also wipe out some of the sleep debt they may have accumulated over the years (Chapter 4). Once this is in place, it may feel appropriate to incorporate some breathing exercises (Chapter 8), or employ some simple mental and behavioural

↓

↓

tools to improve 'coherence' (Chapter 9). The timeframe here may be weeks, months or even longer. The important thing is that progress is being made all the while that is not overwhelming but realistic and sustainable.

OK, back to motivation again for a moment. Let's think about some of the benefits of putting the ideas in *A Great Day at the Office* into practice:

- A greater sense of vitality and wellness

- The ability to be more productive and get more done more quickly

- Improved decision-making ability and creativity

- Improved relationships, both in and out of the workplace

- Improved sleep, and a feeling of being better rested in the morning

- Weight loss, but without hunger, calorie-counting or extensive exercise

- Increased sustainability

- Reduced risk of chronic disease including heart disease and type 2 diabetes

- Improved fitness and strength

- Elevated mood and outlook on life

- Improved image in the eyes of colleagues and clients

- Speedier career progression

This is just a partial list, but these are the common experiences people have from making relatively minor changes to their lifestyle and thinking in some key areas. Even if you did a fraction of these things, you stand to have a richer and more rewarding life as a result.

Who Benefits?

Now, it's obvious that *you* are going to reap significant dividends from the sort of benefits listed above. But think for a moment *who else* might benefit.

I often ask this question at the end of a presentation, workshop or seminar, and the most frequent immediate response I get is: 'The people at home.' Most people have a partner or spouse, and maybe kids too. As I mentioned in the Introduction to this book, none of the people close to you is likely to grumble when you transform yourself into a generally happier and more energized version of the person you currently are.

The benefits on offer here are also likely to benefit your colleagues, staff or team, as you inspire them through being a better role model and leader. The simple fact is that whatever organizations invest in their people to help them optimise their energy and effectiveness returns many, many times over in terms of enhanced productivity, improved business performance and a healthier bottom line. The only people to lose out when you and your colleagues take steps to revitalise yourselves are your *competitors*.

The chances are you work in a demanding and competitive environment. Optimizing your physiological and psychological functioning in a way that makes a tangible and lasting difference to your performance can only add to your competitive edge and boost your chances of success. This is particularly true where effective strategies are adopted by members of a team or more widely disseminated throughout an organization.

Scientific References

Chapter 1

1. Mente A, et al. A systematic review of the evidence supporting a causal link between dietary factors and coronary heart disease. *Archives of Internal Medicine* 2009;169(7):659–669.

2. Brand-Miller J, et al. The glycemic index and cardiovascular disease risk. *Current Atherosclerosis Reports* 2007;9:479–85.

3. Vignini A, et al. Alzheimer's disease and diabetes: new insights and unifying therapies. *Current Diabetes Reviews* 2013;9(3):218–27.

4. Foster-Powell K, et al. International table of glycemic index and glycemic load values: *American Journal of Clinical Nutrition* 2002;76(1):5–56.

5. Harper AE. Defining the essentiality of nutrients. In: Shils MD, Olson JA, Shihe M, Ross AC, eds. *Modern nutrition in health and disease.* 9th ed. Boston: William and Wilkins 1999:3–10.

6. Drewnowski A. Concept of a nutritious food: toward a nutrient density score. *American Journal of Clinical Nutrition* 2005;82:721–32.

7. Ho KS, et al. Stopping or reducing dietary fiber intake reduces constipation and its associated symptoms. *World Journal of Gastroenterology* 2012;18(33):4593–4596.

8. Heizer WD, et al. The role of diet in symptoms of irritable bowel syndrome in adults: a narrative review. *Journal of the American Dietetic Association* 2009;109(7):1204–14.

9. Power AM, et al. Association between constipation and colorectal cancer: systematic review and meta-analysis of observational studies. *American Journal of Gastroenterology* 2013;108(6):894–903.

10. Jacobs ET, et al. Intake of supplemental and total fiber and risk of colorectal adenoma recurrence in the wheat bran fiber trial. *Cancer Epidemiology, Biomarkers and Prevention* 2002;11(9):906–14.

11. Alberts DS, et al. Lack of effect of a high-fiber cereal supplement on the recurrence of colorectal adenomas. *New England Journal of Medicine* 2000;342(16):1156–62.

12. Tan KY, et al. Fiber and colorectal diseases: separating fact from fiction. *World Journal of Gastroenterology* 2007;13(31):4161–7.

13. Biesiekierski JR, et al. Gluten causes gastrointestinal symptoms in subjects without celiac disease: a double-blind randomized placebo-controlled trial. *American Journal of Gastroenterology* 2011;106(3):508–14.

14. Carroccio A, et al Non-celiac wheat sensitivity diagnosed by double-blind placebo-controlled challenge: exploring a new clinical entity. *American Journal of Gastroenterology* 2012;107(12):1898–906.

15. Lajolo FM, et al. Nutritional significance of lectins and enzyme inhibitors from legumes. *Journal of Agricultural and Food Chemistry* 2002;50(22):6592–8.

16. Walker A, Shipman, P. *The Wisdom of the Bones: In Search of Human Origins.* Alfred A Knopf, New York, 1996.

17. Burenhult G. Towards homo sapiens: habilines, erectines, and neanderthals. In: Burenhult, Goran (ed.), *The First Humans: Human Origins and History to 10,000 B.C.* HarperCollins, New York, 1993.

18. Molleson TI, et al. Dietary changes and the effects of food preparation on microwear patterns in the Late Neolithic of Abu Hureyra, northern Syria. *Journal of Human Evolution* 1993;24:455–68.

19. Angel LJ. Health as a crucial factor in the changes from hunting to developed farming in the eastern Mediterranean. In: Cohen MN and Armelagos GJ (eds), *Paleopathology at the Origins of Agriculture.* Academic Press, Orlando, 1984.

20. Cordain L, et al. Plant-animal subsistence ratios and macronutrient energy estimations in worldwide hunter-gatherer diets. *American Journal of Clinical Nutrition* 2000;71(3):682–92.

21. Willett WC, et al. Dietary fat is not a major determinant of body fat. *American Journal of Medicine* 2002;113(9B):47S-59S.

22. Pirozzo S, et al. Advice on low-fat diets for obesity. *Cochrane Database of Systematic Reviews* 2002;(2):CD003640.

23. Halton TL, et al. The effects of high protein diets on thermogenesis, satiety and weight loss: a critical review. *Journal of the American College of Nutrition* 2004;23(5):373–385.

24. Foster-Schubert KE, et al. Acyl and total ghrelin are suppressed strongly by ingested proteins, weakly by lipids, and biphasically by carbohydrates. *Journal of Clinical Endocrinology and Metabolism* 2008;93(5):1971–9.

25. Weigle DS, et al. A high-protein diet induces sustained reductions in appetite, ad libitum caloric intake, and body weight despite compensatory changes in diurnal plasma leptin and ghrelin concentrations. *American Journal of Clinical Nutrition* 2005;82(1):41–8.

26. Johnstone AM, et al. Effects of a high-protein ketogenic diet on hunger, appetite, and weight loss in obese men feeding ad libitum. *American Journal of Clinical Nutrition* 2008;87:44–55.

27. Jonsson T, et al. A Paleolithic diet is more satiating per calorie than a Mediterranean-like diet in individuals with ischemic heart disease. *Nutrition and Metabolism (London)* 2010;30(7):85.

28. Keys A. Coronary heart disease in seven countries. *Circulation* 1970;41(supplement 1):1–211.

29. British Heart Foundation Health Promotion Research Group, Department of Public Health, University of Oxford and Health Economics Research Centre, Department of Public Health, University of Oxford, *European cardiovascular disease statistics* (2008 edn).

30. Siri-Tarino PW, et al. Meta-analysis of prospective cohort studies evaluating the association of saturated fat with cardiovascular disease. *American Journal of Clinical Nutrition* 2010;91(3):535–46.

31. Skeaff CM, et al. Dietary fat and coronary heart disease: summary of evidence from prospective and randomised controlled trials. *Annals of Nutrition and Metabolism* 2009;55:173–201.

32. Hooper L, et al. Reduced or modified dietary fat for preventing cardiovascular disease. *Cochrane Database of Systematic Reviews* 2012.

33. Lawrence GD. Dietary fats and health: dietary recommendations in the context of scientific evidence. *Advances in Nutrition* 2013;4(3):294–302.

34. Ray KK, et al. Statins and all-cause mortality in high-risk primary prevention: a meta-analysis of 11 randomized controlled trials involving 65 229 participants. *Archives of Internal Medicine* 2010;170(12):1024–1031.

35. Studer M, et al. Effect of different antilipidemic agents and diets on mortality: a systematic review. *Archives of Internal Medicine* 2005;165(7):725–30.

36. http://www.thennt.com/nnt/ statins-for-heart-disease-prevention-without-prior-heart-disease

37. Redberg R, et al. Diagnostic tests: another frontier for less is more or why talking to your patient is a safe and effective method of reassurance. *Archives of Internal Medicine* 2011;171(7):619.

38. Redberg R, et al. Editor's Note – To make the case – Evidence is required. *Archives of Internal Medicine* 2011;171(17):1594.

39. Weingartner O, et al. Controversial role of plant sterol esters in the management of hypercholesterolaemia. *European Heart Journal* 2009;30:404–409.

40. Danesi F, et al. Phytosterol supplementation reduces metabolic activity and slows cell growth in cultured rat cardiomyocytes. *British Journal of Nutrition* 2011;106(4):540–8.

41. Rubis B, et al. Beneficial or harmful influence of phytosterols on human cells? *British Journal of Nutrition* 2008;100:1183–1191.

42. Ratnayake WM, et al. Vegetable oils high in phytosterols make erythrocytes less deformable and shorten the life span of stroke-prone spontaneously hypertensive rats. *Journal of Nutrition* 2000;130:1166–1178.

43. Jakobsen MU, et al. Intake of carbohydrates compared with intake

of saturated fatty acids and risk of myocardial infarction: importance of the glycemic index. *American Journal of Clinical Nutrition* 2010;91(6):1764–8.

44. Jakobsen MU, et al. Major types of dietary fat and risk of coronary heart disease: a pooled analysis of 11 cohort studies. *American Journal of Clinical Nutrition* 2009;89(5):1425–32.

45. Weber PC. Are we what we eat? Fatty acids in nutrition and in cell membranes: cell functions and disorders induced by dietary conditions. In: *Fish fats and your health*. Svanoy Foundation, Norway, 1989:9–18.

46. Raheja BS, et al. Significance of the n-6/n-3 ratio for insulin action in diabetes. *Annals of the New York Academy of Sciences* 1993;683:258–71.

47. Simopoulos AP. The importance of the ratio of omega-6/omega-3 essential fatty acids. *Biomedicine and Pharmacotherapy* 2002 56(8):365–79.

48. The IBD in EPIC Study Investigators. Linoleic acid, a dietary n-6 polyunsaturated fatty acid, and the aetiology of ulcerative colitis: a nested case-control study within a European prospective cohort study. *Gut* 2009;58:1606–11.

49. Simonopoulos, AP and Cleland LG (eds.) *Omega-6/Omega-3 Essential Fatty Acid Ratio: The Scientific Evidence*, World Review of Nutrition and Dietetics, Karger, Basel, 2003 (92).

50. Pedersen JI, et al. Adipose tissue fatty acids and risk of myocardial infarction – A case-control study. *European Journal of Clinical Nutrition* 2000:54:618–25.

51. Ascherio A, et al. Dietary fat and risk of coronary heart disease in men: Cohort follow up study in the United States. *British Medical Journal* 1996:313:84–90.

52. Hu FB, et al. Dietary fat intake and the risk of coronary heart disease in women. *New England Journal of Medicine* 1997:337:1491–9.

53. Oomen CM, et al. Association between trans fatty acid intake and 10-year risk of coronary heart disease in the Zutphen Elderly Study: A prospective population-based study. *Lancet* 2001;357:746–51.

54. Bakker N, et al. The Euramic Study Group: Adipose fatty acids and cancers of the breast, prostate and colon: An ecological study. *Cancer* 1997;72:587–97.

55. Christiansen E, et al. Intake of a diet high in trans monounsaturated fatty acids or saturated fatty acids. Effects on postprandial insulinemia and glycemia in obese patients with NIDDM. *Diabetes Care* 1997;20:881–7.

56. Alstrup KK, et al. Differential effects of cis and trans fatty acids on insulin release from isolated mouse islets. *Metabolism* 1999;48:22–9.

57. Salméron J, et al. Dietary fat intake and risk of type 2 diabetes in women. *American Journal of Clinical Nutrition* 2001;73:1019–26.

58. Jakobsen MU, et al. Intake of ruminant trans fatty acids and risk of coronary heart disease. *International Journal of Epidemiology* 2008;37(1):173–82.

59. Bendsen NT, et al. Consumption of industrial and ruminant trans fatty acids and risk of coronary heart disease: a systematic review and meta-analysis of cohort studies. *European Journal of Clinical Nutrition* 2011;65(7):773–8.

60. Gillman MW, et al. Margarine intake and subsequent coronary heart disease in men. *Epidemiology* 1997;8(2):144–9.

61. Willett WC, et al. Intake of trans fatty acids and risk of coronary heart disease among women. *Lancet* 1993;341(8845):581–5.

62. Ramsden CE, et al. Use of dietary linoleic acid for secondary prevention of coronary heart disease and death: evaluation of recovered data from the Sydney Diet Heart Study and updated meta-analysis. *British Medical Journal* 2013;346:e8707.

63. Rohrmann S, et al. Meat consumption and mortality – results from the European Prospective Investigation into Cancer and Nutrition *BMC Medicine* 2013;7(11):63.

64. Samaha FF, et al. Low-carbohydrate diets, obesity, and metabolic risk factors for cardiovascular disease. *Current Atherosclerosis Reports* 2007;9(6):441–7.

65. Austin MA, Low-density lipoprotein subclass patterns and risk of myocardial infarction. *Journal of the American Medical Association* 1988;260(13):1917–21.

66. Faghihnia N, et al. Changes in lipoprotein(a), oxidized phospholipids, and LDL subclasses with a low-fat high-carbohydrate diet. *Journal of Lipid Research* 2010;51(11):3324–30.

67. Volek JS, et al. Modification of lipoproteins by very low-carbohydrate diets. *Journal of Nutrition* 2005;135(6):1339–42.

68. Bischoff-Ferrari HA, et al. Milk intake and risk of hip fracture in men and women: A meta-analysis of prospective cohort studies. *Journal of Bone and Mineral Research* 2011;26(4):833–9.

69. Bischoff-Ferrari HA, et al. Calcium intake and hip fracture risk in men and women: a meta-analysis of prospective cohort studies and randomized controlled trials. *American Journal of Clinical Nutrition* 2007;86(6):1780–90.

70. Winzenberg T, et al. Effects of calcium supplementation on bone density in healthy children: meta-analysis of randomised controlled trials. *British Medical Journal* 2006;333:775–8.

71. Lanou AJ. Bone health in children. *British Medical Journal* 2006;333:763–4.

72. Loones A. Transformation of milk components during yogurt fermentation. In: Chandan RC (ed). *Yoghurt: nutritional and health properties.* National Yoghurt Association, McClean, Virginia, 1989:95–114.

73. Beshkova DM, et al. Production of amino acids by yoghurt bacteria. *Biotechnology Progress* 1998;14:963–5.

74. Östman EM, et al. Inconsistency between glycemic and insulinemic responses to regular and fermented milk products. *American Journal of Clinical Nutrition* 2001;74(1):96–100.

75. Zemel MB, et al. Regulation of adiposity by dietary calcium. *FASEB Journal* 2000;14:1132–8.

76. Teegarden D. Calcium intake and reduction of fat mass. *Journal of Nutrition* 2003;133:249S–51S.

77. Zemel MB, et al. Dairy augmentation of total and central fat loss in obese subjects. *International Journal of Obesity* (London) 2005;29(4):391–7.

78. Zemel MB, et al. Effects of calcium and dairy on body composition and weight loss in African-American adults. *Obesity Research* 2005;13(7):1218–25.

79. Bryan NS, et al. Ingested nitrate and nitrite and stomach cancer risk: an updated review. *Food and Chemical Toxicology* 2012;50(10):3646–65.

80. Archer DL. Evidence that ingested nitrate and nitrite are beneficial to health. *Journal of Food Protection* 2002;65(5):872–5.

81. Andújar I, et al. Cocoa polyphenols and their potential benefits for human health. *Oxidative Medicine and Cell Longevity* 2012;2012:906252.

Chapter 2

1. Jequier E, et al. Water as an essential nutrient: the physiological basis of hydration. *European Journal of Clinical Nutrition* 2010;64:115–23.

2. Kraft JA, et al. The influence of hydration on anaerobic performance: a review. *Research Quarterly for Exercise and Sport* 2012;83(2):282–92.

3. Barr SI. Effects of dehydration on exercise performance. *Canadian Journal of Applied Physiology* 1999;24(2):164–72.

4. Schliess F, et al. Cell hydration and mTOR-dependent signalling. *Acta Physiologica (Oxford)* 2006;187: 223–9.

5. Ganio MS, et al. Mild dehydration impairs cognitive performance and mood of men. *British Journal of Nutrition* 2011;106(10):1535–43.

6. Armstrong LE, et al. Mild dehydration affects mood in healthy young women. *Journal of Nutrition* 2012;142(2):382–8.

7. Sansevero AC. Dehydration in the elderly: strategies for prevention and management. *Nurse Practitioner* 1997;22:41–42,51–57,63–72.

8. Sagawa S, et al. Effect of dehydration on thirst and drinking during immersion in men. *Journal of Applied Physiology* 1992;72:128–34.

9. Armstrong LE, et al. Urinary indices of hydration status. *International Journal of Sport Nutrition* 1994;4:265–79.

10. Lim JS, et al. The role of fructose in the pathogenesis of NAFLD and the metabolic syndrome. *Nature Reviews Gastroenterology and Hepatology* 2010;7(5):251–64.

11. Johnson RK, et al. Dietary sugars intake and cardiovascular health. A scientific statement from the American Heart Association. *Circulation* 2009;120(11):1011–20.

12. Vartanian L R, et al. Effects of soft drink consumption on nutrition and health: a systematic review and meta-analysis. *American Journal of Public Health* 2007;97:667–75.

13. Sánchez-Lozada LG, et al. How safe is fructose for persons with or without diabetes? *American Journal of Clinical Nutrition* 2008;88(5):189–90.

14. Livesey G, et al. Fructose consumption and consequences for glycation, plasmid triacylglycerol, and body weight: meta-analyses and meta-regression models of intervention studies. *American Journal of Clinical Nutrition* 2008;88:1419–37.

15. Aeberli I, et al. Low to moderate sugar-sweetened beverage consumption impairs glucose and lipid metabolism and promotes inflammation in healthy young men: a randomized controlled trial. *American Journal of Clinical Nutrition* 2011;94(2):479–85.

16. de la Peña C. Artificial sweetener as a historical window to culturally situated health. *Annals of the New York Academy of Sciences* 2010;1190:159–65.

17. Swithers SE. Artificial sweeteners produce the counterintuitive effect of inducing metabolic derangements. *Trends in Endocrinology and Metabolism* 2013;24(9):431–41.

18. Swithers SE, et al. A role for sweet taste: calorie predictive relations in energy regulation by rats. *Behavioral Neuroscience* 2008;122(1):161–73.

19. Feijó Fde M, et al. Saccharin and aspartame, compared with sucrose, induce greater weight gain in adult Wistar rats, at similar total caloric intake levels. *Appetite* 2013;60(1): 203–7.

20. Swithers SE. Artificial sweeteners produce the counterintuitive effect of inducing metabolic derangements. *Trends in Endocrinology and Metabolism* 2013;24(9):431–41.

21. Humphries P, et al. Direct and indirect cellular effects of aspartame on the brain. *European Journal of Clinical Nutrition* 2008;62:451–62.

22. Van Den Eeden SK, et al. Aspartame ingestion and headaches: a randomized, crossover trial. *Neurology* 1994;44:1787–93.

23. Lipton RB, et al. Aspartame as a dietary trigger of headache. *Headache* 1989;29(2):90–2.

24. Walton RG, et al. Adverse reactions to aspartame: double-blind challenge in patients from a vulnerable population. *Biological Psychiatry* 1993;34(1–2):13–7.

25. Schernhammer ES, et al. Consumption of artificial sweetener – and sugar-containing soda and risk of lymphoma and leukemia in men and women. *American Journal of Clinical Nutrition* 2012;96:1419–28.

26. Soffritti M, et al. First experimental demonstration of the multipotential carcinogenic effects of aspartame administered in the feed to Sprague-Dawley rats. *Environmental Health Perspectives* 2006;114:379–85.

27. Lemus-Mondaca R, et al. *Stevia rebaudiana Bertoni*, source of a high-potency natural sweetener: A comprehensive review on the biochemical, nutritional and functional aspects. *Food Chemistry* 2012;132(30):1121–32.

28. Gardner EJ, et al. Black tea – helpful or harmful? A review of the evidence. *European Journal of Clinical Nutrition* 2006;61:3–18.

29. Larsson SC, et al. Coffee and tea consumption and risk of stroke subtypes in male smokers. *Stroke* 2008;39:1681–7.

30. Cabrera C, et al. Beneficial effects of green tea – a review. *Journal of the American College of Nutrition* 2006;25(2):79–99.

31. Greenberg JA, et al. Coffee, diabetes and weight control. *American Journal of Clinical Nutrition* 2006;84:682–93.

32. Odegaard AO, et al. Coffee, tea, and incident type 2 diabetes: the Singapore Chinese Health Study. *American Journal of Clinical Nutrition* 2008;88(4):979–85.

33. van Dam RM, et al. Coffee consumption and risk of type 2 diabetes: a systematic review. *Journal of the American Medical Association* 2005;294(1):97–104.

34. White IR, et al. Alcohol consumption and mortality: modelling risks for men and women at different ages. *British Medical Association* 2002;325:191.

35. Lukasiewicz E, et al. Alcohol intake in relation to body mass index and waist-to-hip ratio: the importance of type of alcoholic beverage. *Public Health Nutrition* 2005;8(3):315–20.

36. Dallongeville J, et al. Influence of alcohol consumption and various beverages on waist girth and waist-to-hip ratio in a sample of French men and women. International Journal of Obesity and Related Metabolic Disorders 1998;22(12):1178–83.

37. Wannamethee SG, et al. Alcohol and adiposity: effects of quantity and type of drink and time relation with meals. International Journal of Obesity (London) 2005;29(12):1436–44.

38. McCann SE, et al. Alcoholic beverage preference and characteristics of drinkers and nondrinkers in western New York (United States). Nutrition, Metabolism and Cardiovascular Diseases 2003;13(1):2–11.

39. Tjonneland AM, et al. The connection between food and alcohol intake habits among 48,763 Danish men and women. A cross-sectional study in the project 'Food, cancer and health'. Ugeskr Laeger 1999;161(50):6923–7.

40. Barefoot JC, et al. Alcohol beverage preference, diet and health habits in the UNC Alumni Heart Study. American Journal of Clinical Nutrition 2002;76(2):466–72.

Chapter 3

1. Gailliot MT, et al. The physiology of willpower: linking blood glucose to self-control. Personality and Social Psychology Review 2007;11(4):303–27.

2. Gailliot MT, et al. Self-control relies on glucose as a limited energy source: willpower is more than a metaphor. Personality and Social Psychology Review 2007;92(2):325–36.

3. Sabaté J. Nut consumption and body weight. American Journal of Clinical Nutrition 2003;78(3 Suppl):647S-50S.

4. Mattes RD, et al. Nuts and healthy body weight maintenance mechanisms. Pacific Journal of Clinical Nutrition 2010;19(1):137–41.

5. Harvie MN, et al. The effects of intermittent or continuous energy restriction on weight loss and metabolic disease risk markers: a randomized trial in young overweight women. International Journal of Obesity (London) 2011;35(5):714–27.

6. Varady KA. Intermittent versus daily calorie restriction: which diet regimen is more effective for weight loss? *Obesity Reviews* 2011;12(7):e593–60.

Chapter 4

1. Takahashi Y, et al. Growth hormone secretion during sleep. *Journal of Clinical Investigation* 1968;47(9):2079–90.

2. Goel N, et al. Neurocognitive consequences of sleep deprivation. *Seminars in Neurology* 2009;29(4):320–39.

3. Meerlo P, et al. Restricted and disrupted sleep: effects on autonomic function, neuroendocrine stress systems and stress responsivity. *Sleep Medicine Reviews* 2008;12(3):197–210.

4. Axelsson J, et al. Beauty sleep: experimental study on the perceived health and attractiveness of sleep-deprived people. *British Medical Journal* 2010;341:c6614.

5. Sundelin T, et al. Cues of fatigue: Effects of sleep deprivation on facial appearance. *Sleep* 2013;36(9):1355–60).

6. Meier-Ewert HK, et al. Effect of sleep loss on C-reactive protein, an inflammatory marker of cardiovascular risk. *Journal of the American College of Cardiology* 2004;43(4):678–83.

7. Donga E, et al. A single night of partial sleep deprivation induces insulin resistance in multiple metabolic pathways in healthy subjects. *Journal of Clinical Endocrinology and Metabolism* 2010;95(6):2963–8.

8. Schmid SM, A single night of sleep deprivation increases ghrelin levels and feelings of hunger in normal-weight healthy men. *Journal of Sleep Research* 2008;17(3):331–4.

9. Spiegel K, et al. Impact of sleep debt on physiological rhythms. *Revue Neurologique (Paris)* 2003;159(11 Suppl):6S11–20.

10. Hogenkamp PS, et al. Acute sleep deprivation increases portion size and affects food choice in young men. *Psychoneuroendocrinology* 2013;38(9):1668–74.

11. Reynolds AC, et al. Impact of five nights of sleep restriction on

glucose metabolism, leptin and testosterone in young adult men. *PLoS One* 2012;7(7):e41218.

12. Hursel R, et al. Effects of sleep fragmentation in healthy men on energy expenditure, substrate oxidation, physical activity, and exhaustion measured over 48 h in a respiratory chamber. *American Journal of Clinical Nutrition* 2011;94(3):804–8.

13. Nedeltcheva AV, et al. Insufficient Sleep Undermines Dietary Efforts to Reduce Adiposity. *Annals of Internal Medicine* 2010;153(7):435–41.

14. Van Cauter E, et al. Metabolic consequences of sleep and sleep loss. *Sleep Medicine* 2008;9 Suppl 1:S23–8.

15. Cappuccio FP, et al. Sleep duration and all-cause mortality: a systematic review and meta-analysis of prospective studies. *Sleep* 2010;33(5):585–92.

16. Ebrahim IO, et al. Alcohol and sleep I: effects on normal sleep. *Alcoholism: Clinical and Experimental Research* 2013;37(4):539–49.

17. Sagawa Y, et al. Alcohol Has a Dose-Related Effect on Parasympathetic Nerve Activity During Sleep. *Alcoholism: Clinical and Experimental Research* 2011;35(11):2093–100.

18. Lamber GW, et al. Effect of sunlight and season on serotonin turnover in the brain. *Lancet* 2002;360(9348):1840–42.

19. Gooley JJ, et al. Exposure to room light prior to bedtime suppresses melatonin onset and shortens melatonin duration in humans. *Journal of Clinical Endocrinology and Metabolism* 2011;96(3):E463–72.

20. Wood B, et al. Light levels and duration determines the impact of self-luminous tablets on melatonin suppression. *Applied Ergonomics* 2013;44(2):237–40.

21. Burkhart K, et al. Amber lenses to block blue light and improve sleep: a randomized trial. *Chronobiology International* 2009;26(8):1602–12.

22. Amin MM, et al. The effects of a mid-day nap on the neurocognitive performance of first-year medical residents: a controlled interventional pilot study. *Academic Medicine* 2012;87(10):1428–33.

23. Milner CE, et al. Benefits of napping in healthy adults: impact of nap length, time of day, age, and experience with napping. *Journal of Sleep Research* 2009;18(2):272–81.

24. Samel A, et al. Bright light: A countermeasure for jet lag? *Chronobiology International* 1997;14:173–83.

25. Herxheimer A, et al. Melatonin for the prevention and treatment of jet lag. *Cochrane Database of Systematic Reviews* 2002.

Chapter 5

1. Miller AL. Epidemiology, etiology, and natural treatment of seasonal affective disorder. *Alternative Medicine Review* 2005;10(1):5–13.

2. Lamber GW, et al. Effect of sunlight and season on serotonin turnover in the brain. *Lancet* 2002;360(9348):1840–2.

3. Strong RE, et al. Narrow-band blue-light treatment of seasonal affective disorder in adults and the influence of additional non-seasonal symptoms. *Depression and Anxiety* 2009;26(3):273–8.

4. Glickman G, et al. Light therapy for seasonal affective disorder with blue narrow-band light-emitting diodes (LEDs). *Biological Psychiatry* 2006;59(6):502–7.

5. Rastad C, et al. Improvement in fatigue, sleepiness, and health-related quality of life with bright light treatment in persons with seasonal affective disorder and subsyndromal SAD. *Depression Research and Treatment* 2011:543906.

6. Partonen T, et al. Bright light improves vitality and alleviates distress in healthy people. *Journal of Affective Disorders* 2000;57:55–61.

7. Mills PR, et al. The effect of high correlated colour temperature office lighting on employee wellbeing and work performance. *Journal of Circadian Rhythms* 2007;5:2.

8. Viola AU, et al. Blue-enriched white light in the workplace improves self-reported alertness, performance and sleep quality. *Scandinavian Journal of Work, Environment and Health* 2008;34(4):297–306.

9. Lee TM, et al. Pathophysiological mechanism of seasonal affective disorder. Journal of Affective Disorders 1997;46:25–38.

10. Avery DH, et al. Dawn simulation and bright light in the treatment of SAD: a controlled study. Biological Psychiatry 2001;50:205–16.

11. Avery DH, et al. Dawn simulation treatment of winter depression: a controlled study. American Journal of Psychiatry 1993;150(1):113–7.

12. Avery DH, Dawn simulation compared with a dim red signal in the treatment of winter depression. Biological Psychiatry 1994;36(3):180–8.

13. Avery DH, et al. Is dawn simulation effective in ameliorating the difficulty awakening in seasonal affective disorder associated with hypersomnia? Journal of Affective Disorders 2002;69:231–6.

14. Norden MJ, et al. A controlled study of dawn simulation in subsyndromal winter depression. Acta Psychiatrica Scandinavica 1993;88(1):67–71.

15. Urbach F. Incidence of nonmelanoma skin cancer. Dermatologic Clinics 1991;9(4):751–5.

16. Crombie IK. Distribution of malignant melanoma on the body surface. British Journal of Cancer 1981;43:842–9.

17. Garsaud P, et al. Epidemiology of cutaneous melanoma in the French West Indies (Martinique). American Journal of Epidemiology 1998;147:66–8.

18. Le Marchand I, et al. Sun exposure, diet and melanoma in Hawaii caucasians. American Journal of Epidemiology 2006;164:232–45.

19. Armstong K, et al. The epidemiology of UV induced skin cancer. Journal of Photochemistry and Photobiology 2001;63:8–18.

20. Crombie IK. Variation of melanoma incidence with latitude in North America and Europe. British Journal of Cancer 1979;40:774–81.

21. Weinstock MA, et al. Nonfamilial cutaneous melanoma incidence in women associated with sun exposure before 20 years of age. Pediatrics 1989;84:199–204.

22. Tucker MA, et al. Melanoma etiology: where are we? Oncogene 2003;22:3042–52.

23. Berwick M, et al. Sun exposure and mortality from melanoma. Journal of the National Cancer Institute 2005;97:195–9.

24. Veierød MB, et al. A prospective study of pigmentation, sun exposure, and risk of cutaneous malignant melanoma in women. *Journal of the National Cancer Institute* 2003;95:1530–8.

25. Oliveria SA, et al. Sun exposure and risk of melanoma. *Archives of Disease in Childhood* 2006;91:131–8.

26. Elwood JM, et al. Cutaneous melanoma in relation to intermittent and constant sun exposure – the western Canada melanoma study. *International Journal of Cancer* 2006;35:427–33.

27. Grant WB. Ecological studies of the UVB-vitamin D-cancer hypothesis. *Anticancer Research* 2012;32(1):223–36.

28. Giovannucci E, et al. 25-hydroxyvitamin D and risk of myocardial infarction in men: a prospective study. *Archives of Internal Medicine* 2008;168(11):1174–80.

29. Liu PT, et al. Toll-like receptor triggering of a vitamin D-mediated human antimicrobial response. *Science* 2006;311:1770–3.

30. Wang TT, et al. Cutting edge: 1,25-dihydroxyvitamin D3 is a direct inducer of antimicrobial peptide gene expression. *Journal of Immunology* 2004;173:2909–12.

31. Sabetta JR, et al. Serum 25-hydroxyvitamin D and the incidence of acute viral respiratory tract infections in healthy adults. *PLoS One* 2010;14;5(6):e11088.

32. Salehpour A, et al. A 12-week double-blind randomized clinical trial of vitamin D3 supplementation on body fat mass in healthy overweight and obese women. *Nutrition Journal* 2012;11:78.

33. Hyppönen E, et al. Hypovitaminosis D in British adults at age 45 y: nationwide cohort study of dietary and lifestyle predictors. *American Journal of Clinical Nutrition* 2007;85(3):860–8.

34. Vieth R, et al. Randomized comparison of the effects of the vitamin D3 adequate intake versus 100 mcg (4000 IU) per day on biochemical responses and the wellbeing of patients. *Nutrition Journal* 2004;19;3:8.

35. Vieth R, et al. Efficacy and safety of vitamin D3 intake exceeding the lowest observed adverse effect level. *American Journal of Clinical Nutrition* 2001;73(2):288–94.

36. Mocanu V, et al. Long-term effects of giving nursing home

residents bread fortified with 125 microg (5000 IU) vitamin D(3) per daily serving. *American Journal of Clinical Nutrition* 2009;89(4):1132–7.

37. Vainio H, et al. Cancer-preventive effects of sunscreens are uncertain. *Scandinavian Journal of Work and Environmental Health* 2000;26(6):529–31.

38. Berwick M. The good, the bad and the ugly of sunscreens. *Clinical Pharmacology and Therapeutics* 2011;89(1):31–3.

39. Autier P. Sunscreen abuse for intentional sun exposure. *British Journal of Dermatology* 2009;161 Suppl 3:40–5.

Chapter 6

1. Morton R, et al. Heart rate prescribed walking training improves cardiorespiratory fitness but not glycaemic control in people with type 2 diabetes. *Journal of Sports Sciences* 2010;28:93–9.

2. van Uffelen J, et al. Feasibility and effectiveness of a walking program for community-dwelling older adults with mild cognitive impairment. *Journal of Aging and Physical Activity* 2009;17:398.

3. Roussel M, et al. Influence of a walking program on the metabolic risk profile of obese postmenopausal women. *Menopause* 2009;16:566.

4. Nicklas B, et al. Effect of exercise intensity on abdominal fat loss during calorie restriction in overweight and obese postmenopausal women: a randomized, controlled trial. *American Journal of Clinical Nutrition* 2009;89:1043.

5. Williams PT, et al. Walking versus running for hypertension, cholesterol, and diabetes mellitus risk reduction. *Arteriosclerosis, Thrombosis and Vascular Biology* 2013;33(5):1085–91

6. Voss MW, et al. Plasticity of brain networks in a randomized intervention trial of exercise training in older adults. *Frontiers in Aging Neuroscience* 2010;26:2

7. Shnayderman I, et al. An aerobic walking programme versus muscle strengthening programme for chronic low back pain: a randomized controlled trial. *Clinical Rehabilitation* 2012;27(3):207.

8. Miyashita M, et al. Accumulating short bouts of brisk walking reduces postprandial plasma triacylglycerol concentrations and resting blood pressure in healthy young men. *American Journal of Clinical Nutrition* 2008;88(5):1225–31.

9. Schmidt WD, et al. Effects of long versus short bout exercise on fitness and weight loss in overweight females. *Journal of the American College of Nutrition* 2001:20(5):494–501.

10. Bravata DM, et al. Using pedometers to increase physical activity and improve health: a systematic review. *Journal of the American Medical Association* 2007;298(19):2296–304.

11. Shaw K, et al. Exercise for overweight or obesity. *Cochrane Database of Systematic Reviews* 2006, Issue 4. Art. No: CD003817.

12. Finlayson, G, et al. Acute compensatory eating following exercise is associated with implicit hedonic wanting for food. *Physiology & Behavior* 2009;97(1):62–7.

13. Goran MI, et al. Endurance training does not enhance total energy expenditure in healthy elderly persons. *American Journal of Physiology* 1992;263:950–7.

14. Meijer EP, et al. Effect of exercise training on total daily physical activity in elderly humans. *European Journal of Applied Physiology and Occupational Physiology* 1999;80:16–21.

15. Morio B, et al. Effects of 14 weeks of progressive endurance training on energy expenditure in elderly people. *British Journal of Nutrition* 1998;80:511–9.

16. Manthou E, et al. Behavioral compensatory adjustments to exercise training in overweight women. *Medicine and Science in Sports and Exercise* 2010;42(6):1121–8.

17. Melanson EL, et al. Exercise improves fat metabolism in muscle but does not increase 24-h fat oxidation. *Exercise and Sport Sciences Reviews* 2009;37(2):93–101.

18. Bouchard C, et al. The response to exercise with constant energy intake in identical twins. *Obesity Research* 1994;2(5):400–10.

19. Heymsfield SB, et al. Rate of weight loss during underfeeding: relation to level of physical activity. *Metabolism* 1989;38(3):215–23.

20. Phinney SD, et al. Effects of aerobic exercise on energy expenditure

and nitrogen balance during very low calorie dieting. *Metabolism* 1988;37(8):758–65.

21. Woo R, et al. Voluntary food intake during prolonged exercise in obese women. *American Journal of Clinical Nutrition* 1982;36(3):478–84.

22. Rönn T, et al. A six months' exercise intervention influences the genome-wide DNA methylation pattern in human adipose tissue. *PLoS Genetics* 2013;9(6):e1003572.

23. Boutcher SH, et al. High-intensity intermittent exercise and fat loss. *Journal of Obesity* 2011;12(7):e593–601.

24. Trapp EG, et al. The effects of high-intensity intermittent exercise training on fat loss and fasting insulin levels of young women. *International Journal of Obesity (London)* 2008;32(4):684–91.

25. Heydari M, et al. The effect of high-intensity intermittent exercise on body composition of overweight young males. *Journal of Obesity* 2012;2012:480467.

Chapter 7

1. McCraty R, et al. The effects of different types of music on mood, tension, and mental clarity. *Alternative Therapies in Health and Medicine* 1998;4(1):75–84.

2. Pelletier CL. The effect of music on decreasing arousal due to stress: a meta-analysis. *Journal of Music Therapy* 2004;41(3):192–214.

3. Rickard NS, et al. The effect of music on cognitive performance: insight from neurobiological and animal studies. *Behavioural and Cognitive Neuroscience Reviews* 2005;4(4):235–61.

4. Mammarella N, et al. Does music enhance cognitive performance in healthy older adults? The Vivaldi effect. *Aging Clinical and Experimental Research* 2007;19(5):394–9.

5. Allen K, et al. Effects of music on cardiovascular reactivity among surgeons. *Journal of the American Medical Association* 1994;272(1):882–4.

6. McCraty R, et al. Music enhances the effect of positive emotional states on salivary IgA. *Stress Medicine* 1996;12(3):167–75.

7. Karageorghis CI, et al. The BASES Expert Statement on use of music in exercise. *Journal of Sports Sciences* 2012;30(9):953–6.

8. Karageorghis CI, et al. Psychophysical and ergogenic effects of synchronous music during treadmill walking. *Journal of Sport and Exercise Psychology* 2009;31(1):18–36.

9. Padmanabhan R, et al. A prospective, randomised, controlled study examining binaural beat audio and pre-operative anxiety in patients undergoing general anaesthesia for day case surgery. *Anaesthesia* 2005;60(9):874–7.

10. Lane JD, et al. Binaural auditory beats affect vigilance performance and mood. *Physiology and Behavior* 1998;63(2):249–52.

Chapter 8

1. Bott J, et al. Guidelines for the physiotherapy management of the adult, medical, spontaneously breathing patient. *Thorax* 2009;64(Suppl I):i1–i51.

2. Clark ME, et al. Effects of paced respiration on anxiety reduction in a clinical population. *Biofeedback and Self-Regulation* 1990;15(3):273–84.

3. Hegde SV, et al. Diaphragmatic breathing exercise as a therapeutic intervention for control of oxidative stress in type 2 diabetes mellitus. *Complementary Therapies in Clinical Practice* 2012;18(3):151–3.

4. Martarelli D, et al. Diaphragmatic breathing reduces postprandial oxidative stress. *Journal of Alternative and Complementary Medicine* 2011;17(7):623–8.

5. Martarelli D, et al. Diaphragmatic breathing reduces exercise-induced oxidative stress. *Evidence-Based Complementary and Alternative Medicine* 2011;2011:932430.

Chapter 9

1. Dekker JM, et al. Heart rate variability from short electrocardiographic recordings predicts mortality from all causes in middle-aged and elderly men. The Zutphen Study. *American*

Journal of Epidemiology 1997;145(10):899–908.

2. Dettoni JL, et al. Cardiovascular effects of partial sleep deprivation in healthy volunteers. Journal of Applied Physiology 2012;113(2):232–6.

3. Routledge FS, et al. Improvements in heart rate variability with exercise therapy. Canadian Journal of Cardiology 2010;26(6):303–12.

4. Kulur AB, et al. Effect of diaphragmatic breathing on heart rate variability in ischemic heart disease with diabetes. Journal of the Brazilian Society of Cardiology 2009;92(6):423–9.

5. McCraty R, et al. The impact of a new emotional self-management program on stress, emotions, heart rate variability, DHEA and cortisol. Integrative Physiological and Behavioral Science 1998;33(2):151–70.

6. McCraty R, et al. Impact of a workplace stress reduction program on blood pressure and emotional health in hypertensive employees. Journal of Alternative and Complementary Medicine 2003;9(3):355–69.

7. Bradley RT, et al. Emotion self-regulation, psychophysiological coherence, and test anxiety: results from an experiment using electrophysiological measures. Applied Psychophysiology Biofeedback 2010;35(4):261–83

8. Lloyd A, et al. Coherence training improves cognitive functions and behavior in children with ADHD. Alternative Therapies in Health and Medicine 2010;16(4):34–42.

9. Courtney R, et al. Relationship between dysfunctional breathing patterns and ability to achieve target heart rate variability with features of 'coherence' during biofeedback. Alternative Therapies in Health and Medicine 2011;17(3):38–44.

10. McCraty R, Tomasino C. Emotional Stress, Positive Emotions, and Psychophysiological Coherence. Chapter published in: Arnetz BB and Ekman R (eds.), Stress in Health and Disease. Wiley-VCHm, Weinheim, Germany, 2006:342–365a.

About the Author

DR JOHN BRIFFA BSc MB BS (Lond) is a practising doctor, journalist, author and international speaker. After graduating with honours from University College London School of Medicine he specialized in the application of dietary and other lifestyle factors for the treatment and prevention of illness, and is a leading expert in the optimization of health and wellbeing.

Dr Briffa has written for a wide range of publications, including *The Times*, the *Telegraph*, and *Reader's Digest*, and is a former columnist for *Men's Health*, the *Daily Mail* and the *Observer*. He is a regular guest on radio and TV including Channel 4 News, ITV News, BBC 5 Live and BBC Radio 4. Dr Briffa has authored eight previous books, including the bestselling *Waist Disposal* (Hay House) and *Escape the Diet Trap* (4th Estate).

Dr Briffa is the founder of DR BRIFFA WELLNESS, a specialised consultancy that provides speaking and corporate training services to organisations globally, including the UK, Europe and North America. Clients include Deloitte, PwC, Clifford Chance, Skandia, Wincanton, Baker and McKenzie, Norton Rose Fulbright, Menzies Aviation, Anglian Water, Morgan Stanley, BP, RWE, Allen and Overy, Grant Thornton, British Gas, Freshfields Bruckhaus Deringer, Cushman and Wakefield, FTI Consulting, the Institute of Chartered Accountants in England and Wales, and IBM.

For more details, visit www.drbriffawellness.com

Contact:

DR BRIFFA WELLNESS
Woolaston House
17–19 View Road
Highgate
London
N6 4DJ
UK

Telephone: +44 (0)20 8341 3422

Email: contact@drbriffa.com

Acknowledgements

I'd like to thank Robert Kirby, my fantastic agent, and all at United Agents, for being a pleasure to work with.

Special appreciation goes to Dr Pete Robbins, who read through multiple drafts of the manuscript and offered constructive advice and suggestions at every stage. Others I'd like to thank for providing invaluable input during the writing of this book include Hilary Gallagher, Jonathan Calascione, Carlo Gagliardi, Paul Woolston, Deborah Vandepeer, Lindsay Camp and Sara Neill.

I'm indebted to my parents – Dr Joseph Briffa and Dr Dorothy Burgess – for their support and encouragement. And finally, my heart-felt gratitude and appreciation go to Sandra, for her enduring love, caring and understanding.

Index

By the same author:

Escape the Diet Trap
Waist Disposal

DR JOHN BRIFFA BSc MB BS (Lond) is a practising doctor, journalist, author and international speaker. After graduating with honours from University College London School of Medicine he specialized in the application of dietary and other lifestyle factors for the treatment and prevention of illness, and is a leading expert in the optimization of health and wellbeing.

Dr Briffa is the founder of DR BRIFFA WELLNESS, a specialised consultancy that provides speaking and corporate training services to organisations globally, including the UK, Europe and North America. Clients include Deloitte, PwC, Clifford Chance, Skandia, Wincanton, Baker and McKenzie, Norton Rose Fulbright, Menzies Aviation, Anglian Water, Morgan Stanley, BP, RWE, Allen and Overy, Grant Thornton, British Gas, Freshfields Bruckhaus Deringer, Cushman and Wakefield, FTI Consulting, the Institute of Chartered Accountants in England and Wales, and IBM.